SPY SYSTEM IN ANCIENT INDIA

SPY SYSTEM IN ANCIENT INDIA

Manila Rohatgi

KALPAZ

Published by

Kalpaz Publications
C-30, Satyawati Nagar,
Delhi – 110052
Ph.: 011-47034999, 9811692060
www.kalpazpublications.com
E-mail: kalpaz@hotmail.com

Distribution Network
gyanbooks.com
India, USA, Canada, UK, Australia, France

ISBN: 978-93-5722-913-5 (PB)

First Published, 2024

Printed at: Gyan Press, Delhi.

Spy System in Ancient India
Author: Manila Rohatgi

Contents

A Vedic Hymn

"The mighty Lord on high, our deeds, as if at hand, espies:

The gods know all men do, though men would fain their deeds disguise,

Whoever stands, whoever moves, or steals from place to place,

Or hides him in his secret cell, the gods his movements trace.

Wherever two together plot, and deem they are alone,

King Varuna is there, a third, and all their schemes are known.

This earth is his, to him belong those vast and boundless skies;

Both seas within him rest, and yet in that small pool he lies.

Whoever far beyond the sky should think his way to wing,

He could not there elude the grasp of Varuna the king.

His spies descending from the skies glide all this world around,

Their thousand eyes all-scanning sweep to earth's remotest bound.

Whate'er exists in heaven and earth, whate'er beyond the skies,

Before the eyes of Varuna, the king, unfolded lies.

The ceaseless winkings all he counts of every mortal's eyes:

He wields this universal frame, as gamester throws his dice.

Those knotted nooses which thou fling'st, OF god, the bad to snare,

All liars let them overtake, but all the truthful spare."

Preface

When the creative brain of man makes its contributions, no institution is liable to remain static or dogmatic. Espionage—due to the role of polity makers assumed a dynamic nature.

Man has a keen desire to know the unknown. Owing to this curiosity he gains knowledge by exposing the mysteries of nature. When we make an open effort to know some mystery, it is called 'research'. If an effort is done secretively or without bringing it into others knowledge, it is called 'spying'.

> *"A Ruler of the earth having the spies for his eye, is to awake even when he is asleep".*

In ancient India spy-system had developed into a sophisticated political art. When the expansion of states from petty settlements into larger kingdoms was taking place, an organised system of espionage attracted great attention. In fact possibly no political department seemed to have received so much attention from the ancient statesmen as the organisation of the spies. It is no wonder that it attracted such attention. In this connection we must take into consideration the fact that while we are at present accustomed with the press, radio, telegraph, telephone and other organs supplying the government with plenty of information to act upon, the ancient states had to maintain their safety on the strength of the information supplied by the spies. Therefore, an attempt is being made here to give an analytical and realistic picture of the glorious spy-system of ancient India.

Rigveda, the most ancient of human text, gives the references of '*Spasas*'. Later *Samhitas*, *The Brahamanas*, *The Puranas*, *The Epics*, *Smritis*, Sanskrit Kavyas and Dramas, Tamil literature etc. contain valuable information of spying. The *Arthasastra* of Kautilya presents a high watermark of state craft—a model of perfection of espionage.

The elegant features of espionage of ancient India will certainly serve as an useful guide in comparing the modern intelligence system with that existing from the Vedic age, tracing the evolution and growth of it to suit the changing ideas and need of the contemporary political system.

Now when the functions and techniques of espionage are emphasised upon by most of the nations in the modern world, it is of utmost importance to unravel the achievements of ancient spy system of India which can be of great inspiration and model to the administration not only of modern India but also of the modern world.

Being influenced with this important role of spies in the administration, I choose this topic for my research. From my school times, I had read about the spies as an important part of administrative machinery in a concised form, but I felt a keen desire to go through in it. So I found this topic 'Spy-system in Ancient India' appropriate for my research work. Moreover today it becomes more important to know about the ancient system, if we want to go in the depth and the background of the modern intelligence system and to know how far these modern secret techniques are the advanced form of those old techniques.

The topic has been divided into nine chapters to provide a systematic form.

First chapter is the Introduction that contains two parts, first deals with the contemporary political and social condition from Vedic period to the Gupta period. Spying was an important aspect of administration and social order as well during this period.

Second part contains the origin and development of secret services in historical perspective, and literature related to prescribed periods testify the presence and development of spy system in ancient India.

Second chapter shows the well developed organization of spies. The state was riddled from top to bottom with secret agents. The *Arthasastra* devotes two chapters to its organization. Spies were mainly classified in two divisions called the '*Samstha*' and '*Sancara*', These groups were further divided into many sub-categories. This chapter also mentions of their salaries, basis of recruitment and officers of the department.

Third chapter details the functions of spies. Their functions were manifold. They informed the king about every minute news of native state as well as of foreign. Security of state, and security of the king and royal dignitaries were their main functions.

Fourth chapter deals with the techniques of spies. According to the individual behaviour spies adopted various techniques. Many polity makers unanimously excepted that, 'in the work of espionage all methods were admissible—lying, bribing, poisoning, women's' wile, etc.' They practised the techniques of motivation, temptation, blackmailing, dissension, double agent operation and secret codes to use their target.

Fifth chapter throws light on the various 'covers' of spies. Espionage requires utmost secrecy. Because their work is secret and that secrecy must be preserved, secret agents must appear to be other than what they actually are. So they worked under some kind of 'covers'. These 'covers' provides them with a plausible and legitimate reason for staying in the target country location while it hides their real reason for being there. The most common covers were those of ascetic, mendicant, merchant, artisan, cook, animal trainer, blind, deaf, dumb, etc. as they worked as professional workers. King, Women, Duta and Visakanya also worked as spies in covers.

Sixth Chapter throws light on the Visakanya, the poisonous beauty in Ancient India. The *Katha Sarit Sagara* and Visakhadutta's *Mudra-Rakshasa* give the references of Visakanya. Chandragupta, the Mauryan ruler with the help of his minister Chankaya used this poison—damsel against the king Parvata. Although her appearence in Sanskrit literature is rare yet it is sure that the concept of 'Visakanya' was prevailing in ancient India as well as in Europe also. 'Secretum Secretorum' is a work appeared in European literature in the Latin language, which is a collection of the most important and secret communications sent by Aristotle to Alexander the Great when he was too aged to attend his pupil in person. The idea of poison-damsel is found in it.

Seventh Chapter deals with the diplomacy and diplomatic agents. Espionage as well as diplomacy also play a very important role in the administration and the realm of international relations. The epics are full of the examples of diplomacy. Many of the modern principles and politics of diplomacy were not unknown to the Indian mind. One such masterly genius was Kautilya. In his celebrated and most modern principles of diplomacy are present in abundance, the mission of which was political unification of India. Diplomatic agents, ambassadors or duta were the main agency for carrying out the diplomacy and the inter-state relationship. The services of both the secret agents or '*chara*' and diplomatic agents (*duta*) were essential for the success and growth of the state.

Eighth chapter relates to the position and contribution of spies. They got different position in different periods.

Whether it is political field, military, economy or society, all were benefited with their estimable services. That is why, they were called the eyes and ears of the king.

Ninth chapter is the conclusion of the proposed study. As 'spy system' was originated in the Vedic period, further this institution was developed during the several centuries of political evolution until it was codified by the political genius Kautilya. But whenever, 'spy system' lost its strictness or slackened, India become a hunting ground of barbarians and foreign hordes.

The basic concept of modern intelligence system is rooted in the ancient spy system with its new scientific techniques. So an attempt is made to show the relevancy of ancient spy system in modern intelligence services as a conclusive part. Though the modern India may have claim of advancement of espionage under the foreign impact and also by the modern cultivation of indigenous system but the spy system of ancient India may constantly afford abiding and perennial source of inspiration on more useful basis.

The 'spy system in ancient India' shows the wide range of the minds of politicians. It is needless to say that 'spy system' greatly contributed to the security and stability of the empire.

Shantiparvan declares, "**A kingdom, is said to have its roots in spies and its strength is said to lie in the counsels of policy**".

Manila Rohatgi

Acknowledgements

The commencement of this work needed collecting and consolidating of small bits of information from scattered sources and right approach to the subject was an essential necessity.

In scanning the syp system in ancient India, I have myself availed of learned contributions of the ancient scholars as well as modern historians in this field. My indebtness to their labour is incalculable. It is of course, not claimed that, have been able to read everything written so far on the subject, I hope however, that I have not missed their important work.

I beholden to my parents for their affection and continuous motivation during the composition and completion of this book. Special thanks are due to Mr. Vipin, my husband for his valueable criticism.

I am grateful to Dr. Sangh Mitra, Deputy Director of I.C.H.R., New Delhi, who offered all possible help and encouragement whenever I needed. I also express my gratitude most respectfully to Dr. (Mrs.) Gita Srivastava, my supervisor, Head of the Department of History, C.C.S. University.

I would also like to place on record the assistance I received from the libraries of 'Indian Council of Historial Research', New Delhi, 'Archeological Survey of India', New

Delhi, National Museum Library, New Delhi, Teen Murti House Library, Delhi University (North Campus) Library.

I am thankful to many other heart wishers who sent me cuttings of newspapers and magazines related to the topic, when I used to talk to them in bus while travelling. I also discussed the topic with my grandma and she told me many incidents of the Ramayana related to 'guptacharas' and 'dutas'.

I dedicate this book to my late mother-in-law Smt. Anita Rohatgi whose blessings are always with me.

Manila Rohatgi

Abbreviations

AHI	Ashoka and His Inscriptions, B.M. Barua
APIIAI	Aspects of Political Ideas and Institutions in Ancient India, R.S. Sharma
AS	The Arthashastra
Artha	The Arthashastra
AV	The Atharva Veda
EI	Epigraphia Indica
IHQ	Indian Historical Quarterly
JBBRAS	Journal of the Bombay, Branch of Royal Asiatic Society, Bombay
JBORS	Journal of the Bihar and Orissa Research Society, Patna
MBH	The Mahabharata

MPE	Minor Pillar Edict of Ashoka
MRE	Minor Rock Edict of Ashoka
PE	Pillar Edict
RE	Rock Edict
RV	The Rigveda

1

Introduction

(a) Contemporary Political and Social Condition

In ancient India the Politics was known by several terms like the *Rajadharma*, *Rajyasastra*, *Dandaniti*, *Nitisastra* and *Arthasastra*. Systematic literature on the science of polity, does not go back to a time earlier than 500 B.C. Vedic literature throw considerable light on contemporary political and social life. *The Ramayana*, *The Mahabharata*, *The Arthasastra*, *The Manusmriti* possess a huge work on the science of politics.[1]

Some Sanskrit *Kavyas* and *dramas* i.e. the *Kumar Sambhava*, the *Raghuvamsha* and the *Mudraraksasa*, respectively, etc. also give a comprehensive picture of the administrative machinery in ancient India.

Of all the human organizations that of the 'state' is undoubtedly of the greatest consequence. It is the keystone of the gigantic structure of the organization of a society. From the time of the *Rigveda* to the *Shuraniti* people have been wondering about how the state came into existence and how it survived the numerous and constant challenges to it ? In fact, the state is "an association of associations" which, acting through "Law as promulgated by a government endowed to this end with coercive power, maintains with in a community, territorially demarcated, the universal external conditions of social order ."

In the relation we have enough references of the evolution of state. But for the age of the Harappan culture, there are no such sources for a reconstruction. Of the nature of the state and government in the Harappan period only guesses can be made in the absence of generally accepted decipherment of its inscriptions. There was a remarkable degree of uniformity in aspects of material culture. This can be presumed only on the basis of an unvarying authority, such as that of a temple or some form of religious control. But there is question about it, After long discussion, some scholars have decided that, "as a conclusion, there was a rigid and highly evolved bureaucratic machine, which was capable to organize and distribute surplus wealth and to defent it but it was little conducive to political liberty of the individual". Now question arises whether priest rule existed in the Harrapan culture ? But excellent town planning, public sanitation, weights and measures, determinants of length and weight and architecture reveal the efficient administrative apparatus as far as civic matters and aspects of economic life were concerned thus, it is concluded that the basic obligations of the state, security of life and property, law and order were fulfilled with a remarkable degree of efficiency.

After the Harappans, came the Indo Aryans, probably in the opening centuries of the 2nd Millennium B.C. The Indo Aryan society was a congeries of the tribes and clans that coalsced in opposition to their perceived opponents. The non-Aryans but also thought each other as occassion demanded. There existed a primeval dread of disorder or anarchy called "*matsyanyaya*" the law of big fish devouring the small. War had been the reitmotif in the early history of these tribes. The leader in war was naturally accepted as the ruler in peace time at which stage the *Rajanya* was coming into his own. He was the first among the Kshatriyas-leter to become the lord of the fields. Gradually, as the early Aryans began to spread in East Punjab, Delhi regions and Uttar Pradesh, conditions of production, pressure of population and an emerging diversity of ethnic-cultural groups began to pose their own challenges to the early Aryan polity. The tribal lineages began to be replaced by King, ruling over heterogeneous populations and the process of state formation was set into motion. This became an irreversible process and the only direction into which it could move was the transition from kingdom to empire. The Vedic insitutions of the *sabha* and *samiti* rapidly became an inadequate and obsolete only to be replaced by the royal ministerial councils. The constant threat of wars and their active occurance led to the establishment of standing armies, far different from the tribal and clan levies of the old times. Another factor in strengthening royal authority was the emergence of a new kind of bureaucracy, completely controlled by the king and owing loyalty to him. The culmination came with the formation of the *mantri parishad* of the ratnas-"jewels" at the court. Thus the state arises to end this condition of anarchy in order to restore order which is synonymous with law, justice and equality.

As the state increased its size the number of bureaucrats and their functions also grew proportionately. The state now began to oversee, if not control, almost all aspects of social life-material, spiritual and artistic. The judicial functions of the administration became exlusive and a hierarchy of judges and courts began to work dispensing justice at all levels. Kings now began to demand and receive extraordinary privileges as the various titles birudas signify.

In the *Mahabharata*, when, Yudhishthira asks Bhisma, 'Whence arose the powers of a king ? The two replies, put in the mouth of Bhisma in two chapters, really elaborate the theory of the divine origin of kingship and the theory fo social contract. The theoryof divine origin can be traced in the Brahmana period. It is stated in its most developed form in the following, verses in Manu Samhita.

"The lord created a king for a protection of this whole creation, taking eternal particles of Indra, of the Wind, of Yama, of the Sun, of Varuna, of the Moon, and of a lord Wealth (Kubera)."

But although this extreme theory of divine origin was destined to prevail in the long run, the theory of social contract also exercised great influence during this priod. Its genesis may be traced to the *Sutra* period for, according to Baudhayana, the king was to protect his subjects, receiving as his paya sixth part (of their grains). *The Mahabharata* and the Kautilya also sware of this situation, Kautilya expresses it, that, people were suffering from anachy. Thefts, strife and insecurity replaced order and mutual respect for life, property and the institutions of marriage and family. The law of the jungle became the law of the land where the strong and the mighty oppressed the weak. The gods were disturbed and when men prayed to them to deliver them from their corporate and individual misery, Bramadeva, the creator, brought forth a code of law and enforced it though Manu. Thus was the state born and thus was established the first king. This king was armed with *Danda* the Sceptre - the authority to inflict pu nishment on the wicked in order to protect the law-abiding and the virtous. "*Praja Rakshayita Sadhurdanitivisheradah.*

Kautilya is primarily concerned with the phenomenon of political power, its acquisition, preservation, augmentation and its ultimate use. He of cource, pays his homage to the ideals of *dharma, artha* and *karma*, and as every other moralist, fervently grants that the state should serve moral ends. But after the homage is paid he turns to the very practical problems of rulership, its demands and rewards. He envision the state as being *Saptanga* or *Sevenlimbed.* These limbs are the king, minister, territory, fort, treasury, army and ally/allies. He gave importance to the monarchical form of government in state, while oligarchic republics also existed in ancient India. The king has an awesome responsibility created by his almost total power. Kautilya was very much concerned with the preparation of the prince for such an august office. The training, moral and practical of the prince is dealt with in an important section in the '*Arthasastra*". The coronation ceremony indicated the transformation in the person of the prince who now became the embodiment of power to be exercised through his office.

The theory is also repeated in slightly different version in the Buddhist canonical texts, according to which, there was of course, the hypothetical golden age when men and women were inherently good and virtuous. Then came a change in the human nature, peace gave place to fear and violence. In such oppressive conditions, people elected a king not Manu, but the '*Mahasammata*' the most handsome, gracious and powerful individual from among them to restore law and order, on condition of giving his a portion o their agricultural produce. What happened then was the *bali*, the voluntary tribute, became *Kara*, a tax. This accound implies that the state comes into being as a voluntary bilateral contract between the government and the governed where by the governed agree to pay taxes in return for prescribed services. The general rule, found in the *Sutras*, the *Smiritis* and the *Arthasastra*, that if the king cannot recover stolen property, he must compensate the owner, may be regarded as a logical corollary to this theory. The ideal Buddhist king strives to enforc *dharma* and as a cakravartin (universal ruler) exercises his authority, not with the help of *danda* but has the power of the *Chakra*.

As time passed the Brahmanical theory come to associate elements of divinity with the state or kingship. The evolution of state and kingship was the result of the evils of anrchy and of wickedness inherent in human nature. So more stress is laid on the importance of '*danda*'. The term more or less refers to the powers of punishment or chastisement vested in the ruler. The '*danda*', according to Manu, "alone governs all created beings, protects them, watches ever them while they sleep, and the wise declare it the law." Kautilya alo admire '*danda*'. He says, 'on *danda* depends the progress of the arts and sciences and the well being of mankind'. Hence the science of government is called by him '*dandaniti*'.

But while the necessity of a strong king is stressed by all, no one is ready to vest in him the absolute authority of doing whatever he likes. The theory of divine origin did not carry with it the divine right which the stuart kings, for example, claimed to exercise over their subjects at their pleasure, being accountable to none but God. Thus Manu declares that while a just king prospers, one who is voluptuous, partial and deceitful will be destroyed. The very *danda*, which is a symbol of royal authority, strikes down the king who swerves from his duty, together with his relatives.

The king was not the state but merely a part of it. The state was conceived as an organic whole, its different constituent parts being called '*anga*' or limbs. These are generally described as the king, the minister, the country, the fort, the treasury, the army, and the friendall of which must operate in unison for the kingdom to survive and prosper.

So in later times divinity came to be associated with the king but this divinity was enshrined more in the office than in the personality of the king. As Manu has earlier declared the boundations applied on the king, he also states that a bad king must be destroyed as a mad dog. Though possessed of almost absolute power the ancient king was seldom uncontrolled despot, for various cheeks, those of *dharma* and *Vyavahara* (tradition, custom, usage) as well as geography and want of technolgical means put an effective restraint on the exercise of absolute power Finally, there was always the fear of rebellion provoked by an illegitimate use of power.

The functions of the state are envisioned as constituent and ministrant. The former comprised law and order, security of person and property, prevention and/or suppression of internal commotion or external aggression. The ministrant functions called for relief to the poor and the destitute, support to education and culture, economic security and progress and help to spiritual endeavour regardless of differences in theologies and sects. The reach of the Maurya or Gupta administration extended far and wide and there were very real safe guards against royal absolutism and in this the theoretical back is worse then its practicle bite. Thre were very real constraints on the practice exercise of royal despotism. Like geography and the primitive means of transportation and communication, secondly, the king had very limited legislative authority which was secured by the *Dharmashashtras* and the *Brahmanas*, one more was, that he had to live constantly under the fear of sword of *dharma* and there was always the possibility of rebellion from below brought on by his oppression. Thus the duty of the state is frequently summed up as protection. The state protects the religion, the morality, the customs and the tradition which have been derived from the gods or evolved by society. Protection also means that it is one the prime functions of the state to defend its territory against all possible enemies and to protect the people against internal disorder or injustice. It undertakes accordingly to maintain law and order and to administer justice. Besides these, the state must protect the people from the effects of natural calamities like floods, earthquakes, famine, disease, fire, etc. All these functions of state are clearly mentioned in kautilya's concept of 'good governance' theory of welfare state. Kautilya says that he state should see that husband and wife, father and son, brother and sister, uncle and nephew, teacher and pupil are faithful to one another. The state itself should provide support to the poor, the women, their new born offspring, orphans, the aged, the infirm and the helpless. The state should facilitate, regulate and control public amusements and entertainments, including gambling. Kautilya gave an excise policy in which state was responsible to regulate life, detecting thieves and spies and securing some revenue. All professions and occupations are to be controlled by the state. Like physicians should report all cases of grave illness to the government. The same was with the goldsmiths, weavers of various descriptions, washermen etc. According to Kautilya the state is to provide, manage and regulate the *Rajamarga* or the king's highway, *Rashtra-palha* or the state road, and paths for animals, shoppath etc.

The normal form of government in India was nonarchical but it was different from that which flourished in Europe during the Roman Empire, for the most part during the Middle Ages, and in the Modern period up to the outbreak of the French Revolution. The Hindu state rarely presented that high degree of centralization which is associated with the Roman Empire and the Modern nation-state.

As a general rule, monarchy was the system of government prevailing in Vedic Age. The term 'Rajan' king or chieftain, is of frequent occurrence in the *Rigveda*.[6] The country which the Vedic Aryan occupied, was split up into numerous tribal principalities. One passage of the *Rigveda* speaks of a king living on the banks of the Sindhu, and another refers to a king Chitra and other nobles as residing in the neighbourhood of the river Sarasvati. Ten kings are described as having fought in the historic battle against Sudas.[7]

In the *Danastutis* and elsewhere, a very large number of 'Rajas' are also mentioned. The Patriarchal organization of Aryan society and the state of constant warfare with their neighbours (aboriginal and not rarely Aryans) also prove that the form of government was normally monarchical.[8]

But in the *Rigveda* we come across with the terms which in later times were undoubtedly applied to non-monarchical constitutions. Thus there are references to the '*Gana*' with the '*Ganapati*' or '*Jyestha*' (elder) at its head. The last probably corresponds to the '*Jethaka*' of the Pali texts, and it is not impossible that these were even in this early period, the germs of the republican states of the type we meet with in early Buddhist times.[9]

There existed many tribal principalities during this period. There are references in the *Rigveda* in which a king subdued the other kings. *Rigveda* speaks of king Kasu, making a gift of ten kings to a *Rishi*. The expression of '*Samrat*' and also the idea of a universal monarch also find in *Rigveda*. These expression shows that the size of kingdoms was not small but considerably large with minorities and rituals he was beseated on the throne.

The conception of a sovereign that is reflected in the *Rigveda*, has been described as 'the unequal lord' and the 'sole lord' and having no superiors. Thus, there was a gradation of kings, is palpable from the expression king of kings, the idea of a sovereign lord having vassals under him.[10]

The king occupied a highly dignified and supreme position. This was the King usually hereditary in accordance with the rule of primogeniture, living in high style and a blaze of glory, in enjoyment of an immense revenue from private and public property. Political theory which usually, though not uniformly, approached political questions from the ethical stand-point, expected the king to lead a blameless life, disciplined to ceaseless administrative labour and consecrated to the public good. If laid heavy responsibilities, temporal and spiritual, on him, promised him lasting bliss in heaven or threatened him with all the tortures of hell in accordance with success or failure in the great moral and political venture. The king was to see the material welfare and spiritual advancement of his subject. King was assisted by many officials, chief among them were *Purohita, Senani* and *Gramini.*[11]

In later Vedic period there is reference of '*Ratnins*' or "*Jewels*".[12] Though the office of the king was hereditary, yet he governed with the consent of the people. Two assemblies called '*Sabha*' and '*Samiti*' formed an essential feature of the government. *Sabha* was a small institution which dealt with the local problems and *Samiti* discussed the problems at national level.

Sabha enjoyed some judicial powers and it acted as the national judicature.[13] The king did not maintain a regular army, but every person had to do military service in times of necessity.[14]

Administration of justice was quite advanced. Dr. R.K. Mukherjee in this respect remarked, "The judicial system was advanced beyond the primitive system of eye for eye and tooth for tooth."[15]

Spies (*Spasah*) were engaged by the king to secure information about the kingdom and the people. The *Rigveda* often speaks of the spies of Varuna as sitting around their master at the time of his holding the court.[16] *Dutas* were also principle means of communication between the different states.

The common form of government during the epic period was monarchical but there were some republics as well. Under monarchical system all the powers of the government rested with the king but he was not despot. The people enjoyed the right to dispose a wicked king.

The conception of sovereignty had also crystallised during the Epic age. In the *Mahabharata,* the seven constituent elements of sovereignty had been clearly mentioned. They were "the king, the ministry, the country, the fort, the treasury, the army and the ally".[17] The *Mahabharata* shows clearly the dynamic theory of state and eulogy of force : "Wise man acquainted with Kshatriya duties declared that they who stand in the way of the person taking the sovereignty of the earth, should be slain, guilty of that fault those that stood as enemies of our kingdom have all been slain by us. World was to be enjoyed by the strong".[18]

The *Mantriparisad* and the *Sabha* (assembly of the people) also acted as a check on the authority of the king. Even the coronation oath taken by the king also restricted his authority. He was assisted in administration by several officials. Some of the *mantrees* were *Purohita, Chamupati, Devarpala, Karagaradhikari, Yuvraja, Nagar Adhyaksha, Durgapala, Dharma Adhyabshya*, etc. The epics tell us that "the king was dependent on the advice of the Minister in the some matter as the cattle is dependent on the rains, the Brahamanas on the *Vedas* and the women on their husbands."[19]

The village was the lowest unit of administration. The king was the highest judicial authority. The kings maintained regular army and paid them either in cash or kind. Various types of taxes were collected from the people. Generally the Brahamanas had not to pay any taxes.

An elaborate account of spies is to be met with in the *Ramayana* and in the *Mahabharata*. The government of those days in eliminating corruption was depended largely on the services of spies."[20]

The *Mahabharata* praises the king who appoints the spies to know the secret of enemies and to create the dissension among their ministers and other officials.[21]

In the '*Santiparvan*' of *Mahabharata*, reference of republics are found. The sovereignty was in the hands of few dignitaries. Many '*ganas*' used to form a 'sangha' and lord Krishna was the leader of a confederation.[22]

The Maurya period constitutes a distinctive landmark in the history and cultural development of India.[23]

The Rise of Mauryan dynasty ushered in a new era in the political history of India. It was in the Mauryan age that whole of India was politically united for the first time under one head and rule.[24]

Patliputra actively, controlled the administration of the empire's far-flung provinces. Ashoka's inscriptions have been found in all the principal areas of the subcontinents which may provide one of the bases of the assumption of a unified imperial system. Another indication is contained in Ashoka's admonition to his administrators to be just and compassionate in their dealings with all the subjects of the empire, especially in the tribal areas such as Orissa.

The Mauryan emperors claimed supremacy not only in India but over lands beyond the border of India. Political unity of their period led to historical unity. The Mauryan state was organised with a full supply of departments. The Mauryas, on the contrary, had a regular civil administration and maintained a huge standing army paid directly by the crown.[25] During Mauryan period, the normal form of government was monarchical. In the monarchies, the king controlled the whole administration and his spies kept watch upon every part of it.[26]

King was undoubtedly treated with great respect but at least, in the views of the upper classes that respect was not solely derived from their divinity. The king's over-riding duty was to preserve the order of the society. *The Arthasastra* suggested only four and half hour's sleep and three hours for meals and recreation.[27]

There was no separation of executive and judicial functions. The king presided over them. Normally a king was succeeded by his elder son but there was nothing rigid about the order of succession. According to the *Arthashastra* if a king died without heir, the principal figures in the kingdom the courtiers, merchants and religious leaders, would sometimes meet and choose the king.[28] Thus in Kautilyan polity, a virtuous, learned and generous king spent his life in serving his people. The Kautilyan king had to promote morality, encourage righteousness and patronise education as well as foster the feelings of piety and generosity in the heart of his people by promoting virtue and morality.[29]

Existence of oligarchic and republican states side by side with the kingdoms was one of the most important features of Mauryan period.

Megasthenese, reported that in the time of Chandragupta Maurya, cities also had councils. The city governors were sometimes the military as well as and controlled local troops, police and spies. He recorded that the empire was divided into provinces under governors, and that district administration was under officers called '*Agronomoi*'.[30]

The *Arthasastra* insisted that the government must keep a careful check on everybody. This was done through officials who were responsible for the supervision of forty households each. These officials controlled taxes, recorded birth and death.[31] The system of espionage was the remarkable feature of the administration of Mauryan rulers. It was Chandragupta Maurya who usurped the throne from the hand of the last of Nandas, introduced this system with vigour and efficiency under the guidance of Kautilya. Under this espionage system informers and reporters evalved out methods of communication in languages, symbols and signs of their own unknown to others. These persons were drawn from both the sexes and were spread over amongst all classes of society. Through this agency, the king remained well informed about the activities of his servants and subjects, thus lessening the chances of revolt and conspiracy against him. Some of the informers were specifically appointed to look after the personal safety of the king.

Vincent smith writes that, 'the government relied on a highly organised system of espionage, pervading every department of the administration and every class of population. The formal rules concerning spies occupy a prominent place in the treatise, every chapter of which assumes that the working of the machinery of the government depends mainly on the successful utilization of secret information.'

The smallest unit of administration was the village. In the village itself the lowest level of all in the pyramid of government were the headman and the council. Usually the headman inherited his position but could be replaced at the king's discretion. His salary consisted of tax free land or some benefit in kind. In large village, the headman would be assisted by a small staff; book-keeper, watchman and such like who paid in the same way.

The political system of Kautilya was based on *Dharma*.[32] *Dharma* was the principle that sustained all existence, embodies the whole truth and covered all the forms, institutions and practices of social life. It was felt that *Dharma* stood above all the rules of the world and was binding upon them. Dharma was conducive to the highest good."[33]

According to the *Arthasastra*, all professions and occupations were to be controlled by the state. For instance, a physician should report all cases of grave illness to the government. If death occurred in an unreported case, the physician should be punished with the first emercement.[34]

Protection was also one of the prime functions of the state. The state was to defend its territory against all possible enemies and to protect the people against internal disorder or injustice."[35]

The Mauryan period was characterized by continuous foreign invasion in north-west and the rise and fall of many small kingdoms and petty empires. Invasions, unwidely size of the kingdom, local fissiparousness, the ambition of regional administrators and treachery all played a part in the break-up of Mauryan period.[36]

In Post Mauryan age, the administration did not change substantially from that of the Mauryan age. The official machinery of the Mauryan period continued to function in the period of Sungas, Kanvas and Satvahanas covered whole of the ocean and spread far into northern India.[37] The provincial government of the Sungas and Kanvas was a continuation of the Mauryan system. They also continued the political organization of the Imperial Mauryas.[38]

Local administration left largely to feudatories subject to general control of royal officials. Feudatories were of three grades *Rajas*, *Mahabhojus*, and *Mahasenapati*.[39]

In the north-west India, some changes were introduced in the political system by the foreign invaders. The period that opened with the downfall of Mauryan empire and closed with the foundation of the Gupta empire, was a vast one punctuated by brilliance and gloom as also by great endeavours and relentless conflicts.[40]

Sunga dynasty was founded by Pushyamitra Sunga, which is said to have lasted for a hundred and twelve years.[41] Pushyamitra stemmed the tide of foreign invasion and maintained his authority over a large part of the empire. He thus arrested, for the time being, the disintegration of the Magadha empire which throughout the country of Sunga rule, extended as far as Bhilsa in Madhya Bharat, if not further to the west. The Bactrian Greeks maintained friendly relations with them. The Sunga period saw the revival of the Brahmanical influence. Sungas were Brahmans of the Bharadvaja gotra, who belonged to Vidisa near Ujjain. In the *Asvalayana Srautasutra*, the Sungas were known as teachers."[42]

Pushyamitra was succeeded by his son Agnimitra. Sujyeshtha and Vasumitra were another rulers. The tenth or last Sunga king according to *Puranas* was Devabhuti. According to Bana he was the victim of a conspiracy engineered by his Brahman minister Vasudeva and was killed by a slave girl who approached him in the guise of his queen.[43] The Sungas were succeeded by the Kanvas. According to the Puranas "after Kanvas the earth was to pass to the Andhras, whose dominion extended over the Deccan from Arabian Sea to the Bay of Bengal and included Berar and Malwa."[44]

This shows the weak espionage system of later Sungas and uses of female spy as a queen to kill the king. After the downfall of Sungas and Indo-Greeks rule in West India, Scythian (the Sakas, Parthians, Kushanas) rule, the title is known about the administration of the Scythian epoch leaves no room for doubt that the institution of that age were not haphazard and improvi*Sati*ons of military starts, having no relation with the past, but a developed and organized system, the fruit of the labours of generation of political theories and political statesmen.[45] In Deccan, the Mauryan Empire was followed by the rule of the Satvahanas. At its height Satvahanas empire covered the whole of the Deccan and spread far into Northern India.[46]

Kushanas, under the leadership of Kadphesis-I crossed the Hindukush and made themselves masters of Kabul and Kandhara. The system of government feudal lords continued during the reign of Kushanas. Kanishka believed in the divine origin of kingship, this idea is embodied in the portrayal of his body emerging from clouds with flames rising from his shoulders and the assumption of the title of "*Devputra*".[47]

Politically, the Gupta age was the age of integration in India. After more than three hundred years of fragmentation and foreign domination, northern India was again under the vigorous rule of a powerful monarch of versatile talents.[48]

Between the age of the Mauryas and that of the Guptas great changes seem to have occurred in the constitution and working of kingdoms and empires. The *Satrapa* system of the Sakas became an innovation that was to have continued influence in the state craft. The empire of the Guptas was much smaller in size than that of the Mauryas and it is reasonable to assume that the Gupta administration was much less direct in the outlying provinces than in the empire's heartland. This was especially so after the career of Chandragupta II. The presence of feudatories with their own armies and administrative apparatus created spheres of quasi-independent powers with the frame-work of the empire itself.

Another sign of the increasing feudalization of the polity, is the large number of land grants issued during the Gupta and Post-Gupta periods. These land grants were charters of gifts of parcels of land individuals, groups or institutions to whom were made over the revenues of the land and the grantees were exempted from payment of traditional taxes to the state. In such cases these lands were alienated from the state in matters of ownership rights, land revenue and taxation and in requirements to furnish *corvee* labour for public works. It is obvious that in such lands the state transferred its administrative and judicial authority to the grantee. The rise of quasi-independent states such as the Maitras of Valabhi and the extensive prevalence of land grant authorities in the North as well as in the South indicated the gradual erosion of the authority of the state and its effective transfer to regional and local centres of power.

The reigns of Samudra Gupta and Chandra Gupta covering nearly three quarters of a century, once more brought about the political unity of northern India. Inspite of numerous wars, people enjoyed prosperity and security of life and property.[49] Criminal law was mild. Spies were engaged to know the secrets of enemies.

Hereditary monarchy was the prevailing type of government during Gupta period. There was no trace of autocracy in their mode of conduct and administration. They respected the established laws of the land and acted in the interest of the subjects committed to their charge. The Gupta rulers were bound by a system of checks and balances. They were controlled by their councils of Ministers and others.[50]

Succession being hereditary the eldest son usually succeeded the father. Chandra Gupta I was succeeded by his son Samudra Gupta. Generally it was an accepted custom that the eldest son of the family was to be crowned *Yuvaraja*.[51]

In case of Chandra Gupta II, his nomination by his father was indicated in the expression '*tatparigrihita*'. He was also described as the 'Satputra' of his father.[52]

The doctrine of the divinity of the king had become more popular in this period. *Samritis* and inscriptions of this period emphasised[53] that a king could become a successful ruler only if he waited upon the elders studied the art of government and cultivated righteousness.

The law was above the king, and the king was not a lawmaker. At the most, he could administer the law without least violating the spirit underlying it.[54] Protection of the people depended upon the king. In the Gupta polity the *Yuvaraja* had his separate establishment, both civil and military. Queens and princes usually did not take active part in the administration.[55]

The Great *Dharma* sustained everything and this was the very basis of the state.[56]

Thus, the political set-up of the Rigvedic period was of an advanced type. Hereditary monarchy that was first introduced in this period, prevailed in other periods also in different ways.

The Mauryan government in short, was a highly organised and thoroughly efficient autocracy, capable of controlling a vast empire.

We have an imperfect picture of the political condition and their administration of the kingdoms that flourished in India during post Mauryan period from 200 BC to 300 AD.[57]

The Gupta period represents a distinct phase of Indian history and culture. The main theme of the Gupta history was the foundation of Gupta empire which at full maturity brought unity, peace and prosperity over nearly the whole of northern India.[58]

Social Condition

The society during the early Vedic period was highly organised. Settled life implied a greater degree of internal social stratification within the tribe or village. The family was patriarchal in character with the eldest male member enjoying absolute control over other member of the family".[59] Joint family system was prevalent from Vedic period to Gupta period. In epic age it was considered improper for younger brother and sister to marry before their elders. Family was a close unit of society, bound together by the tie of natural affection.

Existence of caste system in the early Vedic age is a disputable matter. Different scholars have tried to assert on the testimony of certain mantras in the *Rigveda* that a hereditary caste system existed in the society. They refer to a mantra in the *tenth mandla of Rigveda* which says, "Brahmans sprang from the head of Brahma, Kshatriyas from his arms, the Vaishyas from his thighs, and the Sudras from his feet".[60]

Thus, the Brahmans were men of learning and are described as head, the Kshatriyas who were concerned with the use of physical force are described as arms, the Vaishyas for trade and commerce and the Sudras for the service of human society. Thus, principle of division of labour was prevailed in the whole period.

Besides another reference *Rigveda* indicates the non-existence of rigid caste system during this period.[61] This hymn says, "I am a poet, my father is a physician, my mother grinds can no stone".[62]

According to Dr. R.C. Dutta, "Society was not divided into hereditary castes". Hence, caste system based on heredity was unknown in the early Vedic period. Division were based on occupation but the society was still tribal and largely egalitarian.[63]

In epic time, the caste system had become very rigid and works of all the four castes were fixed. However, there were a few exceptions too, such as Dronacharya being a Brahman, had accepted the duties of Kshatriyas and Vishwamitra being a Kshatriya performed the duties of Brahmans.

In epic society, Brahamanas did not enjoy the supreme position, instead the Kshatriyas came to occupy a dominant position.[64]

During the Maurya-Period, society was based on orthodox Brahminical system which divided it among four

Varnas together with many lower castes (*averavarna*). The Brahmans were highly respected and next in order came Kshatriyas and Vaisyas and Sudras.[65]

The *Arthasastra* accords a special position to the Brahmans in society. It prescribes the worship of Brahmans along with that of gods to ward off calamities.[66] It is to be recalled that the Mauryan empire begin with a Brahman. A Brahman was exempting from all sorts of bodily punishments, regardless of the nature of the crime.[67] But Kautilya did not gave place the *'dharma'* in politics or administration.[68]

A graphic account of caste system was given by Megasthenese. He enumerated seven classes or castes into which the society was divided. viz.—(1) philosopher, (2) husbandmen, (3) herdsmen, hunter, (4) artisans and traders, (5) military personnel, (6) overseers or spies, and (7) Councillors."[69] They were put in different *varna*. From the account of Kautilya it also appears that some people in the Hindu society begin to attach greater important to the principle of birth rather than that of occupation and temperament.

Varnashramadharma, as governing the life of the individual was recognised and the rulers were supposed to safeguard it to secure social solidarity.

In post Mauryan period, the triumph of the Brahmans meant that the organization of *Varnas* received support from the state. The foreigners were freely accepted into the fold of society.[70]

This was the age of Brahmanical revival. It was supported by the Sungas, Kanvas and Satvahanas. Since Brahmanical revival depended upon royal power, rulers adopted such titles such as '*Maheshvara*' and '*Sarvalokashvara*'.[71]

Social laws were becoming rigid under Guptas. King as well as *Abhayadatta*, *Rajastheniya* and *Dharmadosha* were described as checking the mixture of the Varnas.[72]

Ashram system was a notable feature of the later Vedic period and a fairly comprehensive account of it is in the *Dharmasutras*. Presuming the life of an individual to be 100 years. It was divided into four *Ashramas*, i.e. *Brahmacharya Ashrama*, that of a student from 1 to 25 years, *Grihastha Ashrama*, that is marriage or family life from 25 to 50, *Vanprastha Ashrama*, that of a retired life in the forest from 50 to 75 years and *Sanyasa Ashram*, the life of complete renunciation from 75 to 100 years. But it was not strictly adhered to in this time. In epic period also there existed no rigidity in it. Vedvyasa in the *Mahabharata*, regarded the *Ashramas* as the four stairs to reach the *Brahmaloka*.[73]

This account, based on the Brahmanical religious tests, is fully corroborated by Kautilya's *Arthasastra*,[74] which describes in detail the duties assigned to the four Asramas. The scheme of the four Asramas was designed to give wide scope to individuals in the choice of a vocation in life which was best ruited to their intellectual capacity and mental inclinations. It was not necessary that one should strictly follow the four stages one after another. Though this might be regarded as a normal procedure by the orthodox section, and one that was largely followed in practice, still the choice was left to every individual, who was not forced either to lead a house holder's life or to renounce it against his will.[75]

A.L. Basham writes in his book, The wonder that was India, that, this scheme, of course, represents the ideal rather then the real. Many young men never passed through the first stage of life in the form laid down, while only a few went beyond the second. Many of the hermits and ascetics of ancient India were evidently not old men, and had either shortened or omitted the stage of householder. The series of the four stages is evidently an idelization of the facts.[76]

Kautilya also Makes some restrictions. He does not at all approve of a premature renunciation of the world and the duties of domestic life waithout the formal sanction of the legal authorities and without making provision for son and wife.Later on its integrity was threatened by the haterodox sects like Jainism and Buddhism and various astetic orders. But on the whole this voluntary system worked well and the different stages very well reflect the different ideals which inspired society.

Marriage was regarded as a sacred and divine institution and performed with the recitation of hymns. Girls had freedom in the choice of their husbands. Marriage with *Dasyu Varna* was prohibited. Dowry and bride prices were in vogue. Monogamy was the common form of marriage. But polygamy was also prevalent amongst the members of higher classes. Polyandry was non-existent. Widow marriage was also allowed during this period. The evils like *Sati* system, *pardha* system and early marriage of the girls belong to later period.[77]

In epic age eight types of marriages had developed, but the most interesting form of marriage described in the epics is the *Svayamvara*, confined originally to the Kshatriya class, where in, a princess selected her husband of her own free will from among the assembled suitors, or as a result of a tournament in the use of war like weapons. Polygamy and polyandry were practised. Widow marriage is not mentioned in the two epics.[78]

In Mauryan period, marriage between member of the same class (*Varna*) was preferred, though as noted intermarriages between different castes were prevalent. Kautilya[79] has mentioned eight kinds of marriages : (1) *Brahma*, (2) *Daiva*, (3) *Arsya*, (4) *Prajapatya*, (5) *Asura*, (6) *Gandharva*, (7) *Rakshasa*, (8) *Paishacha*. Kautilya called *Brahma*, *Daiva*, *Arsa*, and *Prajapatya* forms of marriages as approved (*dharmya*) marriages. It is interesting to note that according to Megasthenese the Indian's marriage is marked by the gift of "a yoke of Oxen". This proves the popularity of the *Arsha* form of marriage in the 4th century B.C.

Kautilya permitted divorce where both the husband and wife agreed to it but only in *adharmya* marriages, not in *dharma* because in it marriage was a sacrament in which divorce was not permissible.

In post Mauryan period, these eight form of marriages were prevalent and accepted. *Anuloma*, *Pratiloma* and inter-racial marriages also took place.[80] The *Arthasastra* and a few *Dharmasastras* permitted the remarriages of widows.

The efficacious practice of *Sati* was not present in the earlier period. It is believed that this practice was prevalent among ancient Greeks, Germans, seaves and other races and influenced India considerably, confining mainly to nobles and princesses in the intial stages. But it appears in Vedic India that the *Sati* sacrifice was discouraged and no vedic passage, induabitably reffered to the barouring of the widow alive as then current. The *Sutras* that follow the Brahmanas give sparse references to *Sati*.[81] The *Manusmriti* is entirely silent about it. The *Ramayana*[82] describes a Brahmana woman who committed *Sati* when molested by Ravana. In the *Mahabharata*,[83] Madri wife of pandu is shown as performing *Sati*. So the *Ramayna* and the *Mahabharata* record a few cases of *Sati*. The Jain literature does not speak about *Sati* system. The Buddhist Probably deterred it.[84] The *Manusmriti* is entirely silent about it. The Epigraphical evidences in support *Sati* are numerous and throw lurid light on the '*Sati*' Practices. The earliest of them is found in 191 AD of the Gupta era.

Women during the early Vedic period were held in high esteem. No religious rite and ritual could be completed without her presence. They were sufficiently educated and civilized. But in later Vedic period position of women considerably declined. Though they were permitted to receive education and engage in intellectual pursuits, they were not permitted to take part in the politics and in the tribal assembly, *Sabha.*"[85] In later vedic period, the idea grew that women were periodically subject to defilement because of their menstruation which made them ineligible for the recilation of the sporitual texts. There are evidence that women married on attainment of adulthood and could choose mates where as by the time of Manu they were to be married off before puberty. Manu perhaps with his tongue in his check, declares that where the women are honoured, there the gods are pleased bu hastens to add that a woman does not deserve independence.[86] The father's property was intrarited by his son and not by his daughter, unless she was the only issue. The right of adoption was recognised.[87] The position of women during the epic period generally continued to be quite respectable. Description of Draupadi as '*Brahamavadini*' testifies the position of respect enjoyed by the women in the society.

In Mauryan period, after marriage a woman was confined to her home. Offences against women of all kinds were severely punished. The offence of killing a woman was equal to that of killing a Brahman.[88]

Prostitutes were recognised and they had to attend court and were regularly employed in the royal household on a big salary. The *Arthasastra* suggested the appointment of a Superintendent of prostitutes and levy of tax. Kautilya and Megasthenesee said that a close contact should be kept on brothel for security purposes and recommended the employment of skilled prostitutes as spies.[87] Women were sometimes known to have carried on administrative work. According to Megasthenese the Pandaen nation was governed by females."[89]

In post Mauryan period, women were prominent in social life and held property in their own right. It was seen from records of their lavish charity, mentioned in inscriptions. In sculptures, we see them worshipping Buddhist emblems, taking part in assemblies and entertaining guests.[90]

During the Kushana period, women enjoyed great freedom in India. They did not use any veil.[91]

Under the Guptas, for the first time, the right of a woman to inherit was fully recognised in the '*Yajnavalkya Smriti*.' But Manu, Narada and Katyayana were against it.[92]

Thus, women in Gupta period continued to enjoy freedom, respect and honour.

Great importance was attached to education during Vedic period. The education was mainly oral and religious in character. Whether the art of writing was known to them cannot definitely be said. At the *Ashram* the child was provided free lodging and boarding. They paid only '*Gurudakshina*'. The girls received education from women teachers, usually girls of rich families received education. Education during Vedic period covered quite a wide field and aimed at physical, moral, intellectual as well as spiritual development of the students. In epic period, education was generally imparted by the private teachers who did not charge any fees.[93]

During the Mauryan period, education was fairly and widely spread. Ashokan edicts indicate that literacy prevailed among the common people. The establishment of nunneries must have been a great step in this direction.[94]

Girls of aristocratic families were imparted some instruction in fine arts such as music, dance and painting but some of them even in this period continued the study of Mimansa philosophy. Medium of higher education must have been Sanskrit in those days.

As against this bright picture of the high intellectual moral and physical education of women, there were also steadily gowing disabilities. Formerly the girls were went through the *Upanayana* ceremony like the boys, but this gradully canre to be merely formal. Manu prescribes that in the case of women *Upanayana* should be performed without the recitation of sacred texts. Yajna vakya laer on denied to perform the *Upanayana* ceremony at all for the girls. The wife wife formerly performed Vedic sacrifices, was denied the right to do so[95] and could not, even recite the vedic mentras. Thus was the woman, reduced at least spiritually, to the status of the Sudra. The Bhagavadgita clearly reflected this position of women.

Slavery also existed in Vedic period, it may be observed that slavery was not confined to any particular class and persons belonging to all castes could become slave. An Arya could become a slave. The *Mahabharata* tells Lis that according to the law of war the vanquished could be enslaved by the victor. Slavery was perpetuated by making the children of slaves in to slaves of their parent's masters.[96] According to Manu and Narada, slaves could be acquired by birth in the masters house, by purchase, by gift, by inheritance, by maintenance during famine, by pledge, by release from a heavy debt, by capture in war, by voluntary surrender of freedom, by connection with a female slave, and by many other processes. Slavery was also the judicial punishment for crime.[97] A slave is not entitled to any property according to Manu and is not to be a judicial witness except in the last resort.

In Ancient India an army was knows as *chaturangini* constituting cavalry, elephants, chariots and infantry. In addition to these well known four divisions the Mahabharta has mentioned four other departments connected with the military organization. The first was 'visti' or the department of transport and commissariat; the second was 'Nava' or

'Navyi', the third 'chara' or espionage and the last Daisika or the department of scouts and guides for army.

Megasthenesee, the seleucid ambassador at the Mauryan court had commented on the absence of slaves in India but it is contradicted by Indian sources. He amplifies it by stating that, "the Indians donot even use aliens as slaves and much less a country man of their own." Slavery was a recognised institution and legal relationship between master and slave was clearly confined.[98]

The people in early Vedic age were both vegetarian and nonvegetarian but in later Vedic period meat eating become quite popular. A Verse in the *Udyoga-Parvan* says that the food of the rich consists of flesh, that of the middle class, of milk and its products, and that of the poor, of all preparations. But rice barley and wheat were the chief foodgrains.

In spite of the growing spirit of *ahimsa.* In Mauryan times, various kinds of fish and meat, not excluding beef, were extensively taken by the people.

Madyapana, or drinking was prevalent in ancient India. The two intoxicating drinks mentioned in the Veda are, *Soma* and *sura.* Of these, *soma* was most probably a hieratic drink, while *sura* was the popular drink, not usually offered to gods. The *Smritis* condemn drinking *sura* by *brahamanas.*[99] Kautilya gives a detailed description of various kinds of liquor, which was a state monepoly. Megasthenese rays that the Indians donot drink wine except at sacrifices but it seems to be an Bramanical ideal which did not coincide with actual practice in life, for even apart from the festimony of Kautilya's *Arthasastra,* there is enough evidence to show that the habit of drink was common special among the Ksatriyas-male and female.

Games were a part of social life. Both indoor and outdoor games were played. In vedic age, Chariot-race, horse race were popular. The word *'Samaja'* is used for several times in different contexts. In Mahabharata, the tournament in which the young Pandava and Kaurava princes displayed their feat of arms is called *Samaja*, whereas, the tournament, which Drupada had arranged to sebet a husband for Draupadi, is called *Samaja*. In the Ramayana it is compound with '*Utsava*' indicating a special type of festival. The word Samaja is also mentioned in Asokas incriptions as a great festival, while samaja seems to have accuired an evil reputation, for Manu, directs that a thief should be scarched for in a brothel, wine shop and *Samaja* etc. But finally *Samaja* included sports such as wrestling, and tournaments along with some other forms of entertainments like dance and drama.

Among indoor games, the most popular and most ancient was gambling away at dice. The Vedic people were addicted to this form of gambling. The Rigveda deleniates the dicer as "leader of agreat horde." However, Vedic literature do not mention the use of the dice-board. But dice was thrown on the depression (adnidevana) or (Irina) in the ground. Jatakas and Buddhist literature also make mention of gambling wth dice. The Vedic and Smirti literature vividly points out that gambling houses were menaged by the state. The *Arthasastra* advocates the strict control of gimbling.[100]

The Vedic period serves as the basis of present social system. Many customs are still existed. People lived a religious life. The social life during the ancient India was highly organised.

In Mauryan period, people frugal life and observed good order. People were mild, and truthful. Theft was a rare occurrence. Thus, the keynote in social life was a joy for life.[101]

From the social point of view, the post Mauryan period was a period of crisis. Society was now divided into a number of castes. Many foreigners had now settled down in the society.

Like Mauryan period, the social condition of Gupta period show-up people happy, well pleased in life. The country, as a whole, was a sound economic footing and there was a general feeling of security, well being and progress.[102]

(b) Secret Services in Historical Perspective

The spy system of early India is the consequence of the geo-political conditions of the times, when there was prevailing the rule of anarchy. The condition of the community of states was very unstable. Each big state was trying to cover run the small states and there was an incessant fight for supremacy.[103]

Although king was responsible to check these fightings and to establish peace and security yet the threats by the marauders could not be effectively restrained by the king in view of poor communications, continued foreign invasions and internal disorders.

Victory was naturally sought to be achieved through diplomacy.[104] For, the state made massive use of 'secret services' for diverse purposes. In order to ascertain whether the country was loyal and free from conspirators and with the prime object of ensuring the security of state and protection of the people, spies were freely engaged. Thus, every state was in imminent danger of external interference and sabotage.[105]

Secret agents were utilized to collect reliable information about the tribal settlements, their movements and dispositions, which were extremely important in the context of expanding the Vedic society.[106] Besides it, spying was practiced in the Vedic period for the security of the state, to uphold the moral order and for the eradication of criminals.[107]

The earliest references to the activities of secret agents are available in the *Samhitas*. Firstly, the word '*Spasa*' is found in first *Mandala of Rigveda,* where king is compared with the sun. The spies have always filled a very important place in the kings council right from the days of the Rigveda.[108] The Rigveda often points out the spies (spasah) of Varuna as sitting around their master at the time of his holding the court. Varuna was urged to plant his spies everywhere so that they could visit every place and watch everything increasingly.[109]

Varuna's spies surveying the two worlds, are extolled as being, blessed with wisdom and piety. He knows the flight of birds in the sky, the path of ships in the Ocean, the course of the far traveling wind, and beholds all the secret things done. No creature can wink without him, and he witnesses truth and falsehood. His agents were watchful, moved extensively to collect information.[110] They helped him in the discharge of his duties and informed him about the happening of the state.[111] Nothing that happened remained unknown to him. His '*pasa*' was the instrument of coercion with which, he used to bind all culprits.[112]

Varuna was assisted by '*sarama*' the '*spybitch*' which goes around in search of criminals. Indra sent *Sarma*, to trace out the treasure of Panis.[113] There is also reference of 'Sarama' as a lady ambassador in the *Rigveda* in *Pani Sukta* (10108). She was sent to Pani with an ultimatum for war or for peace on the order of Indra.[114]

The Rigvedic traditions of Varuna's agents were carried on in the later *Samhitas*. Other deities of the Vedic pantheon heavily depended on the secret agents for overseeing the activities of the people, and for taking pre-emptive measures against the '*dasas*' and '*dasyus*'.

Further evidences in regard to spies are supplied by the *Atharvaveda*. Soma is described to have rays like spies that would never close their eyes and were present everywhere;[115] ready with fetters for trying the offender. Whereas Varuna's spies are said to have thousand eyes to watch the whole world.[116]

It may be suggested, on the basis of the employment of spies by Varuna, the divine counterpart of the human being, that spies were often employed by the Vedic monarchs with a view to keeping themselves well informed of the happenings of various kinds within their kingdoms.[117]

The spies have been attributed to Mitra (VIII, 61, 3), to Agni (VI, 4, 3), to Soma (IX, 43,47), to demons combated by Indra (X.10.8)[118]. The spies of the celestial deities were reflected on the earth when the Vedic king imbibed their qualities and attributes.

Spasah is described thrice with the Agni. Spies of Soma were appointed in a systematic way. They are spreaded everywhere to arrest wicked. They were alert, sweet tongued, possessed with high character and beautiful in appearance.[119] The institute of Vishnu (III, 35) enjoins that, "the king must explore, by means of spies, both the state of his own kingdom and of his foes".

The Sanskrit dictionaries use different terms for spies of various shades depending upon the nature of work and mode of their operation.

Amarkosa mentions several words for secret agents, i.e. *Cara*, *Pranidi*, *Prahita*, *Apasara*, *Spasa*, *Gudhapurusha*, *Apta*, *Pratyagita* and *Yathahivarna*. *Vaijayantikosa* and *Abhidhana Chintamani* also describe these nomenclatures.[120] *Amarkosa* defines Cara as an agent sent abroad to collect strategic and tactical information. The reference to secret agents in the '*Astadhyayi*' of Panini, shows that this institution had come to be recognised as an important aspect of administration even before Kautilya.[121]

Patanjali also mentions '*Dutas*' and Karnejapas' or *Suchakas*. These '*Karnejapas*' worked as 'secret servicemen' who collected information from urban areas. Kamandaka devotes twelfth section regarding the qualities, functions and importance of the embassies and the spies in *Nitisara*. He says, "spies are" the eyes of the ruler of the earth; he should always look through their medium, he who does not look through their medium, stumbles down, out of ignorance, even on level grounds, for he is said to be blind.[122]

The *Jatakas* also mention the secret agents as '*Upanikkitta purisas*'. The Jataka texts create the impression that by the post Vedic period there developed a regular network of spies in most of Indian kingdoms. They reported to their kings, to whom they owed their appointment, the military preparations as well as the evil designs of foreign rulers. It was evidently on the basis of such reports, secretly conveyed to them, that kings would decide their line of action to counteract enemies' movements.[123]

In the '*Mahaummaga Jataka*', a spy dispatched an important report to his master from a distant kingdom. Another Jataka text informs how the secret agents of a king of Kampilla, even at the time of war, outmaneuvered the enemies to enter the city of Mithila by its postern gate, and successfully carried all sorts of useful news about the hostile camp of his master.[124]

The Jain texts describes five kinds of council of a king : Puranti, Chattanti, Buddhi, Mantri and Rahassiya. The member of 'rahassiya' council pacified the angry queen, carried the news of the dates of the purificatory bath after monthly course of various queens; they also informed the king the names of his daughters who were eligible for marriage. They also informed him of the love affairs of the queen and also talked with the king in private on various topics pertaining to his sexual life.

During the Sodsa Mahajanapadas, the rulers of these regions were always trying to annex the kingdoms of their neighbours. Peace was a short truce, all aiming for the next onslaught. Espionage was common in Buddhist period. Many shrewd diplomats sought to win their policy by crooked methods and taking recourse to stratagems.[126] Spies were also employed to thwart enemies' plans by creating a breach of trust between the latter and their army.

The spies came to be equated with the eyes of the king, in the epic and post epic period.[127] An elaborate account of spies is to be met within the *Ramayana.* The government of those days in eliminating corruption from within, depended largely on the service of spies, is evident from Rama's inquiries of Bharata if the latter was keeping an eye on the fifteen '*tirthas*' of the kingdom and eighteen '*tirthas*' of foreign countries through these spies.[128] Their list has been given by commentator Nilkantha, who says that a king need not to employ spies to guard the conduct of own *Mantris, Purohits* and *Camupati* (*Senapati*).[129]

The *Lankakanda* speaks of spies, who were full of confidence, courage and zeal and were fearless. Ravana sent spies in camps of Rama to know the secrets and nature, number and movements of forces.[130] Because it is said, that, a wise monarch that discovers all that concerns his adversary through his spies, needs to 'exert himself only to a moderate degree to overcome his enemy in the field of battle.[131] So spying was the most important activity during the war period in Ramayana age. It was felt that a spy should collect secret information about the enemy. Moreover, a spy was also a warrior who participated in the battle field and often commanded, guided, supervised and controlled the army.[132]

The *Ayodhyakanda* further shows that the king should not initiate any action on the basis of the report, submitted by a single spy. Actions could only be taken if the information received from three different sources independent of each other, was found to concur.[133]

But Ravana's secret service department was not active in early Lanka. Ravana was himself not interested in it. It was the result of Supernakha's conver*Sati*on with Ravana, when Laxmana cutted down the nose and ears of Supernakha, being annoyed she rebuked to her brother Ravana, that, "the king who does not appoint the spies for the security of subject in his state, such king is rejected by the people as an elephant remains away from the mud of river".[134]

She further says, that, "you are surrounded with ill-mannered and faithless ministers, so you are unable to appoint the spies. And this is the reason that your relatives were killed and palaces are isolated and you are unknown to situation.[135] Later on he maintained an organised spy system. So, it is sure that Anaryas also adopted the spy system.[136]

The *Mahabharata* provides us with a more elaborate account of spies, as compared to the *Ramayana*. In emphasizing the importance of the institution of espionage the *Santiparvan* describes "spies as constituting one of the eight linbs of the army".[137] In the Udyogaparvan they are described as the very eyes of the king.[138] and states that, "cows see by smell, priests by knowledge, king by spies, and other men through eyes". A preceding verse also inculcates that, "a king may learn wisdom from a fool, as one gets gold from a rock, and should geean information from spies, as a gleaner gets ears of corn". The Vanaparva also stress on the fact that "a king must employs spies on every district and every fort".

The *Santiparvan* further states that, "the spies were expected to report the public opinion to their ruler, a king should plan to murder his enemy after getting the correct information and should know his weaknesses through the spies."[139]

They were planted in every nook and corner of the kingdom, in shops, places of amusement, holy places, rural areas, public places, the king's assembly hall, the houses of citizens, business centres, secretariat, etc.[140] Anxious to know the whereabouts of the Pandavas, during the period of the '*ajnatavasa*', Karna suggested that spies should be asked to wonder through the kingdoms and populous provinces, prying into assemblies of the learned and delightful retreats of ascetics, in the inner apartments of places, in shrines and holy spots, in mines and diverse regions.[141]

During the war of Kurukshetra, Jayadratha came to know, with the help of spies that Arjuna had planned to kill him and they were also the spies, who informed Krishna about the Kauravas' reaction against Arjuna's plan. Bhisma says that king should know the public opinion about himself from his confidant spies.[142]

Besides the monarchy, espionage, system existed in republics also.[143] To discard the evils in republics, Bhisma orders that in secret matters, secret services should be maintained by the heads of republics.[144] These instances are sufficient to prove the existence of an efficient and active intelligence department or the system of espionage in the *Mahabharata*.

The *Sangam* age in South India spread over the early centuries of the Christian era has ample evidences to show that the institution of 'Secret Service' had come to be recognised as an important component of the state machinery.

Spies were employed in large number by the ancient Tamil kings. The spies were called 'Orrar' and espionage was called '*Vey*' or '*Orru*'. It was an elaborate system organized with considerable attention to detail. Espionage was a permanent institution in the Sangam polity and was not suspended during peace time but only became more intense in war time. Traditionally, an ancient conventional war started with preliminary 'offense' of cattle lifting.[145]

Describing the early stage of cattle lifting, it is stated that those who lifted cattle as well as those who attempted to recover the cattle employed spies. The Tamil classic '*Tirukkural*', about the date[146] of which there is divergence of opinions among scholars mention about the spies.[147] It says, "the spies were verily the eyes of the king for through his spies, the vision of the king could reach the places which his own eyes could never hope to reach." N.M Mudaliar has summarised the accounts of spies, provided by Tiruvalluvar, "Spies can disguise themselves as ascetics and holy men and should wear a suspicious appearance. The spy should bring reliable information that is hidden, and the information brought by one spy should be got checked by that of another."[148]

Spies should not know each other and if the reports of three agree, reliance could then only be placed on them.[149] The *Kural*, contains some significant verses relating to spies—

These two; the code renowned and spies,

In these let king confide as eyes,

Each day, of every subject every deed,

'Tis the king's duty to learn with speed.

His officers, his friends, and enemies,

All these who watch are his faithful spies,

Of unsuspected men and all unfearing eyes,

Those who let no secret out are worthily called spies.

As monk or devotee though every obstacle makes way.

A spy, Whate'er men shall do, must a watchful mind display.

A spy must search each hidden matter out,

And render full report, without a doubt.

Spying by spies, the things they say,

To test by other spies will pay.

One spy must not another see, contrive it so,

And have things thrice confirmed so truth you'll know.[150]

Thus, the spies were the essential servants as the king must know all that happens in his and other courts in *Sangam* Age.[151]

The virtues of organising the secret service have been greatly elaborated in the *Arthasastra*. Dependence on spies, is a striking feature of the practical character of Kautilya's Statecraft.[152]

The necessity of espionage was especially intense in the Mauryan empire that extended from the border of Persia to the south of Mysore. That is why Kautilya envisaged a well knit system of espionage.[153]

Kautilya devoted two chapters to the enumeration, definition and organization of spies. The *Arthasastra* is a mine of valuable information in this respect.[154] Spies have been classified into two broad divisions, called the '*Samsthas*' stationary spies and the '*Sancharas*', wandering spies. Several terms are used for spies and agents depending on their suitability and situational requirements. These are '*apasarpa*', '*pathika*', '*utpathika*', *upanisada*, *ubhayavetana*, *gudhpurusa*, and *cara* besides the expressions used for their various categories.[155]

In the *Arthasastra*, the espionage system became a permanent feature of the state and it was organised in the most uninhibited manner. People were overshadowed by spies, who were to wander everywhere under the covers, of actors, artisans, dancers, singers, craftsmen, players of musical instruments, snake charmers, beggars, joker, astrologers, etc.[156]

The tentacles of the department of espionage were spread far and wide. The envoys proceeding to a distant state with an important duty to discharge had, in times of apprehension of foul play from the king whom he went to visit to fall back upon the aid of the secret agents.[157] Kautilya emphasized on diplomatic espionage. That was carried out by envoys, who were '*Prakasa dutas*', (open emissaries), as well as '*caras*' who were '*gudhapurusas*' (spies).[150] In order to foil the intrigues of foreign envoys, counter envoys, spies and visible as well as invisible watchmen were appointed.[159]

A strange and inexplicable facet of the administrative history of ancient India is that while in Kautilya, we find a highly developed and complicated system of governance including an all pervasive espionage system. Very little information is available on the stages of its development in the pre Mauryan times. What Kautilya has delineated could not have been the creation of one man or one period.[160]

The historical evidences of the existence of spies along with that of Kautilya is found from the contemporary works of Greek historians and the Asokan edicts.[161]

Arrian refers to a class of officers called 'Episcopal' 'Superintendents' who spy out what goes on in country and town, and report everything to the king where the people have a king, and to the magistrates where the people are self- governed. They kept watch on the officer's functions and their report, whether it is false or true, but indeed no Indian is accused of lying. To judge from the nature of their work the superintendents of Arrian could be identified with spies.[162]

Strabo speaks of different class of '*Ephori*' or 'inspectors.' He describes the spies as inspectors. He says, "They are entrusted with the superintendence of all that is going on, and it is their duty to report privately to the king..... The best and the most faithful persons are appointed to the office of Inspectors." He further says that the city inspector employed as their courtesans, and the inspectors of the camp, the women who followed it. The employment of women of easy virtue as spies is also alluded to by the Kautilya's *Arthasastra.*[163] These inspectors were to inspect what is going to happen and to report secretly to the king.

H.C. Raychaudhry named 'overseers' to the spies of Arrian, while other historians say them 'superintendents' according to Arrian.[164]

Megasthenese found them numerous enough to be considered a special class of society, of them he says, "The sixth class consists of the 'overseers' to whom is assigned the duty of watching all that goes on and making reports secretly to the king."[165]

Some were entrusted with the inspection of the city, and others with that of the army. The former were employed as their coadjutors the courtesans of the city, and the latter the courtesans of the camp.[166]

The class of overseers may well contain administrative officials in its number, the *adhyaksas* of the *Arthasastra.*[167] The 'overseers' of Arrian and the 'inspectors' of Strabo may correspond to the *'Rashtriya'* of the Junagadh inscription or to the '*Pradeshtri*' or '*Gudhapurushas*' of the '*Arthasastra*'. '*Pradeshtri*' may be derived from *'pradis'* which means 'to point', to communicate.[168] But Romila Thapar makes a different view on the words ephoroi (strabo), episcopoi (Diodorus) or episcopal (Arrian), which are used for spies by Greek writers. She mentions that most earlier writers argue that this was a class of spies.

Spies are not described working as inspectors or overseers. Their purpose is to merge themselves within the group that they are sent to spy upon, and identify themselves completely with members of the profession which will give them the closest access to the matter which concerns them.

In the light of the text, this is an exaggerated interpretation of the terms used by the Greek writers. The literal meaning of the two terms is more that of an overseer or a superintendent rather than a spy. The fact that they were asked to make secret reports to the king does not imply that they belonged to the espionage service. The mention of these reports may be better interpreted as indicating that they had direct access to the king, and that their important reports could reach him without having to go through the many channels of bureaucratic organisation. Furthermore, it seems hardly feasible that spies could be distinguished as a class, apart from the rest of the population. The purpose of having spies is lost if their numbers and activities are widely known.

The sixth class was that of officials junior in rank to the councillors. They would thus be the same as the *adhyaksas*, the superintendents of various departments mentioned in the *Arthasastra*. These officials were responsible for the efficient working of a particular department under their charge. It would be unsual that in the course of their charge. It would be unusual that in the course of their work they would be expected to make reports either to the king or to the higher officials. The institution of spies as described in the *Arthasastra* is not similar to this sixth class.

Indeed, members of their department must had been very influential and powerful so as to attract the notice of a foreign ambassador watching their status and significance in the administration, he referred to them by mistake as a caste engaged in 'Special tasks'.

The testimony of these writers, made clear that spies were the eyes and ears of the government, monarchical as well as republican, keeping watch on everything that happened in the kingdom, and reporting their discoveries to the king or to any other suitable authority, as the case may had been. The evidences of these spies would always bear the stamp of authenticity.[170]

Besides the *Arthasastra*, and the foreign accounts, edicts of Asoka give the true portrayal of the system of espionage in Mauryan kingdom.[171]

In Pillar edicts I, IV and VII a class of officers called 'Purusas' divided broadly into high, middle and low ranks. V.A. Smith equated them with the '*Gudhapurusas*' of the *Arthasastra*.[172]

B.M. Barua took them as corresponding to the *Amatyas* of the *Arthasastra*. He kept '*Purusas*' in top ranking officers as they controlled the '*Rajukas*' who were the executive heads of districts. They were also identified with the '*Purusas*' or '*Rajpurusas*'.[173] But Dikshitar mentioned them as the 'members of subordinate services.[174]

According to Romila Thapar, in the inscription of Asoka, the word *tpulisani*, or kings agent is mentioned. They functioned in a similar way as modern public relation officers. They were acquainted with public opinion which they reported to the king, and the king in trun used them to ensure that his policy was being made known even in the remote parts of the kingdom.

Owing to the nature of their work they were not all of the same grade. Asoka mentions that they were appointed to three grades.

Those closest to the king who may have contributed to decision on policy, must have belonged to the highest grade.

Associated with the *Pulisani* were the *Pativedakas* or special reporters, also mentioned in the edicts.

Pillar Edict IV indicated that '*Purusas*' knew the mind of the king. They inspected officers to watch the loyalty of probationary officers and maintained contact with common people so as to study public reaction with regard to 'the various policies of the government.[176] For Asoka, these officers were of use as a vast propaganda machine in addition to their other functions.

Pillar Edicts I and VII also mentioned their duties consisted of the dissemination of '*Dhamma*'. The policy of *Dhamma* for instance would be explained by them to the population, and the reaction of the latter ascertained. This reaction may well have been the basis for some of the edicts. Open preachers as they were, it would remain 'inexplicable how they could remain undetected as they should, if they were to play the role of spies effectively.'

Rock Edict VI speaks of a class of royal agents called '*Prativedakas*' who were to keep the king abreast of the affairs of the people at all times.[177] Asoka allowed these spies access to him at any hour of the day. In his famous edicts .... he states, "In the past, state business was not translated or reports made at all hours of the day, I have therefore made arrangements that officials may have access to me and may report on the affairs of my people at all times and in all places—when I am eating, when I am in the harem or my inner apartments, when I am walking or engaged in religious exercises.[178]

The *'Prativedakas'* to judge from the nature of their work as well as from the etymology of the term itself, were evidently spies or informers, who were, no doubt, employed in large number to report to the king what was happening in the kingdom ?[179] The '*prativedakas*' of Asoka have been taken by

Louis Renou to indicate 'agents of the court' sent on confidential mission. They were identified with '*Pravritiyaprta*' of the Jain literature who reported to the king on the actions of Mahavira.[180]

Both the Pulisani and the Pativedakas must also have served as a link between the central administration and provincial administration. Romila Thapar states, that the... Pativedakas may be compared with the institution of spies mentioned in the *Arthasastra* (cara and gudha Purusa). The Asoka organization does not appear to be as complex as that envisaged by Kautilya. In the work of the latter the espionage system is of the utmost importance. Spies are sent all over the country disguised as ordinary citizens in every walk of life. Even ministers were watched by spies. Asoka on the other hand admits in the edicts that he employs both agents and reporters. They may have been travelling inspectors (those of high grade), who were known to the population and the administration, who went from place to place examining the governmental organization and making reports to the king.

Asoka speaks of the *Pradesikas* who have been doubtfully identified with the *Pradesikas*. They have been sometimes been equated with spies or reporters on the ground that the word '*Pradesa*' occurs in the *Arthasastra* in the sense of 'report'. But D.K. Ganguly makes difference between them, saying as, '*Pradesikas*' were the persons who went out on tour every five years, as stated in Rock Edit III, could hardly been spies who, while on duty, had to move regularly from place to place. In a Pallava inscription word '*Sanjar-antaka*' is used for spy.[181]

Such type of officials or secret agents are not unknown to the administration of other empires. The Achaemenids sent an officer every year to make a careful inspection of each province. He was known as the king's eye or the king's ear and the king's massenger. His work was an additional control on the part of the king over the administration. Charlemange had evolved a similar but even more efficient system. Two officials known as the Missi were sent each year to tour the country. One was secular representative and the other was the representative of the Church. They usually travelled in pairs, thus acting as a check on each other's work. They had the power to dismiss lower officials if any were found to be inefficient. They insisted on the king's decrees being read out at public meetings, and wherever necessary these decrees were translated from Latin to the vernacular. It is quite probable that the *pulisani* were also expected to read aloud the edicts of Asoka whenever opportunity demanded. Of the two Missi the clerical representative investigated the work of monks and nuns, and the secular official examined the judicial and financial records of the administration. In the case of Charlemagne, the *Missi* acted as a check on the growing feudal power of local lords. In the case of Asoka the king's agents curbed the ambition of provincial rulers.

So alike Maurya's espionage system was prevailing in other countries. Charlemange and Asoka's mode of spying had similarity in some matters.

Julius Caesar also appointed the secret agents. They were called 'Explotrates'. Alexander used a different method of spying to know the opinion of soldiers in the army. He came to know about the traitor, who was exciting the soldiers against him, through mail system.[182]

In later periods secret agents were employed to verify reports received by the king from diverse sources. King Yasaskara of Kashmira used secret agent to counter check reports that were coming to him. They were known as *Cakrika*, *Pisuna* and *Pumscalaka*.[183]

In Kushana period also, the states continued to make extensive use of the secret services. Spies were appointed in districts to keep an eye on the village officials who used to collect the taxes from the people.[184]

During the Age of 'Puranas' there was an efficient spy system. The king could see everything in his kingdom through spies.[185] "A blind prince may see through the eyes of his spies, but an ignorant king is always in the dark", wrote the writer of *Garudapurana.* In this Purana, the king is called blind. As the man without knowledge is ignorant or blind, the king without spies is also blind. But a king can see through his 'charas'. While an ignorant man is unable to see the reality.[186] Even enemy kings were said to move about in disguise to know the affairs in other states and so a king was to be particular in choosing a minister. In *Agnipurana,* the head of the spies is called 'charadhyaksha'. These Charadhyaksha never disclose their secrets.[187] In *Matasya Purana* (215, 9) head of spies is called 'Janadyaksha' and in Vishnu Dharmottar Purana he is called 'Ganadhyaksha' (II, 25, 9). The Agnipurana compares the king with the Vayu. As Vayu (air) is present every where, king is also omnipresent through his 'charas'.[188] In the '*Vishnu Dharmottar Purana*', the king is called 'Charchakshu[189] and he is said to appoint more than one spies for a single job, who are unknown to one another. (24, 66-67).

Manusamhita describes the *Rajdharma* in seventh chapter. Here many references of spies are found. Manu has used word '*Maya*' for the spy.[190]

To look over the activities of spies, is one of the duties of a king. Manu speaks of as many as five categories of spies and called them '*Panchvarga*'. But unfortunately does not specify them.[191]

Kalluka gives the name of these '*Panchvarga*' in his commentary. They were the *Kapalikas*, *Udasthias*, *Grhapaties*, *Vaidehikas* and *Tapasas.* These divisions of spies would compare well with the five divisions of the '*samstha*' group of spies, as enumerated by Kautilya in the *Arthasastra*. But Manu is silent on the '*sancaras*'.[192]

Manusamhita mentions that king should personally visit the different parts of the state and keep a close watch on his administrative services with the aid of espionage services.[193] It does not mention how spies were appointed? What their caste was? Whether they spied on the kings' ministers as well, and the guises they adopted to mislead people while they were on duty.[194] Manu speaks about the '*Vayuvarta*' of king. That means like the air, king is also present everywhere through his spies.[195]

Yajnavalkya samhita also mentions the spies in thirteenth chapter '*Rajdharma Prakaran*' dealing with the daily activities of king. It is the duty of king to have contact with the spies everyday.[196] Just after the war, and later on after the evening worship, he should be with them to listen to their secret talks.[197] Yajnavalkya says that the king is to protect his subjects against scribes, check on officers with spies, honour the honest, punish the corrupt.[198]

It appears from Yajnavallekya's work that to keep the king well informed of the doings of his feudatories and other rulers and to watch his officers in order that they might be rewarded or punished as they deserved. A detailed account of spies is to be met with in the '*Duta-Cara-Vikalpa-Prakaranam*' section of the contemporary Sanskrit work the *Kamandakiya Nitisara*. Like Kautilya he has divided spies into two broad heads, the Samsthas and the Sancaras.

The *Sukraniti* throws light enough on spying, and its importance. A king should know about the officers, soldiers, relatives, enemies and women of palaces through the spies.[199] The '*Gudhachara*' should be worthy and truthful.[200]

The Sanskrit Dramas and '*Kavyas*' emphatically advocate that the institution of espionage was well developed and was constituted and nurtured with care.

The *Mudraraskasa* of Vishakadatta presents a well knitted espionage system. Political conspiracies, dissensions, tactics used during the foundation of Mauryan empire and destruction of Nanda dynasty, are perfectly mentioned in it. It describes the functions, various covers, techniques of different types of spies. This drama is a game of spies.[201] In *Mudrarakshasa*, Chanakya appoints spies in the capital to get the information of internal and external departments.[202] It bears witness to the important role that spies used to play by bringing about discord among enemies and finding out what going on in the kingdoms.

The *Mrichhakatika* of Sudraka speaks of spies in seventh and ninth chapters, as frequently thoroughfares for scooping news to be reported to king. In the Ninth Chapter Charudutta presents a description of 'Nyaya Mandap' that here the ministers are like water, diplomats are like waves and spies are like crocodile and.

The writings of Kalidasa would bear witness to the prevalence of the system of espionage in India during the imperial Guptas. The system of spies was an essential part of government machinery as it is even in the present times.[204]

All over the kingdom was maintained a regular network of spies who were called upon to bring everything to the kings notice. Such spies were asked to keep watch not only on hostile elements but also on friends. In Raghuvansa, there is a king 'Atithi.' He had perfect knowledge of politics and diplomacy. He had spreed the net of spies in his kingdom the every minute events thropugh his spies.[205] He had appointed spies on his officers and enemies, they were also unknown to one another and the king was always a wake while sleeping.

Kalidasa agree that spies enjoyed the rare privilege of being granted audience by the supreme head of the state.

The testimony of *Kadambari*, by Bana and the *Sisupalavadham* of Magha give knowledge of spies during post Gupta period. *Kadambari* speaks of the employment of many thousands of spies by a minister for keeping himself alive to every whisper of tributary kings in the kingdom, as though uttered in his own palace. Bhasa discusses about the spies in his drama '*Pratigyayogandharayan*'. Vatsaraj was helped by a spy to get the Vasavadutta.[206]

In the *Kumarsambhava* there are references of female spies. A female spies tells that Parvati is serving the Mahadeva on the Himalayas.[207]

The *Sisupalvadha* of Magha speaks of the spies as the eyes of the king. Famous Nitimaker Samdev Suri, also mentions the spies, as they must be appointed to know the activities of their country and other countries and they should be *Sati*sfied, active, truthful, and thoughtful.[208]

The *Panchatantra* discusses the very important role played by spies. There is a passage in the *Panchatantra* in which it is stated that cow recognises things by smelling them, scholars see through Vedas and the king knows all matters through his spies.[209]

The absence of notices on secret agents in epigraphs can perhaps be explained by the fact that the Indian epigraphs even till the medieval phase are almost silent on the intimate aspects of the security of the state. That's why, having an institutional form of secret service department, the officers have generally been left out. But all the literary evidences indicate not only that spies existed, but that they were numerous and important part of the government.

Espionage ranked among the main instrument of Statecraft in ancient India and the '*pranidhi*' or spy was regarded by experts on polity as all indispensable adjunct to sound government.

Throughout history the espionage system was through and ruthless in its operation, and worked with a remarkable efficiency.[210]

Thus, the art of spying was handed down from the past. Spyism euphemistically considered as the second oldest profession of the world finds mention in the Vedas, the most ancient of the human texts.[211]

References

1. A.S. Altekar, State and Government in Ancient India, Delhi, 1977, p. 1.
2. B.C. Gokhale, Ancient Indian History and Culture, Popular Prakashan, 1995, p. 93.
3. *Ibid.,* pp. 98-99.
4. Artha. 1.12.1, 2.1.26.
5. R.C. Majumdar, The Age of Imperial Unity, B.V.B. Bombay, 1953, p. 311.
6. A.S. Altekar, *op. cit.,* p. 37.
7. R.C. Majumdar, The Vedic Age, Vol. I, Bombay, 1965, p. 355.
8. R.C. Majumdar, The Vedic Age, Vol. I, Chapter XVII, p. 355.
9. R.C. Majumdar, The Age of Imperial Unity, Vol. II, Chapter I, Bombay, p. 3.
10. T.B. Mukherjee, Inter State Relations in Ancient India, Meerut, 1967, p. 11.
11. S.C. Raychaudhary, History of India, Delhi, 1995, p. 52.
12. R.C. Majumdar, Vedic Age, Vol. I, Chapter XXI, Bombay, p. 436.

13. S.P. Sharma, History of Ancient India (from Earliest Times to 1000 A.D.) New Delhi, 1996, p. 51.
14. *Ibid.*, p. 52.
15. B.P. Saha and K.S. Behera, Ancient History of India, New Delhi, 1988, p. 71.
16. D.K. Ganguly, "Aspects of Ancient Indian Administration", New Delhi, 1979, p. 282.
17. T.B. Mukherjee, *op. cit.*, p. 50.
18. *Mahabharata, Shantiparvan*, X, 6-7.
19. S.C. Raychaudhry, *op. cit.*, p. 91.
20. D.K. Ganguly, *op. cit.*, p. 289.
21. द्वित छिद्र द र्गी नपतिर्नित्यमेव प्र ास्यते।
    त्रिवर्गेविदितार्थ च युक्तचारोपधि चय चः।।
    Santiparvan, 57/7
22. S.P. Sharma, *op. cit.*, p. 85.
23. G.M. Levin Bongard, Mauryan India, New Delhi, 1985, p. 1.
24. K. Nilakanta Shastri, Age of the Nandas and Mauryas, Bihar, 1967, p. 171.
25. V.A. Smith, Oxford History of India, Oxford, 1970, p. 100.
26. R.C. Majumdar, *op. cit.*, p. 235.
27. Michael Edwards, Everyday Life in Ancient India, London, 1969, pp. 43-44.
28. R.C. Majumdar, ed., The Age of Imperial Unity, Bombay, 1980, Vol. II, Chapter XVII, p. 312.
29. H.S. Bhatia, Political and Legal and Military History of India, Delhi, 1984, Vol. II, p. 77.
30. I.W. Mabbet, Truth, Myth and Politics in Ancient India, New Delhi, 1971.
31. Edward Michael, 'Everyday Life in Early India', London, 1967, p. 47.

32. H.S. Bhatia, Political, Legal and Military History of India, New Delhi, 1984, Vol. II, p. 14.
33. R.C. Majumdar, ed., The Age of Imperial Unity, Bombay, 1980, Vol. II, p. 301.
34. R.C. Majumdar, *op. cit.*, pp. 309-310.
35. S.R. Goyal, Kautilya and Megasthenese, Meerut, 1985, pp. 54-55.
36. I.W. Mabbett, *op. cit.*, p. 10.
37. N.Q. Pankaj, State and Religion in Ancient India, Allahabad, 1983, p. 101.
38. A.K. Sinha, Provincial Administration in Ancient India, Patna, 1981, p. 392.
39. K.A. Nilakanta Shastri, The History of South India, Madras, 1966, p. 92.
40. N.Q. Pankaj, *op. cit.*, p. 101.
41. V.A. Smith, The Oxford Students History of India, London, 1954, p. 59.
42. भरद्वाजाः गुड़ा कताः ौ ि रियः ।

    Asvalayana Srautasutra XII, 13, 5.
43. R.C. Majumdar, *op. cit.*, p. 98.
44. Tarachanda, 'Short History of Indian People from Earlier Time is the Present day, London, 1953, p. 64.
45. H.C. Ray Chaudhry, *op. cit.*, p. 454.
46. K.A. Nilkanta Shastri, *op. cit.*, p. 92.
47. Baldev Kumar, The Early Kusanas, Sterling Pub. Ltd., Delhi, 1973, p. 106.
48. R.C. Majumdar, ed. The Classical Age, Bombay, 1970, Vol. III, p. 103.
49. R.C. Majumdar, Ancient India, Delhi, 1974, p. 235.
50. V.R.R. Dikshitar, The Gupta Polity, Madras, 1952, p. 112.

51. अविनीत कुमार हि कुलमा ु विव यति।
विनीत मौरस पत्र यौव राज्यडभिषचयेत।।
Kamandaka Nitisara, VII, 5, 6.

52. R.K. Mookerji, The Gupta Empire, Delhi, 1969, p. 150.

53. A.S. Altekar, State and Government in Ancient India, Delhi, 1977, p. 340.

54. V.R.R. Dikshitar, *op. cit.*, pp. 114-115.

55. A.S. Altekar, *op. cit.*, p. 334.

56. V.A. Smith, *op. cit.*, p. 100.

57. V.A. Smith, *op. cit.*, p. 100.

58. R.C. Majumdar, Ed. *op. cit.*, p. XII.

59. H.C. Raychaudhary, *op. cit.*, p. 53.

60. ब्रह्णोडस्य मुखमासीत बाहू राजन्य कतः।
उरू तदस्य पदवै य पदभ्याम ुद्रो अजायते।।
Rigveda, X Mandla.

61. R.C. Majumdar, Vedic Age, Vol. I, Chap. XIX, p. 390.

62. कारूरहं ततोभि पगुपल प्रक्षिणी नना। *Rigveda.*

63. S.C. Ray Chaudhary, *op. cit.*, p. 55.

64. S.C. Raychaudhary, *op. cit.*, p. 43.

65. R.K. Mookerji, Chandra Gupta Maurya and His Times, Delhi, 1993.

66. S.R. Goyal, Kautilya and Megasthenesee, Meerut, 1985, p. 63.

67. R. Sharmasastri, Kautilya's *Arthasastra*, Mysore, 1967, p. 189.

68. S.P. Sharma, *op. cit.*, pp. 208-209.

69. R.C. Majumdar, The Age of Imperial Unity, Vol. II, Chapter XXI, p. 549.

70. Tara Chand, Short History of Indian People from Earlier Times to the Present Day, London, 1953, p. 69.

71. R.G. Bandarkar, A Peep into the Early History of Mauryan Dynasty to the Fall of the Imperial Gupta Dynasty, BC 322-500 AD, J.B. BRAS, Vol. XX, Bombay, 1902, pp. 356-408.
72. R.K. Mookerji, The Gupta Empire, Delhi, 1973, p. 147.
73. चतुष्पदी हि निः श्रेणीब्रहाब्येष्ठा प्रतिष्ठितः।
    एतां आरूहा निः श्रेणीम ब्रहमलोके महीयतं।।
74. Artha., Book, I, Ch. III.
75. R.C. Majumdar, Age of Imperial Unity, p. 553.
76. M.L. Bhagi, Ancient Indian Culture and thought. The Indian Pub., Ambala. p. 32.
77. S.C. Ray Chaudhary, *op. cit.*, p. 55.
78. S.P. Sharma, History of Ancient India, New Delhi, 1996, p. 91.
79. (1) कन्यादानं कन्यामूलंकत्य ब्राह्मो विवाहः (2) सहधर्मचर्या प्राजापत्यः (3) गोमिथुना दानादार्षः (4) अन्तर्वेधामत्विजे दानाद्वैवः (5) मिथः समवायाडान्धर्वः (6) उुल्कादानासुर (7) प्सद्वादानाद्रारक्षाः (8) उुप्तादानातं पै ााचः।

    Kautilya's *Arthasastra*, III-Chapter 11.
80. M.L. Vidyarathi, India's Culture Through the Ages, Meerut, 1970, p. 100.
    V.N. Hari Rao, History of India upto 1526 AD, Madurai, 1982, p. 66.
81. K.K. Murty, Social and Cultural life in Ancient India, 1982, p. 81.
82. Ramayana, Uttarakanda-11-53.
83. Mbh. Adiparvan, 95.65.
84. Encyclopaedia, Britanica, USA, 1957, Vol. 21, pp. 624-25.
85. R.C. Majumdar, Vedic Age, Bombay, 1965.
86. M.L. Baght, *op. cit.*, p. 41.
    R.C. Majumdar, The Age of Imperial Unity, Bombay, 1980, Vol. II, pp. 562-565.

87. R.K. Mookerji, Hindu Civilization. B.V.B. Bombay, 1977, p. 74.
88. V.N. Hari Rao, *op. cit.*, pp. 66-67.
89. *Ibid.*, p. 569.
90. K.A. Nilkanta Shastri, *op. cit.*, p. 92.
91. Baldev Singh, The Early Kushanas, New Delhi, 1973, p. 220.
92. Om Prakash, Religion and Society in Ancient India, Delhi, 1985, p. 158.
93. S.C. Raychaudhry, *op. cit.*, pp. 57-94.
94. K.M. Panikkar, A Survey of Indian History, Bombay, 1963, pp. 39-40.
95. Manu, IV, 205-206, IX 18, XI 36.
96. Michael Edwards, Everyday Life of 1969, p. 30.
97. R.C. Majumdar, Age of Imperial Unity, p. 570.
98. Macrindle, Megastenese, p.
99. A.K. Majumdar, Concise History of Ancient India. Munshiram Manoharlal Pub., New Delhi, 1983, pp. 135-136.
100. K.K. Murthy, Social and Cultural Life in Ancient India. Sundeep Pub., Delhi, 1982, pp. 68-71.
101. R.C. Majumdar, The Age of Imperial Unity, 1980, Vol. II, p. 579.
102. R.N. Dandekar, The Age of the Guptas and other Essays, Delhi, 1982, p. 67.
103. J.W. Spellman, Political Theory of Ancient India, Oxford, 1984, p. 137.
104. T. B. Mookerji, Interstate Relations in Ancient India, Meerut, 1967, p. 73.
105. P. Saran, Ancient Indian Political Thought and Institution, Delhi, 1983, pp. 537-538.
106. P.L. Bhargava, India in Vedic Age, Ed., II, Lucknow, p. 261.

107. Dr. B.K. Majumdar, Role of Secret Services in Ancient India, I.H.C., Vol. 19, p. 119.

108. Major S. K. Bhakri, Indian Warfare, New Delhi, 1981, p. 86.

109. Rigveda, I, 25, 13, Trans. Maharishi Dayanand Saraswati, Sarvadeshik Arya Pratinidhi Sabha, New Delhi, 1972.

110. उतेयं भूमिर्वकणस्य राज्ञउतासौ द्यौवंहती दूरे अन्त।
उतो समुद्रौ वरूणस्य कुक्षी उतास्मिन्नल्प उदके निलीनः।।3।।
Atharvaveda, 4.16.3, Trans. Maharishi Dayanand Saraswati, Sarvadesh Arya Pratinidhi Sabha, New Delhi, 1972.

111. Raghvendra Vajpeyi, 'Varuna Hymns' and the Origin of Monarchy, I.H.C., Vol. 33, 1972, p. 51.

112. सर्व तद्राजा वरूणों वि चष्टे यदन्तरा रोदसी यत्परस्तात।
संख्याता अस्य निमिषो जनानामक्षानिव स्वध्नी नि मिनोति तानि।5।
Atharvaveda, 4.16.5.

113. Major S.K. Bhakri, *op. cit.*, p. 86.

114. T.B. Mookerji, *op. cit.*, p. 25.

115. *Atharvaveda*, V, 6, 3; *op. cit.*

116. दिव स्प ाः चरन्तीदमस्य सहस्त्रक्षा अति प यन्ति भूमिम।।4
Ibid., IV, 16, 4.

117. D.K. Ganguly, Aspects of Ancient Indian Administration, New Delhi, 1979, p. 282.

118. Macdonell, Vedic Mythology, pp. 23-24.

119. सहस्रधारे वितते पवित्र आ वाचं पुनन्तिकवयो मनीषिणः
रूद्रास एषमिषिरासो अद्रहः स्प ाः स्वच्चः सुद ाे नचक्षतः।।
Rigveda, 9, 73, 7.

120. S.D. Trivedi, Secret Services in Ancient India, New Delhi, 1984, p. 17.

121. V.S. Agrawal, India As Known to Panini, 195-31, p. 415.

122. स्वपन्नपि हि जागति चारचक्षुर्महीपति।
चार चक्षु नरेन्द्रस्तु सम्पतेत तेन भूयसा।
अनेनासम्पतन मार्गात पतत्यन्धाः समेअपि हि।।
M.N. Dutta, *Kanandaka Nitisara*, 12/29/30.

123. S.L. Roy, Diplomacy in Ancient India, Charu Pub., Calcutta, p. 185.

124. D.K. Ganguly, *op. cit.*, p. 283.

125. Brhatkalpa Bharya, Pithika, Sanghadasagani, 1933-38, pp. 378-383.

126. T.B. Mookerji, *op. cit.*

127. Major S.K. Bhakri, *op. cit.*, p. 86.

128. काच्चिदष्टा द ान्येषु स्वपक्षे द ा पंचन
तिभिस्त्रिभिरवि ज्ञातै वैत्सि तीर्थनिचारणेः।।100/36
Ramayana, *Ayodhyakand*, trans. Pandey Pandit Ramnarayana Dutta Geeta Press, Gorakhpur.

129. Manorama Jauhari, Politics and Ethics in Ancient India: A Study Based on the Mahabharata, Varanasi, 1968, p. 222.

130. D.K. Ganguly, *op. cit.*, p. 239.

131. चारेण विदितः ात्रुः पण्डिततैर्वसुधाधियैः।
युद्वे स्वत्येन यत्नेन समासादय निरस्यते।।
Yudhakanda, 29/21.

132. Upendra Thakur, Some Aspects of Ancient Indian History and Culture, Abhinav Pub., New Delhi, 1974, p. 174.

133. *The Ramayana*, Ayodhyakanda, 100/36.

134. *Ibid.,* 35, 5.
अयुक्तचारं दुद िमस्वाधीनं नराधिपम।
बर्जयन्ति नरा दरान्नदीपंकमिव भिवाः।।

135. अयुक्तचारं मन्थेत्वां म्राकतैः सचिवैयुर्तः।
स्वजनं च जनस्थानं निहतं नावबुध्यसे।।
Ibid., 33, 11

136. Lallanji Singh, *Ramayankalein Yudhkala*, p. 154.

137. रथा दागा ह्रया चेव पादाता चैव पाण्डव।
विष्टिनवि चरा चैव देाािका इति चाष्टमम।।
Santiparvan, 59,41.

138. D.K. Ganguly, *op. cit.*, p. 290.

139. अप्रमत्तां भवेद राजा छिद्रद र्ाी परात्मनोंः।
Mahabharata, *Santiparvam*, 91, 55.

140. D.K. Ganguly, *op. cit.*, p. 290.

141. *Mahabharata, Virataparvan*, 25, 5-22; 26,8-12. trans. Kesari Mohan Ganguly, Delhi, 1981.

142. *Santiparvan*, 89, 15-16.

143. Vimla Chaudhary, 'Prachin Bharat Mai Gupt Cara Seva', Y.K. Pub., Agra, 1993, p. 42.

144. मंत्र गुप्तिः प्रधानेषु चार चामित्रकर्षन।
न गवाः कत्स्न ाो कत्स्न ाो मंत्रं श्रीतुमर्हन्ति भारत।।
Santiparvam, 107/24.

145. N. Subrahmaniam, Sangam Polity, Bombay, 1966, p. 100.

146. The date of Tiruvalluvar has not yet been finally settled. According to M.R. Ayangar, he flourished in the fifth century A.D., while in the opinion of V.R.R. Dikshitar, he was not far century. A.D. Srinivasa Ayyangar is of opinion that Tiruvalluvar cannot be assigned to any date earlier than the sixth century A.D., p. 100.

147. D.K. Ganguly, *op. cit.*, p. 292.

148. *Ibid.*, pp. 292-293.

149. *Kural*, Verse 589, Quoted from S.L. Roy, *op. cit.*, p. 198.

150. J.W. Spellman, *op. cit.*, p. 138.

151. N. Subrahmaniam, *op. cit.*, p. 101.

152. N.N. Law, I.H.Q, Vol. 36, 1960, p. 238.

153. Parmatma Saran, Ancient Indian Political Thought and Institution, Meerut, 1983, pp. 537-38.

154. Dr. Bimal Kanti Majumdar, Role of the Secret Services in Ancient India, I.H.C., Vol. 19, 1956, p. 119.

155. N.N. Law, Machinery of Administration in the Kautilya, I.H.Q., Dec. 1929, pp. 625-26.

156. Indra, Ideologies of War and Peace in Ancient India, Hoshiarpur, 1957, p. 93.

157. N.N. Law, *op. cit.*, p. 32.

158. S.L. Roy, *op. cit.*, p. 191.

159. *Arthashastra*, I. 16, trans. Udayveer Shastri, Delhi, 1970.

160. S.D. Trivedi, *op. cit.*, p. 15.

161. S.L. Roy, *op. cit.*, p. 185.

162. D.K. Ganguly, *op. cit.*, p. 283.

163. H.C. Raychaudhry, Political History of Ancient India, Oxford University Press, Delhi, 1996, pp. 258-59.

164. H.C. Raychaudhry, *op. cit.*, p. 259.

165. J.W. Mecrindle, Ancient India as described by Megasthenese and Arrian, Bombay, 1877, pp 85-86.

166. J.W. Spellman, *op. cit.*, p. 137.

167. *Ibid.,* pp. 137-138.

168. H.C. Raychaudhry, *op. cit.*, p. 259.

169. Romila Thapar, pp. 111-112

170. D.K. Ganguly, *op. cit.*, p. 284.

171. *Ibid.,* p. 288.

172. D.K. Ganguly, *op. cit.*, p. 288.

173. H.C. Raychaudhry, *op. cit.*, p. 259.

174. V.R.R. Dikshitar, Mauryan Polity, New Delhi, 1993, p. 223.

175. P.E. Bloch, Les Inscription d' Asoka, VII, p. 164.

176. K.A. Nilakanta Shastri, The Chols, Madras, 1955, p. 227.

177. Rock Edict IV.

178. J. Auboyer, Daily Life in Ancient India, Asia Publication House, 1961, p. 41.

179. D.K. Ganguly, *op. cit.*, p. 289.

180. Louis Renou, The Civili*Sati*on in Ancient India, Calcutta, 1959, p. 103.

181. R.K. Chaudhary, *Prachin Bharat Ka Rajnitik Sanskritic Itihas*, Patna, 1970, p. 528.

182. Vimala Chaudhary, *op. cit.*, p. 3.

183. Major S.K. Bhakri, *op. cit.*, p. 88.

184. Bhaskar Chattopadhyay, Kushana State and Indian Society, Calcutta, 1975, p. 122.

185. दर्पो विरोधो नियतं युद्धसाम चसंग्रहः।
परिरवाकमरणचैव चारेण राज्यद निम्।।
Brihaddharm Purana, Uttara Kanda, iii, 2.

186. अन्धो हि राजा भवति यस्तु ाास्त्रविवर्जितः।
अन्धः प यति चारेण ाास्त्रहीनो प यति।।
Garudapurana, Chap. 111, 19.

187. अन्तः पुरचराध्यक्षो वैर भूतौन्निर्राकतैः।
Agnipurana, 221, 3.

188. जगमयाप्नोति वै चारेस्तो राजा समीरणः।
दोषनिम्तह कारित्वाद्राजा दैव स्वतः प्रभुः।।
Agnipurana, 226, 18.

189. राजानः चार चक्षुः।
Vishnu Dharmottar Purana II, 24, 63.

190. मायां चारद्धारेण जानीयात।
Manu Samhita, VIII/104, G.N. Jha, Calcutta, 1922-29.

191. दूत संप्रेषणं चैव.....प्रणिधीनां च चेष्टितम VII/153.
कत्सनं चाष्टविधं कर्म पंचवर्गं च तत्वतः।।154

192. Jai Kumar Jain, *Manu Smriti*, Translation of Kallucabhatta Commentary, *Mavay Muktavali*, p. 307.

193. स तानु परिकामेत सर्वानेव सदा स्वयम।
तेषाम कत परिणयेत सभ्यग्राष्ट्रेषु तच्चरम।।
Manu Samhita, 122/7.

194. Motiwani Kewal, *Manu Dharam Sastra*, Madras, 1958, p. 149.

195. प्रवि च सर्वभूतानि यथा चरति मारूतः।
तथा चारैः प्रवेष्टव्य ब्रतमेतषि मारूतम।।
Manu Samhita, 9/306.

196. Shri Narayan Mishra, *Yajnavalkya Samhita*, The Kashi Sanskrit series.

197. प येच्चरांस्ततो दूतान्प्रषेयेन्मंत्रिसंगतः।। 326/13
संधयामुपास्य ऋणुचाच्चाराणां गुढ़र्भाषितम।।330/13
Yajnavalkya Samhita, *Acharadhaya Rajdharama Prakaran.*

198. I.W. Mabbett, Truth, Myth and Politics in Ancient India, Thomson Press (India) Limited, New Delhi, 1971, p. 50.

199. Vimala Chaudhary, *op. cit.*, p. 85.

200. सावधामनः सिद्धरात्रस्त्रः सल्लिखेच्यतत।
असत्यवादिनम गूढचरं नैव च ान्ति च।।
Sukraniti, Ch.. 1/337.

201. J.C. Mishra, *Mudraraksasa*, Varanasi, 1972.

202. प्रयुक्त च स्वपश्र पर पश्रयोरनुरक्ता.....
बहुविधदे ावेषभाषा चार संचार वेदिनो नानाव्यंज्जनाः प्रविधायः।
Mudrarakshasa, I Part, I Episode.

203. Vimala Chaudhary, *op. cit.*, p. 116.

204. S.A. Sabnis, Kalidasa : His Style and His Times, Bombay, 1966, p. 220.

205.A. न तस्य मण्डले राज्ञो न्यस्तप्रणिचिः दीधितेः।
अदष्टम भवत्किाचेद्धयभ्रस्येव विवस्वतः।।
Raghuvamsa Sarga, 17, 48.

205.B. परेषु स्वेषु च क्षिप्तैरविमातपरस्परैः।
सो पसपैर्जजागार यथाकालै स्वपन्नपि।।
Ibid., 51.

206. Nemichandra Shastri, Mahakavi Bhasa, U.P. Hindi Academy, p. 553.

207. गुरोर्नियोगच्च नगेन्द्र कन्यास्थाणुं तपस्यन्तभधिल्य कायाम्।
अन्वास्त इत्यप्यरसां मुखेम्यः श्रुतं मया मत्प्रणिधिः सवर्गः।।(3, 17).

208. अलौत्यममान्धः षित्वमर्म्यूहकत्वं चारगुणाः।
Ram. C. Malvia, *Somedavsuri*, *Yashastichampu*, *Varanasi*, 1972.

209. Apurka Chandra Barthakuria, India in the Age of the Panchatantra, Punthi Pustak, Calcutta, 1992.

210. Benjamin Walker, Hindu World, Vol. 1, George Allen & Unwin Ltd., Puskin House, Museum Street, 1968, p. 342.

211. N.N. Law, I.H.Q., 1990, N. Delhi, pp. 31-32.

2

Organization of Spies

Thought does not originate in a vacuum and social and political thinking is intimately related to social and political milieu in which it originates. Every thought moreover, bears the stamp of the ethos of the people who give birth to it.[1] Idea of the establishment of an espionage organisation is the result of the contemporary political and social condition. The charge of a pastoral society constantly undergoing violent social and political agitations. With the growth of tribal states and with the insistence on independence of the states was felt the necessity of agents for knowing the activities of enemy states.[2]

In such surroundings secret agents in the form of '*Spasas*' originate. But in the absence of political stability, it could not get a developed form. Varunas spies, of frequent occurrence in the *Rigveda* and elsewhere',[3] testify to the early organisation of state intelligence.

The necessity of espionage was especially intense in the Mauryan empire. Fear of external aggression and internal contentions determined the imperative need for a strong and active espionage in an institutional form.

All modern states have their organisations of secret services and ancient India is no exception.[4] Espionage is supposed to be as old as the *Vedas*. The Epic, the Puranas, the *Arthasastra*, the *Dharmasastra* and other literature of country refer again and again to spies.[5]

Specialists in social sciences and legal experts have come to the conclusion that in all early societies the organisation of espionage was well developed. The department occupied a very important place in the administration of a state in ancient India with its various organs.

Categories of Spies

The Epics, The *Arthasastra*, *Smritis* and other literary works categorise the spies in various ways. Although the *Arthasastra* presents a perfect classification, the *Ramayana* also gives categories of spies viz. Civil spy and Military spy.

In *Uttarakanda*, the spies who gave the information of public criticism of Sita to Rama, were the *civil spies*.[6]

Sugriva sent Hanumana as a civil spy to inquire the feelings of Rama and Laxamana in guise of ascetics.[7] The '*Civil spies*' were also called '*Caras*' because they collected the news of interstate.

The responsibility of *Military spies* was very hard and challengeable. King and Senapatis were depend on them to know the force of enemy.[8] Spies were usefully employed to ascertain the nature of a hostile country and fortified places as well. This was treated as military espionage.[9]

There are mention of three spies for having a look over eighteen *tirthas*. They were unaware of one another.[10]

Regarding their types, the '*Mahabharata*' refers to the '*Vahischarah*' or those who went to other states to gather information.[11]

Antascharah, indicates that they were something different type of spies who worked inside the state and tried to find out the enemies agents or the people's attitude towards the king.[12]

The *Mahabharata* mentions that *Pashandah Tapasah*, fools, deaf and blinds also worked as spies.[13] They carried their business in disguise. The Vavahara Bhasya also throws light on various types of spies. In order to protect the realm from internal disturbances and the invasion of the enemy, a minister is said to have employed a number of spies such as *Sucakas*, *anusucakas*, *pratisucatas* and *sarvasucabas*, who supplied him all sorts of secret information. The *Sucakas* made friendship with the harem officers and found out internal secrets of the harem; the *anusucakas* were employed to detect the foreign spies in the city; the *pratisucakas* sat on the city gate apparently doing some menial work; the *sarvasucakas* gathered information through their assistants and reported it to the amatya. These spies were both males and females and they worked in frontier territories, their own country, cities and the royal harem.[14]

Kautilya refers to many other types and classes of spies, but the epic does not furnish details regarding this.[15]

The combined testimony of the classical authors and Kautilya proves beyond doubt the prevalence of the institution of spies in the Mauryan kingdom.

Kautilya has devoted four chapters as well as a large number of isolated passages, here and there, to a gruesome description of spies who have been classified into two broad divisions, called the '*Samsthas*' stationary spies and the '*Sancaras*' wandering spies.[16]

The agents belonging to '*Samstha*' were stationed in the establishment financed by the state, where as the '*Sancaras*' moved from place to place depending on professional requirements.[17]

The spy masters of the two categories headed their own cadre of agents and controlled their operations. The member of one group were not aware of the existence of the other.[18]

The secret agents of *'samsthas'* has again been subdivided into five heads.[19] It has rightly been suggested that this group of *'Samstha'* consisted of those belonging to one or the other Brahmanical stage of life as well as the hetroden orders of the monks.[20]

The *Kapatikas-Chhatra*, fraudulent disciples. The word *'Kapatikah'* is derived from *'Kapata'*, deceit (*Kapatena Caratiti*). They were capable of guessing the mind of others (*Para marmajnah*) and reported to the king and the Mantri to whom they were responsible, whatever evils they noticed in any persons.[21] They were rewarded with honour and monetary grants.

The *Udasthitas*—apostate monks. They were degraded ascetics, but were still endowed with intelligence and honesty.[22] Equipped with plenty of money and assistance, they should get work done in a place assigned to them, for the practice of some occupation. And from the profits of work, the king should provide all wondering monks with food, clothing and residence and to those, who seek a permanent livelihood, he should secretly propose. 'In this way grab, you should work in the interest of the king and present yourself here at the time of meals and payment'. And all wandering monks should make similar secret proposals to (monk in) their respective orders.[23]

The Grhapatikavyanjanas—house-holder spies. They were agriculturists with depleted resources and without any ostensible means of livelihood. They had fallen from their profession but were possessed of foresightedness and pure character. On being rehabilitated by the state, they ran a network of secret agents. They had to carry on their duty as exactly as the '*Udasthitas*' at a place assigned to them for agricultural work.[24]

Vaidehakavyanjanas—Merchant spies, they were traders, fallen from their profession, but possessed of intelligence and honesty.[25] They were rehabilitated and supported by the state. They handled scores of spies from funds provided by the state; and collected necessary information for the king with the help of fellow merchants, while carrying on the manufacture of merchandise on lands, allotted to them.[26]

Tapasa—Seeming ascetics, they were the hermits with a shaven head or with matted hair, practising austerities.[27] They lived in suburbs of a city in association with a host of disciples with a shaven head or braided hair and pretended as possessing preternatural powers, to live on a handful of vegetables or meadow grass, taken once the interval of a month or two and to foretell future events. And he should pacify with money and honour those who are resentful for good reason, those resentful without reason, by silent punishment, also those who do what is inimical to the king.[28] Thus a *tapasa* is a bogus ascetic who impresses upon the gullible that he is great seer and thus becomes the centre of intelligence work.[29]

These five classes of members of secret service which include disciples, agriculturists, traders, ascetics etc. and thus come from practically all walks of life, can keep watch over various sections of people. Though they belong to the '*Samstha*' it is evident that Kautilya wants these five classes of spies to report not only about internal affairs but about external affairs as well.[30]

The punishments in secret which the *Tapasavyan janas* were capable of imposing obviously included assassination, poisoning, etc.

The '*Sancaras*', on the other hand, were of four types. They were required to keep a strict surveillance on the top officials.[31]

The Sattrin—The classmate spies, agents of par excellence. They were the orphans, fed by the state and they studied science, palmistry, sorcery, legerdemain, the duties of the various orders of religious life and the reading of omens and augury.[32] They were also to keep watch over the seducible and non-seducible parties in these country and in the enemys' country and to make propaganda in favour of the rulers' policy.

The Tiksna—A person of desperate and violent propensity engaged in secretly liquidating elements hostile to the state. They were fearless in disposition and took pleasure in killing. They were the brave doer who had given up all thought of personal safety and would fight (with an elephant or a wild animal), for the sake of money. They were also employed as bearer of umbrella, water vessel, fan, shoes, seat, carriage and riding animals and were supposed to ascertain the outdoor activities of high officials, especially the eighteen *tirthas*.[33]

The Rasada- Poisoners, they were the persons who had no trace of filial affection left in them and they were very cruel, indolent, crooked, devoid of any tender feeling for even their friends and relations, and able, as the name implies, to administer poison.[34] They were employed as cooks, waiters, bath attendants, shampooers, bed-preparers, barbers, valets, water-servers, actors, dancers, singers, professionals and story tellers.[35]

The Bhiksuki or Parivrajika—Female mendicants. They were poor widows of Brahmana caste, very clever and desirous of earning, their livelihood. Honoured in the kings harem, such women would frequent the residences of high officers.[36]

This classification of Kautilya has been followed in India throughout the successive centuries both in the north and the south.[37]

Although, assuming the guises or the qualities essential to their functions, the *Arthasastra* has divided the first set of spies, only into 'five classes'. However, there is no limit to covers which the spies could assume and in fact, Kautilya mentions many more than five. The '*Sancaras*' are divided into four classes though the disguises taken by them depended on situational requirements.[38]

Perhaps, '*Samsthas*', are as a rule, required to do duties that do not directly involve in the acts of violent nature, the '*Sancaras*' may be required to commit acts of violence including murder, arson and looting. Thus the '*samsthas*' may be called secret informants and the '*sancaras*', secret agents. A.L. Basham, however, feels that, "these institutes were not responsible for the whole organisation of espionage, for there were special spies, directly subordinate to the king or a high minister and employed to spy on the minister themselves".[39]

Jain texts mention the use of intelligence for internal security. Spies were called '*Anusuchakas*', '*Pratisuchakas*', and '*Sarvasuchkas*'.[40]

Manu speaks of as many as five categories of spies but unfortunately does not specify them.[41] Kullukabhatta, the commentator of the *Manu Samhita* describes these five spies as they were the *Kapatikas*, *Udasthitas*, *Grhapatis*, *Vaidehikas* and *Tapasas*.[42]

These divisions of spies would compare well with the five divisions of the *Samstha* group of spies as enumerated by Kautilya in his *Arthasastra*.[43]

Medhatithi, a later commentator refers to the five classes of stationary spies accepted by Manu.

Kamandaka classified the secret agents as stationary and wandering, e.g., '*samstha*' and '*sancara*'. His nomenclature for the agents of these categories is slightly different.

In the first category come *Vanika* (traders), Krsivato (farmers), Lingi (ascetics), Bhiksuka (apostate monks), Adhyapaka (teachers) whereas to the second category belong *Tiksna*, *Parivajika*, *Sattrin* and *Rasada*[44] (bravadoes, begging nuns, classmates, poison givers) respectively.

Of these *vanikas* are *vaidehakas* of Kautilya, the *krshikalas* are *grihapatikas*, *linginas* and *bhiksukas* as *udasthitas* and *tapasas* are ascetics. Likewise, in the case of wondering spies, *tiksna*, *sattrins* and *rasadas* are common to both the lists while *Parivrajika* evidently stands for *bhiksuki*.

Kamandaka observes secret agents as '*prakasa*' who carry out their work openly and '*aprakasa*' who are engaged in secret operation. The '*Prakasa*' agents were known as '*dutas*'.[45]

Katyayana distinguishes secret agents on functional basis, these are '*Stobhaka*', who is a part time informer and is paid specific assignments, and '*Suchaka*' who functions as a police informer.[46]

According to Buddhist and Jain cannons, spies were fell into two classes, those who busied themselves with the misdeeds of officials and the opinions of subjects and those who sought to probe the designs and plans of rival monarchs.[47]

The *Ashtadhyayi* of Panini mentions '*Upanisat*' and '*Aupanisadika*' as two classes of spies first were the 'secret means' employed by the king and second were as an agent who made his living by secret means. Also mentioned was *Visenavalhyah*', a person marked out for poisoning.

Patanjali gives the name of '*dutas*' and '*Karnejapa*' or '*suchakas*'. The '*dutas*' used to visit the neighbouring states and collected the information, and to laise with then governments. '*Karnejapas*' were 'secret servicemen' who collected information from urban area.[48]

The *Nitivakya Mitram* also mentions the categories of spies as by the Kautilya, but he does not make any division[49] as '*sancars*' or '*sanstha*'. It gives different names of spies:—

Yampattika — The spy, disguising as a religious man carrying *Yamapatta* (a roll of cloth containing a series of picture of the exploits of Yama and scenes of hell) wonder here and there. Mudraksasa mentions that the agent carrying the *'Yamapata'* conveys intelligence to Chanakya regarding several of Raksasa's secret man and supporters in the city who were surprising by planted by Chanakya himself. The utility of this type of spies comes in the way that they can enter the house of a stronger without any difficulty, showing his *'Yamapatta'* which creates no suspicion.[50]

Aahitupindaka — snake charmer

Shaundika — drink seller

Shaubhika — the spy who used to wear a mask at night.

Patacchar — in guise of thief or prisoner.

Vita — the person who sent the people to the prostitute.

Ganak	—	in guise of learned of Mathematics.
Suda	—	the kitchen cook, etc. names were given according to the functions of spies.

The *Arthasastra* of Kautilya is elaborate in the treatment of espionage and emphatic about its use. Kautilya includes in a chapter on '*Samgramika*' the spies,[51] as the auxiliary limbs of the fighting forces.[52] He mentions various categories of spies:

(1) those who collected information about the enemy's strength or the disposition of his forces, (2) those who were well versed in *Kutayuddha*, (3) who incited enemy forces to revolt, spread false rumours and who set fire to the enemy's camp and murdered the enemy leaders whenever there was an opportunity.[53]

A further class was that of the 'desperado', recruited from professional prize-fighters, whose main duty was the assassination of those enemies of the king.[54]

Salaries: In the epics it is not definitely known whether spies were entitled to a systematic and regular emolument or were favoured with occasional rewards in return for the successful accomplishment of their mission. There occurs in the '*Virataparvan*' a passage which speaks of Dushasana as granting an advance payment to spies with a view to finding out the Pandava brothers at the time of their living in cognito.[55] But in the *Arthasastra* the entire civil service was of different grades and scales of salary. Attaching to each grade, Kautilya gives an account of these grades, which very well show the vastness and complexity of the administrative machinery that was created to look after the manifold interests and requirements of the country.

Kautilya divided the grades of officers of spies in term of salary. Spies of different classes are to get 1,000 panas.[56]

The village staff (spies and washerman) are to get 500 panas. Attendants of spies are to get 250 panas or more in proportion to work (Prayasavriddha vetana). The experienced detectives (Manavakas) were put in the grade of 1000-500 Panas. These spies were recruited from criminal classes.[57]

They were placed under the supervision of heads who determined their wages, rewards and instructions and assignment of work (*vikshepa*). Payments were made to fifth columns in the enemy territory. Army chiefs were paid to create dissensions in the army.[58]

Duta (Couriers) are to be paid 10 *panas* for carrying messages upto ten yojanas, twenty *panas* for a distance up to hundred *yojanas*.

There is a provision (2.8.24-32) for reward to a spy, it was 1/6 of the amount involved if he could render effective help in detecting a fraud.[59]

Reward was also a type of salary. All spies are to be rewarded with money and honours when the results justify it.[60] The spies were not to be rewarded publicly lest they should be recognised.[61]

The salaries given to '*Samstha*' were higher than those to the '*Sancaras*'[62] though the works assigned to the '*sancaras*' spies appear to be more hazardous the spies belonging to '*samasthas*'.

Stationary spies (*Samstha*) got 1,000 *panas*, the wandering spies (*Sancara*) 500 *panas* and servants leading the spies got 250 *panas* or in proportion to the work done.[63]

The group of *samstha* was placed in the sixth grade of pay[64] and the officials of *sancara* were placed in the seventh pay grade.[65]

Kautilya says that the salary of the '*Sancaras*' should be increased according to their efforts.[66]

The salary of the first group is higher probably owing to the fact that while they are expected to organise a network of spies the latter mostly work on their own.[67]

Grahapatika and *Vaidehaka*, etc. (*Samstha*) were financed by the state. They were supported and rehabilitated by the state, if they were fallen from their profession, whereas the '*Sancaras*' moved place to place depending on professional requirements.

Buddhist and Jain cannons also favour that, the spies in various disguises, must be paid adequately.[68]

The *Nitivakyamitram* mentions about the salaries of spies, that only a *Sati*sfactory reward is the salary of spies. Being fascinated to the reward they used to work immediately and with great zeal.[69]

Basis of Their Recruitment: Planning of vital intelligence is essential for the survival of consolidated authority, where loyalties have to be constantly evaluated and opinion has to be constantly checked. Such planning becomes more vital in an age where news service is non existant, Vigilance in administration must be protected by concealed tests of loyalty and constant screening of administrative personnel. These tests are necessary to the grant of suitable assignments to administrative personnel those who pass specific tests are to be given specific assignments. The art of employing spies was thoroughly mastered and almost all ancient literary sources exhaustively deal with this system. But there was no fixed source of recruitment of secret agents.

The employment and direction of spies is one of the prime duties of the king. A king should appoint a faithful spy with the assistance of his council of ministers, who themselves have been carefully tried previously by the spies.[70] Having initiated a person into the espionage, the minister should tell him, "Sworn to the king, and myself, you shall inform us of whatever wickedness you may notice".[71]

The most important point was, to examine them thoroughly before their appointment and to appoint them so secretly that they could not recognize one another.[72]

Regarding their requisites, the *Mahabharata* informs that such persons should be employed as spies who are well trusted and reliable and are the sons of soil. They should be skilful, and expert in doing good to the king. Only those could be employed who may bear the sufferings caused by hunger, thirst, and can do some physical labour. Their outward physical appearance should be like those of fools, blinds and weak persons, but they should be very wise by nature.[73]

Kamandaka requires high qualifications, a spy should be able to read thoughts and have a good memory, endurance, wit and speed.[74]

They must belong to good families with a good social standing. In absence of suitable agents, the king is advised to depute even a lowly person on intelligence errand.[75]

The persons possessing sterling qualities of character and sharp intelligence, polite and soft spoken, alert, agile and swift in action, endowed with a penetrative and keen intellect, incorruptible contended, presence of mind and possessing the capacity to analyse, were recruited in secret services.

Despite these requisites, a person is not to be employed as a spy, if he is not loyal person. Because there is every possibility of leakage of the secrets of the foes. Thus, the kings should employ loyal and wise persons as their spies.[76]

Writers on polity are unanimous in prescribing that agents should be well informed and expert in various arts and sciences, should be keen students of human psychology, be able to gauge the sentiments and feelings of others, should have unflinching loyalty to the king and posses an unblemished character. Prospective recruits should be generally married and have children who could be taken as hostages.[77]

The spies were to be drawn from both sexes and from all grades of society[78] from orphaned children to Brahman widows and Sudra women, including a variety of state employees, and were recruited from all walks of life, students, traders, farmers, merchants, artisans, ascetics and even criminals without any consideration of age, sex and caste, and from all classes and men of all descriptions, including Brahmanas.[79] They could be professional spies.[80]

Brahmanas were supposed to be most worthy, trustful to be spy. From the application of such qualifications as wise, holy, etc. to spies, Ram Shamasastry observes that the spies, in the Vedic period were recruited from among the Brahmanas.[81] The reason for their selection, according to him, is that they may not be harmed by either friends or foes. He further argues that otherwise it is importable that 'the system of espionage would have hardly lasted long and served its purpose'.[82] But it is highly debatable whether spying was approved of as one of recognised duties of the Brahmin community in the Vedic society.

The *Mahabharata* also considered Brahmanas, capable of doing impersonation, cunning skilful and suitable for the risky task of spying.[83]

Ambassadors generally used to be Brahmanas may be inferred from the remark which *duta* threatened with seizure by the enemy is expected to make; even the lowest born among ambassadors must not be killed, what to speak then of the Brahmanas.[84]

Kautilya also preferred Brahmans as to appoint spies. Because he knows that Brahmans are benefitted with the attribute not to be assisinated by any one. If they are caught during spying they could be granted apology of death sentence. The mention of monks, escetics and mendicant women, like Parivrajika (A woman ascetic) and Munda (a man with a shaved head), Jatila (a man with braided hair) as spies provide an eloquent commentary on Kautilya's religious attitude. Though a Brahman, and certainly a believer in the established order of society, he feels no hesitation in advocating an unscrupulous exploitation of the religious susceptibiliti of the people.

The *Mudraraksasa* give reference to the brahmana spy named Indusharma in disguise of '*Chapanaka*' a Jain monk, appointed by Chanakya.[86]

J. Auboyer also mentions that unconnected with their priestly character, Brahmans might be spies,[87] but instead of some of these references, there is lack of details to arrive at any definite conclusion regarding the caste composition of the '*caras*' in the Vedic period.[88]

Regarding to this view, V.R.R. Dikshitar's present his argument that, only men of wisdom and purity were sent on this errand of spying. Thus suggesting that they should be persons above corruption and temptation of any sort.[89]

Later evidences, however, clearly shows that both Brahmins and non-Brahmins, who were capable were appointed to this post.[90] Manu does not mention how spies were appointed or what their caste was?[91]

Poor Brahmana widow could be recruited as a spy, desired earning a good living. According to Kautilya, exploiting her honoured position a Brahmani, of irreproachable conduct could go everywhere, to the houses of ministers, *purohitas*, commanders etc., indeed even to the kings inner quarters, and learn things which no other spy could never dream of.[92] The *Vedas, Dharmasastras,* the *Arthasastra* and Jain literature show that women were appointed as spies in various ways.

But the Epics do not mention about it. Women were considered light hearted, whimsical, eccentric, weak and unable to keep secrets. No secret councils of the state were to be held in women's presence.[93] Women were not regarded even worthy of being entrusted with state-secrets. Generally they were not taken in confidence into transaction of state business.[94]

In the *Mahabharata*, Bhishma told Yudhisthira to appoint the *caras* as his *duta*.[95]

After recruitment, the secret agents were put through a rigorous training in the techniques of adopting disguises, changing appearances, science of signalling, secret writing and creating dissensions in the enemy ranks. The *Ramayana*[96] suggests that agents should undertake decisions on their own initiative without awaiting, directions from the king.

Tamil Mahakavya 'The *Kural*' gives enough information about the espionage. Moreover, chapters 51 and 52 are concerned with methods of recruitment of officers and ways of employing them only.[97] Generally spies were recruited from poor and destitute classes and are thus dependent on the government for their subsistence.[98]

Officers—With the existence of a developed, complicated, comprehensive, all pervasive and ubiquitous institution of spies in ancient India, it must have necessitated very close and personal supervision of the king or his reliable officers.[99]

There was a central espionage department. This controlled the activities of all spies, within the country or in foreign states.[100] It was perhaps directed and supervised by the bureau of general administration and revenue collection which was presided over by '*Samahartra*'.[101] He used all types of spies to check the information collected by the '*gopas*' and to identify the loyal state servants. Both '*samstha*' and '*sancaras*' were under the '*Samahartra*.[102]

The appointment of secret service officers was the main responsibility of the king, though sometimes they were also recruited by ministers and departmental heads. Some check was necessary on the spies as well spies should not know each other.[103]

The king must know the internal and external troubles if the state, for the king appointed certain officials who were directly connected with him and reported secretly about the activities of different groups in the state.[104] He selected '*ubhayavetana*' agents and deployed counter spies.

Mahasandhivigrhaka, the head of foreign affairs department, appointed the spies to know the condition of native and foreign land.[105]

There were a number of informants, and agents who were reporting on corrupt and dishonest government servants, fraudulent businessmen. There would be the members of crime branch. They had to inform at once to their heads or the nearest security officers. In the *Mudraraksasa,* the spies of Chanakya, Raksasa and Malayaketu reported to their respective masters directly.[106]

In various states, there were appointed various 'Spy Mandala' and every *Mandala* had an officer. Women can be appointed on this officer post.[107]

There is mention of the '*Spasadhyaksa*' in *Panchatantra.* Vidhya Sagar pines him 'the officer in charge of cosmetics', etc. used by the king. Bil Kale interprets him as '*Spasadhyaksa*' means 'the officer in charge of the spies'. The critical examination of these terms shows that some royal officers were engaged in defence while the others were connected with the personal security of the king.

The '*Spasadhyaksa*' was apparently in charge of the heavy responsibility of keeping a watch over external and internal enemies endangering the life of the king and the stability or independence of the kingdom.[108]

Kautilya does not mention the institution of spies as an organization functioning under a unified command. The spies and secret agents worked under their respective heads of department, and also directly under the king. The *Agnipurana*[109] created an officer called the 'Superintendent of spies'. *Caradhyaksa*, Somdeva also refers to the appointment of a head of spies called '*Varisthaka*'. He speaks of the head of the organization of envoys whom he calls '*Janghacharikanayaka*'.[110]

In Maurya period the head of spies was called '*Mahamatya sarpa*' or '*Mahamatyasarpa*'. Both stationary and touring officials formed the personal of this cadre, which included tried men from the administration side.[111]

In Gupta period, in the copper plate of *Dharampala* of *Khalimpur*, there is a reference to the spies, they are called '*Khola*' and the head of the espionage department is called the 'Rahasyadhikrita'.[112] 'Khola' has been interpreted by R.C. Majumdar as an officer in charge of the intelligence department or a 'spy'.[113]

Secret meetings—Nothing was considered more important than to maintain the secrecy about the proceedings of the council deliberations : were to be so carried on that "even birds cannot see them".[114] India's imminent polity thinkers, Acharya Sukra, Brispati, Narada, Kautilya, etc.

had emphasised on the night meetings as an important organ of the administration in which there were the king and his confidant advisers in the meetings.[115]

It was the proper time for hearing the reports of the secret agents between 18.00 and 19.00 hours and between 03.00 and 04.30 hours he despatched them on their errands.[116]

Manu suggests evening time for receiving agents and the suitable place is an inner closet.[117]

According to the Buddhist and the Jain Cannons, deliberation on all affairs of high moment requires the utmost secrecy, that is essential for success. Counsel should not be held in places which echo to human voices and should not consult those whose relations you have injured.[118]

Secret agents exhausted all human ingenuity in detecting any breach of faith. Those who disclosed the counsels should be torn to pieces. But no amount of precautions could completely overcome the difficulty. So Kautilya reorganises a kind of informal inner council, consisting of three or four ministers whom the king should consult especially in emergencies.[119]

Secrecy in holding council is enjoyed upon the king by practically all authorities. The king is advised to consult his ministers separately and then jointly, after listening to all advice, he should himself decide what action to follow.[120] Kautilya laid emphasis on the secrecy of policy making. He said that the king must be careful to guard the secret of the deliberations arrived at. The king not only should guard his secret form men but even form talking birds and animals.

Methods of convey—The most important part of the espionage is to convey the collected information properly. The writers on polity had, therefore, devised various means of quick communicating intelligence.

The most common method for spies was to be disguised in '*sadhus*' bard or singer, fortune teller, deaf, dumb, etc. to communicate the message to their heads. They used sign alphabets, codes known as '*gudhalekha*'. The *Mudraraksasa* mention about the secret script. The spies used it to send their information. It was not known except the caras.[121] Records were also maintained of the information collected by spies. They used to sing the poems to excite the people.

Women spy entered the palace in disguised and sent the information through songs, recitations and writing concealed in musical instruments, predetermined codes were used to communicate the gist of intelligence.[122]

The secret agents staying in forest used a relay system for transmission of message from a long distance. They produced identifiable sounds by blowing counches or beating drums by climbing hillocks and trees, so that nobody can see them.[123]

The '*Tolkappiam*' describes that the spies communicate their message by making varieties of noise already agreed upon as signals.[124]

Domesticated pigeons carrying sealed letters and a series of smoke and fire were used to transmit messages.

Several methods of secret communication, such as coded language, secret script and signals also mentioned in the *Mahabharata*.[125] Vidura sent two spies to Yudhisthira to aware him from the mal-intentions of Duryodhana, and they used coded language. Predetermined signals and coded language termed as 'Mlechha Bhasa' was used to escape the Pandavas from the Varnavata.

The *Ramayana* also mentions the use of coded messages, identification signals and signs. When Sita was captured in 'Asoka Vatika', Hanumana presented her a signet ring of Rama and spoke in a particular language.[126]

In the *Mudraraksasa*', the secret agents of Chanakya used a coded signal for their identification.[127]

The secret agents in the *Kamandaka Nitisara* communicated with each other with the help of code words, secret writing and agreed signs and signals.

In ancient period, since intelligence was communicated through '*gudhalekha*', pre-determined signals and with the assistance of pigeons, secret agents must have made elaborate arrangements to interpret these messages. The spies as well other persons, conveying messages, were given priority in transportation, as they were supplied with free travelling passes.[128]

The information given by the secret agents was examined very carefully.[129] The writers on polity had emphasised on the assessment of information. Information given by spies such as actors, dancers and singers was to be tested by the senior spies and verified by others. If there is conflict between the different sources, secret punishment to be meted out.[130]

Moreover, on the safe side, there were also spies to spy on the spies. Obviously, these spies were not to know each other[131] except when cooperation was necessary and all information was checked through three different sources to ascertain its validity[132] and the final verification through spy is desirable, but these three spies are to function independently and be employed without any one of them knowing that he is being spied upon.[133]

Spies of Kalidasa were not only unknown to one another but unwittingly watched each other.[134]

These evidences indicates not only the spies existed, but that they were a numerous and important part of the government. There was a regular central department of espionage set-up that correlate the reports and direct the activities of its agents.[135]

References

1. Beni Prasad, Theory of Government in Ancient India, Allahabad, 1926, p. XIII.
2. T.B. Mookerji, Interstate Relation in Ancient India, Meerut, p. 24.
3. Rigveda, 1-25.13; IV 4.3, VI 67.5; 87-3; X 10.8; AV XVIII. 1. 9.
4. Dr. Bimal Kanti Majumdar, 'Role of the Secret Services in Ancient India', I.H.C., Vol. 19, 1956.
5. N.N. Law, 'Machinery of Administration in the Kautilya', I.H.A., Dec. 1929, p. 625.
6. Dr. Lallaa ji Singh, Ramayan Kalin Yudhkala, Agra, 1982-83, p. 155.
7. कपिरूपं परित्यज हनुमान मारूतात्मजः।
   भिक्षुरूप ततो भेजे रा बुद्धितीया कपिः।।
   Kishkindha Kanda, p. 112.
8. चरनप्रत्यापिकान ूरान धीरान विगत साध्वसान। 6/29/18
9. S.L. Roy, Diplomacy in Ancient India, Calcutta, p. 195.
10. Mahabharata, Sabhaparvan, 5.27.
11. Brajdev Prasad Roy, Political Ideas and Institutions in the Mahabharatas, Calcutta, 1975, p. 366.
12. Manu Bharati, Vol. 38 (1-4), 1990-91, p. 45.
13. Mahabharata, Shantiparvan, 69.8.
14. Vavahara Bhasya, I.P. 130 a Commentary, Malayagiri, Bhava Nagar, 1926.
15. B.R. Roy, *op. cit.*, p. 366.
16. D.K. Ganguly, Aspects of Ancient Indian Administration, New Delhi, 1979, p. 284.

17. चार संचारिणः संस्था गूठाश्रा गूठसंज्ञिताः
Arthasastra,1. 12.16.
18. *Arthasastra*, 1. 12.12.
19. N.N. Law, I.H.Q., Dec. 1929, *op. cit.*, p. 625.
20. U.N. Ghoshal, History of Indian Public Life, Vol. II., p. 136.
21. परमर्मज्ञः प्रगल्भः छात्रः कापटिकः ।।
Arthasastra, 11.11.3
22. प्रव्रज्याप्रत्यवतितः प्रज्ञा ाौचयुक्त उदास्थितः ।।6 ।।
Ibid., A. 1.11.6.
23. D.K. Ganguly, *op. cit.*, p. 284.
24. कर्षकोवत्ति क्षीणः प्रज्ञा ाौचयुक्तो गहपतिकव्यज्जनः ।
स कषिकर्म प्रदिष्टायां भूमाकिति समानं पूर्वेण ।।
Arthasastra, 1.11.12- 13.
25. S.L. Roy, *op. cit.*, p. 183.
26. वाणिजको वत्तिक्षीणः प्रज्ञा ाौचयुक्तो वेदेहकवयज्जनः ।।4 ।।
Arthasastra, 1.11.14.
27. मुण्डो जटिलो वा वत्तिकामस्तापस्त व्यज्जनः ।।6 ।।
Ibid., 1.11.16.
28. *Arthasastra*, 1.11.27.
29. Aradhana Parmar, Techniques of Statecraft—A Study of Kautilya's *Arthasastra*, p. 237.
30. S.L. Roy, *op. cit.*, p. 188.
31. *Arthasastra*, 112, 1-12.
32. ये चाप्यसंबान्धिनो डव यमर्तवयास्ते लक्षमंडगविद्यां जम्भकविधां मायागतमाश्रमधर्म निमित्तमन्तरचक्र मित्यधीयानाः सत्रिणः ।।1 ।।
Ibid., 1.12.1.
33. *Arthasastra*, Bk. I. Ch. 12.7.
34. N.N. Law, I.H.Q., Dec. 1929, *op. cit.*, p. 625.

35. Dr. Aradhana Parmar, *op. cit.*, p. 238.
36. *Arthasastra*, 1. 12.4.
37. S.D. Trivedi, *op. cit.*, p. 25.
38. N.N. Law, pp. 441-450.
39. S.L. Roy, *op. cit.*, pp. 188-89.
40. T.C. Jain, Life in Ancient India as Depicted in the Jain Cannons, Bombay, 1947, p. 59.
41. कत्सनं चाष्टविंध कर्म पच्चवर्गं च तत्तवतः।
    अनुरागापरागो च प्रसारं मण्डलस्य च।। Manu Samhita, 154/7.
42. Dr. Jai Kumar Jain, *Manu Samhita*, Trans. Kulluka-bhatta's, Manvarth Muktavali, p. 307.
43. *Ibid.,* p. 308.
44. M.N. Dutta, Kamandakiya Nitisara, Calcutta, 1896, p. 182.
45. *Ibid.,* XII, 25-29, pp. 187-188.
46. Lingat Robert, The Classical Law of India, p. 220.
47. Beni Prasad, *op. cit.*, p. 237.
48. P.D. Agnihotri, Patanjali Kalin Bharata, Allahabad, 1963, pp. 211-382.
49. Ramchandra Malaviya, Nitivakyanvitram, 1972, Varanasi, p. 74.
50. "यमपदिदटको गलत्रोटिकः।"
51. *Arthasastra*, 10, 1-2, 10-6, 54.
52. B.K. Majumdar, Military System in Ancient India, Calcutta, 1955, p. 64.
53. Dr. Bimal Kanti Majumdar, Role of Secret Services in Ancient India, IHC, Vol. 19, 1956, p. 119.
54. A.L. Basham, The Wonder that was India, 1967, p. 121.
55. D.K. Ganguly, *op. cit.*, p. 291.
56. R.K. Mookerji, Chandra G. Maurya and his Times, Delhi, 1960.

57. *Arthasastra*, B.V., Chap. III, pp. 277-98.
58. T.B. Mookerji, *op. cit.*, p. 74.
59. S.C. Banerji, Aspects of Ancient Indian Life from Sanskrit Sources, Calcutta, 1972, p. 70.
60. J.W. Sepellman, Political Theory of Ancient India, Oxford, 1964, p. 138.
61. N. Subrahamaniam, Sangam Polity, Bombay, 1966, p. 101.
62. N.N. Law, I.H.Q., Dec. 1929, *op. cit.*, p. 626.
63. B.K. Majumdar, *op. cit.*, p. 97.
64. *Arthasastra*, V, 2.22.
65. *Ibid.,* V, 3, 233.
66. *Ibid.,* V, 3.
67. S.L. Roy, *op. cit.*, p. 189.
68. Beni Prasad, *op. cit.*, p. 237.
69. Ranichandra Malaviya, Nitivakyaniritam, Varanasi, 1972, p. 74.
70. *Arthasastra*, 1. 11.
71. S.L. Roy, *op. cit.*, p. 187.
72. Manorama Jauhari, Politics and Ethics in Ancient India, A study based on Mahabharata, Varanasi, 1968, p. 225.
73. प्रणिधीश्र ततः कुर्याज्जडान्धवाधिराकतीन।
पुसः परीक्षितान प्राज्ञान क्षुत्पिपासा श्रम श्रमान।
Shantiparvan, 8/69.
74. I.W. Mabbett, Truth, Myth and Politics in Ancient India, New Delhi, 1971, p. 49.
75. Mahabharata, Shantiparvan, XX.
76. Brajdeo Prasad Roy, *op. cit.*, p. 366.
77. Palmer, Encyclopaedia Britannica, 1982, Vol. 9, p. 26.
78. Beni Prasad, *op. cit.*, p. 140.

79. Bimal Kanti Majumdar, Role of Secret Services in Ancient India, IHQ, Vol. 19, 1956, p. 110.
80. Michael Edwards, *op. cit.,* p. 24.
81. D.K. Ganguly, *op. cit.*, p. 282.
82. S.L. Roy, *op. cit.*, p. 184.
83. Manorama Jauhri, *op. cit.*, p. 225.
84. S.R. Goyal, Kautilya and Megasthenes, Meerut, 1985, p. 67.
85. P.C. Chakervorty, The Art of War in Ancient India, p. 69.
86. Krishna Kumar, Prachin Bharat Ka Sanskritic Itihas, New Delhi, 1993, p. 645.
87. Jeaumine Auboyer, Daily Life in Ancient India, (from approx. 200 BC-AD 100), 1961, p. 25.
88. S.L. Roy, *op. cit.*, p. 184.
89. V.R.R. Dikshitar, War in Ancient India, 1920, p. 127.
90. S.L. Roy, *op. cit.*, p. 184.
91. D.K. Ganguly, *op. cit.*, p. 292.
92. S.R. Goyal, *op. cit.*, p. 69.
93. D. Shakambari Jayal, The Status of Women in the Epics, Delhi, 1966, p. 299.
94. Prof. Indra, The Status of Women in Ancient India, Banaras, 1955, p. 148.
95. चार श्रा प्राविधिश्रौव काले दानममत्सरः |5/59 |
Mahabharata, Shantiparvan.
96. Ramayana, Yudhakanda, Ch. VI.
97. N. Subrahmaniam, Sangam Polity, Bombay, 1966, p. 103.
98. S.L. Roy, *op. cit.*, p. 188.
99. S.D. Trivedi, *op. cit.*, p.
100. T.B. Mookerji, *op. cit.*, p. 177.

101. *Arthasastra*, 4. 4, 3.
102. Aradhana Parmar, *op. cit.*, p. 239.
103. Beni Prasad, *op. cit.*, p. 190.
104. Shanti Prasad Chhangani, Interstate Relations in Ancient India, New Delhi, 1986, p. 59.
105. Krishna Kumar, *op. cit.*, p. 634.
106. J.C. Kishra, *'Mudraraksasa',* Varanasi, p. 19.
107. Krishna Kumar, *op. cit.*, p. 643.
108. A.C. Barthakuria, Panchatantra India in the Age of, Calcutta 1922, pp. 31-61.
109. Agnipurana, 221, 3.
110. S.D. Trivedi, p. 35, *op. cit.*, p. 35.
111. B.N. Puri, *History of Indian Administration*, Vol. 1, Bombay 1968, p. 68.
112. *Prachin Bharat Me Rajnitik Siddhanta aur Lok Shasana*, p. 367.
113. Das Sukla, Crime and Punishment in Ancient India, A.D. 300-A.D. 1100, Delhi, 1977, p. 90.
114. तदुद्दे ।: संवत: कथानामनिस्त्रावी पथिभिरेव्यनालोक्य: स्यात। *Arthasastra*, 1. 15, 3-4
115. Vimala Chaudhry, *Prachin Bharat Mai Guptachara Vyavastha.*
116. *Arthasastra*, 1. 19 1 3, 18, 22.
117. *Manusamhita*, VII, 223.
118. T.B. Mookerji, *op. cit.*, p. 96.
119. Beni Prasad, *op. cit.*, p. 125.
120. J.W. Spellmen, Political Theories of Ancient India, Oxford, 1964, p. 86.
121. Dr. Heeralal Sukla, *Mudraraksasa ka Sanskritic Itihas*, Nagpur, 1976, pp. 21-22.
122. *Arthasastra*, 1.12, 11-14.
123. *Arthasastra*, 12.5, 51.

124. N. Subrahmaniam, Sangam Polity, Bombay, 1966, p. 100.

125. *Mahabharata*, *Virataparva*, VIII, *Adiparva*, XLVIL.

126. *Ramayana*.

127. Dr. Heeralal Sukla, *op. cit.*, p. 22.

128. S.S. Nigam, Economic Organization in Ancient India, pp. 259-60.

129. N. Subrahamaniam, *op. cit.*, p. 101.

130. I.W. Mabbett, Truth, Myth and Politics in Ancient India, New Delhi, 1971, p. 49.

131. यथा न विधुरन्योन्यं प्रणिधेयास्तथा हिते।
Mahabharata, IXIX-9.

132. J.W. Spellmen, *op. cit.*, p. 139.

133. N. Subramaniyam, *op. cit.*, p. 101.

134. Raghuvamsam, XVII, p. 51.

135. J.W. Spellman, *op. cit.*, pp. 137-139.

3

Functions of Spies

In ancient India, espionage had developed into a sophisticated political art and Kautilya views it as an indispensable adjunct of foreign policy and also as an important instrument of serving the government.[1]

A complete network of spies used to be spread throughout the length and breadth of the country. They provided their services in every field of life. Their functions were manifold. In Vedas the functions of '*Spasas*' of Varuna are described in an interesting manner. Sixteen Sukta of fourth kanda of the *Atharvaveda*[2] deals with the functions and qualities of Varuna's spies. They informed the king about every minute news of native state as well as foreign. *Arthasastra*[3] give some chapters on the various functions of *gudhapurushas*. The *Mahabharata* and the *Ramayana* also deal with the wide sphere of their activities. The '*Kural*' gives a detailed account of the nature and functions of the spies of Sangam age.[4] The field of the activities of spies was very large. They collected information about the government personal, functioned as the vigilance and anticorruption squad and also operated in unearthing foreign. They spies on the general populace of the kingdom as well.[5] The secret agents worked for state, administration, polity, economy, military and society. They played an important role in diplomacy. It is through the spies that king acquires the knowledge of the secrets and weak points of his enemy.

1. Security of the State. With the incessant struggles for supremacy among, the oligarchies, the concept for the establishment of a state came forward and later on the question arises of its stability. The security of the state is the prior duty of a king and this necessity gave birth to the spy system. Though the organization of police was established for the safety and security of people but much of the police control was conducted by means of spies who acted as agents and provocateurs. In early India, due to the lack of means of communication, transportation, and press, it was a difficult task to know about kingdom.[6] The ambitions of kings were associated with the advancement of the state and they were fulfilled by the battle. But considering the violence and wastage of sources, some states developed the diplomacy and espionage. Diplomatic espionage was used to know the weaknesses of enemy state or to terrorise them before the waging war, so that victory could be easier for them. So with the help of espionage rulers made the way for the defeat of enemy king and created the measures for the security of the state.

I. The spies used various tricks to destroy the enemy by diplomatic espionage. The power of diplomacy was held to be the most far reaching one. An arrow of a zealous warrior may (even may not) kill only one person, but the policy of a diplomat may uproot a whole kingdom.[7] So secret agents used the policy of diplomacy to defeat their target. In this relation their function were :

(a) To show the omniscience, omnipresence and divinity of king[8]. Doing this the spies used to fill their side with enthusiasm and the enemy side with terror. With the help of spies the king get the secrets of officials and tell them.[9] Besides if he was already informed about the ill-intentions of his own

ministers, and he make them out before them. Thus the king knew the secrets and happenings that were going on in the foreign lands with the help of spies and domesticated pigeons and showed his omnipresence.

To prove his divinity, the king talked to the idols of deities in which, spies were hidden and call themselves the God.[10] Like this, the secret agents operating as ascetics capable of seeing underground objects, holy men staying in water with the support of an underground tunnel or chamber under the river bank for long duration; operating as traders, sages, '*natas*', *acrobats* with their bodies smeared with burning oil, raked in bear skins, emitting magic fire and smoke from mouths or assuming the appearance of '*raksasas*', showing the image of a deity, causing excessive flow of blood from sacred images etc. should frighten the people of the enemy country and at the same time proclaiming, with the help of the same tactics, the omniscience, omnipresence and the invulnerability of own forces and the king. Infact, they acted as propangandists, spreading reports in praise of the ruler.

(b) To sow the seeds of dissension among the enemy's officers. Prior to launching a full scale assault on the enemy fort, Kautilya suggests implementation of secret measures to weaken the enemy. Secret agents infuse the feelings of protest against the enemy king among his subjects, soldiers and officers. An example in *Mudraraksasa*, where Siddharthaka, a spy of Kautilya, infiltrated into the service of Raksasa, and following the plan of his master, aroused suspicion in the mind of Malayketu against Raksasa. They insulted the people calling them donkey who were doing work for their ruler.[11] They impressed upon the mind of the enemy king, his subjects and troops that the gods were against their king, with ominous signals foreboding times of distress, devastation and death for the enemy king.

They excited for revenge those people who were insulted, punished by the enemy king. *Satrins* causes dissension among the people, as the means suggested for removing difficulties in the rear of a king while he is thinking of marching against an enemy, causing troubles by violent methods.[12]

'Somdeva' also suggests creation of dissension among the senior officers and ministers of enemy king. Prolonged siege of the fort, bribing of the personnel responsible for the protection and control of the fort and use of 'fiery spies' to assassinate the enemy king as some of the measures to capture a well protected enemy establishment.[13]

Spies presented rewards and money to those person who were ready to act against the enemy ruler. They provided them with money and food. The near relatives of enemy were also motivated to against him and tempted with royal post in court.

(c) To create fear or to frighten the enemy forces. Secret agents were advised to use occult practices showing miracles by the use of various herbal concoctions to frighten or damage enemy forces. These practices include capacity to see in darkness, ability to move without any shadow and being invisible; making birds and animals invisible; putting people of a house and enemy troops to sleep; making the vessels in a house noiseless and silent; secret means of opening a door without creating any noise and without using tools, ability to penetrate beyond the door-bar and opening door locks; killing enemy troops or occupants of a house by putting near them or burying at their door-step certain organic and herbal preparations, etc.

Manu also mentions this policy to create fear among the enemy's forces as to make them powerless and by creating sounds at nights.[14] To disturb the enemy's army, the trader spies released the hounds of cows, goats and hunter spies release the tigers, lions, snakes and other violent animals in their camps. On the occasion of night battle, secret agents propagated with the help of drums, that we have entered the enemy state and had subjugate their territory. Thus spreading the false news and rumours they frightened the enemy.

(d) To win the confidence of enemy king, and to kill him. It was also a duty of spies to kill the enemy king, adopting the different tricks. Spies, disguised as ascetic, attracted the king with their activities and compelled them to come out from his fort.

Kautilya suggests some methods to impress the king. Shaved and haired '*Tapas*' spies, reside near the city with their disciples and propagated that they are four hundred years old, living in cave since a long time. They will invite the enemy king and his ministers in cave to see the miracles of God, and when king will stay there at night, they should kill him.[15]

Assassins should kill the king by fire when he is in a narrow place, by smoke when he is in a desert, by poison if he is in his residence, by frightful crocodiles or persons moving in water if he is bathing in river water or kill him as he is coming out of his apartment which has been set on fire.

Weakness for sex was successfully exploited by the writers on polity to kill the enemy king and army chiefs and other important dignitaries. Beautiful spy women were provided to them to win them over for accomplishing sensitive assignments later on to murder them.[16]

Mechanical devices such as to drop the heavy stone on the king while he is visiting a temple, or to loose the screws of chariot of king were also practised.

(e) To use poison and smoke. Kautilya advises free and uninhibited use of poison in the articles used by the enemy.

Poison could be administered by agents belonging to *'Mlechha'* communities disguised as hump backs, *Kiratas*, dumb, deaf or blind and idiots. Secret agents introduced lethal weapons in the articles meant for the king's sports, and in the materials from the stores to be used by him.[17]

Different methods are given in the *Arthasastra* to mix poison in wine, cooked food, grass and other articles used by king and people.

"A secret agent appearing at a wine shop to purchase wine as liberation for the departed soul of a man whom he claim to be his son but is actually a person condemned to death, should offer a hundred jars of wine on the first day, the wine should be unadulterated but on the next day deadly poison should be mixed with wine which should then be offered to army chiefs of the enemy.

Women and children under instructions of secret agents, purchasing wine, curd, butter or oil from dealers should pour these in their vessels containing poison; then bargaining on the price or quality they should pour the contents back in the same container of the dealer. The poisoned articles may then be arranged to be sold to enemy troops.

Secret agents should also mix the poison with the fodder and grass intended for elephants and horses and in disguise of dealers of animals, they should sell them to enemy contingents. Thus spies weakened the enemy's army.

Sometimes a secret agent sold cooked poisoned meat and rice to enemy troops by offering it on lower price than the other. So that soldiers could be killed in indirect way.[18]

Kautilya suggests the use of smoke with properties seriously affecting the vision by the secret agents at the time of battle, to create commotion.[19] For this purpose, roots, stems, leaves and powder of deadly plants, and animal waste have been suggested. Water is to be polluted by using the excreta of certain birds and animals mixed with juice of specified plants, Herbal and organic preparations should be administered to the enemy for temporarily affecting sensory organs i.e. causing blindness, paralysis and stupefaction.[20]

These miraculous acts have been suggested by Kautilya in order to demoralise the troops and to disintegrate the allied forces.

Kautilya suggests that, "practices accompanied by *Mantras* and medicines and those that are caused by illusion with them, the king should destroy the enemies and protect his own people.[21]

(f) To destroy the economy of enemy king. Kautilya suggests some ways to weaken the enemy's financial condition and to destroy the monetary resources before attacking him. Secret agents were engaged for this purpose in enemy forts, farms and godowns. Secret agents, serving as guards inside, the fort should place fire-mixture in the tails of ichneumons, monkeys, cats and dogs and let them loose in the stores of seeds, fortifications and houses so that stored foodgrains and armaments could be destroyed.

Besides it, spies were used to cut the supply lines, destroy the crops by fire, pollute the water by mixing poison, spoil the fertile land and killed the domesticated animals mixing poison and other metallic waste in their fodder. Thus adopting these immoral tricks spies destroyed the economy of enemy king and tried to secure their state.

(g) To forecast auspicious signals of the victory of own king. On the basis of dreams, body expressions, birds voices and on the occurrence foreboding good or evil, spies declared that all these presages show the victory of own king and defeat of enemy. They spread these views in public by beating the drums.[22]

When the war was about to commence or was already in progress, the spies in the garb of astrologers, forecast the victory of own forces and failure of the enemy plans.[23] This was done to boost the morale of armed forces and of the civilian population.

II. To test the loyalty and purity of character of officers. One of the main functions of spies is to operate as contact surveys for formulation of suitable policies, which widen the base of loyalty to established authority.[24]

Secret agents helped the king to test the character of administrators employed in departments to be employed by offering temptations.[25] The nature of the temptations (*Upadha*) varied according to the qualifications needed for discharging the duties of the post for which a particular probationer was a candidate. These tests were (a) *dharmopadha*, (b) *arthopadha*, (c) *kamopadha* and (d) *bhayopadha*, relating to religion, wealth, love and fear respectively. Such persons were appointed on the posts whose purity and impurity were tested by *Upadhas*.[26]

A priest is ostensibly insulted or dismissed by the king for not complying with his instruction to officiate at a religious rite performed by an outcast. He sends the *Satrins* under disguised to the officials to test, inciting them to join in a conspiracy against the unrighteous king by saying, "The ruler is outrageous. Let us set up another who is righteous and born of the same family or who is imprisoned. This is agreeable to us what do you think?"[27] Those that agree to the proposal are found wanting under the test. If any or all of the officers refuse the offer, he or they are pure. This is the religious test.[28]

An army officer, really spy ostensibly dismissed for receiving bribe, may by similar agency incite each officer to murder the ruler in view of thus acquiring great wealth. If refuse, the officers are pure. This is *Arthopadha* or monetary temptation.[29]

A woman spy, posing as pious and close to the ruler family may tempt the prime minister (or high officials) by saying : "The ruler's wife is enamoured of you and would receive you into her chamber". If they reject the offer, they are pure. This is love temptation or *kamopadha.*[30]

Another spy, posing as a disciple, may incite each high officer; to test their fearlessness. They says, "The ruler has taken to unwise course. Let us rid ourselves of him and have another. If they refuse, they are proved pure in fear temptation.[31]

Thus, secret agents, wearing the different covers carry out the instruction of the king or any official or officials to test the character of probationers for posts in any of the Government departments by putting temptations in their way.[32]

Those candidates, who are successful in all the tests, are eligible for being appointed as mantris : those that pass the religious test may be selected for the posts in law courts. The overcoming of monetary allurements prove men fit for service in the state departments under Samaharta, etc. where money is handled on a large scale or in revenue or tax work.[33]

The successful resistance to amatory allurements proves the capacity for performing duties in palaces where women reside or could be employed in superintending entertainments. Those who are tried under fear temptation should be employed in administrative service.

Those who have been tested under all temptation should be employed in high ministerial offices[34] and who are proved impure should be employed in mines, forests (timber and elephant) and factories.[35]

Kautilya suggests that, king should not involve himself or his lady to test the character of his advisers. This should be done only through the spies.[36] So it was the important function of secret agents in their field. The ruler should find out purity or impurity of his officers through the agency of spies.[37]

III. To watch the honesty of the heads of the various departments and their subordinates. It was also the duty of spies. The stationing of spies to watch the *tirthas* is mentioned in several old Sanskrit works.

The eighteen *tirthas* exhaust, roughly at least, the whole sphere of work of a state and meet its indispensable requirements providing for the deliberation of state questions and assistance to the sovereign, both secular and spiritual, for his personal safety and convenience for the administration of justice in the country, for its internal peace and external security, for the collection of state dues and their application, and lastly for the supply of material needs of the people by the exploitation of its natural resources, by manufactures, commerce and industries. The information gathered regarding the *tirthas*[38] is sufficient for ordinary purposes to show the inner workings of a state and the direction of its policy.[39]

So it was necessary to appoint the spies on the *tirthas*. According to the *Ramayana* and the *Mahabharata* the first three *tirthas* viz., *mantrin*, *purohita* and *yuvraja* and excluded from the observation of the spies engaged by a king within his own kingdom, while they are not excluded by him so far as other states are concerned. Three spies are unknown to one another are allotted to each *tirtha* in order that their independent reports may check one another, and suggest the necessity of a further verification before action in case of their neutral disagreement. This procedure is also maintained by Kautilya in '*trayanam ekasakye sampratyayah.*'

IV. To watch the various departments in the neighbouring kingdoms. The collection 'of information as to what was going on in the neighbouring kingdoms, in the states within a king's mandala such as '*Satru*' (enemy), '*Mitra*' (friend), '*Udasina*' (the state possessing the greatest strength with in the *mandala*) and '*madhyama*' (the state possessing medium strength within the *mandala*, was a necessity, otherwise a king and his highest officials could never keep themselves apprised of the doings and the policies of the other states, and thus try to make their own position secure by being pre-warned.[40] Hence spies were appointed to watch secretly and report about the workings of the various departments of the surrounding states and about the doing of their authorities.[41] Like Kautilya, Tiruvalluvar also is of the opinion that the spies are required to perform the dual functions of keeping watch over the internal matters as well as informing the ruler about the state of affairs in the neighbouring states.[42]

It was important of supply the important items of correct information about the developments in the administration of the neighbouring states, for the fickle changes in the interstate atmosphere in those days could have been thus forewarned was to have been forearmed. A convenient and probably cheaper method of having reports from other kingdoms through spies was by appointing what were called the *Uhhayavetanas*.[43] They can get information easily from the other state. They were in the pay of the state engaging their services as spies. While at the same time they secured jobs in the departments of the other state where they worked to collect information, receiving salaries for their labour from that state.

Along with it, spies discovered the spies of enemy or neighbouring state, in their own state. They were appointed in markets, public places social festivals, in the groups of hermits, gardens etc. by the king. Generally enemy's spies tried to mixing in public. So that they can't be recognised.[44]

To Maintain Relation with Foreign Land : A special class of spies were appointed on foreign lands by the king. Kautilya mentions three forms of espionage in relation to foreign states viz. political, diplomatic and military. Through political espionage, secret emissaries discover the disconted or disloyal elements in the hostile states.

Diplomatic espionage was carried by ambassadors and diplomatic agents in foreign courts. The duties of these officers in peace-time included not merely the carrying out of negotiations, but also observation of what went on in the kingdoms to which they were accredited. They are specially expected to keep an eye on all matters which, directly or indirectly, affected the interest of the state they represented. Here envoy performs the duty of a spy on foreign land. Kautilya lays down that "the envoy shall make friendship with the enemy's officers such as those in charge of wild tracts, of boundaries, of cities and of country parts. He shall also contrast the military stations, sinew of war, and strongholds of the enemy with those of his own master. He shall ascertain the size and area of the state, as well as strongholds of precious things, and assailable and unassaiable points, with the help of disguised spies". So with the help of spies, envoys work on forcing states and infact these envoys were nothing more than the honorable spies acting under the protection of the customary law unlike modern times. Even when occasional embassies were not on visit in a neighbouring state, spies were always at work to fish out useful information in disguised forms.[45]

Military espionage in relation to foreign states, consisted in the employment of secret agents to procure accurate information regarding the military resources of the hostile state, plans and movements of the hostile army, and self-guarding one's own camp and army from the poisonous, contamination of enemies spies.[46] The Kadambari of Bana shows that without the help of spies; no foreign policy would succeed, even though it followed the best approved line and was blessed with the most judicious employment of men and money.[47]

V. To make aware the king about the opinion of people and condition of his state. The spies, not only worked to find out what was happening in foreign countries but also what was happening within the country. The main function of espionage was to strengthen the position of his king by knowing in advance the designs and moves of his potential enemies.[48]

The Kural says, "The spies are essential servants as the king must know all that happens in his and other courts".

To know the public opinion, spies were to pretend to take sides in public debate about the government's virtues, inducing other people to reveal their views, they are to report rumours and signs of discontent and they are to bring round the disaffected by the standard diplomatic methods of liberality, division and punishment.[49] The *Mahabharata* mentioned that, The spies were expected to report the public opinion to their ruler.[50]

In this reference, Ram himself is represented in the *Raghuvamsa* as questioning a spy, named Bhadra as to any rumour about his own conduct.[51]

Greek writers also stress upon this function of spies. They refer to a class of man called overseers (spies), (Episkopoi) who "overlook throughout the country and in the cities, and make reports to the king where the Indians are ruled by a king" Strabo says, "it is their duty to report privately to the king, that is going on in the state."[52]

It was the duty of the spy to win the loyalty of the people through propaganda. There seems to have been a fear of republican uprising and the people were to be enamoured of the utility of loyalty and its religious sanction too.[53]

Another method of internal spying was to have two spies argue over the relative merits of the king. The one who praised the ruler would no doubt win, but it would not be without interest to both spies to observe which side of the dispute was taken by the local people. While truthful and loyal spy was rewarded, punishment and ever execution was the fate of the spy, who abused this position of considerable importance.

They watched the citizens who were dissatisfied in the kings own dominion as also those who were *Sati*sfied or against him in the neighbouring states in order that, when necessary, the dissatisfied may be won over by conciliation or gifts, or kept in check through dissension among themselves or recourse to violence.[54] In short their duty is to watch the *Krtyas* and *Akrtyas* in the king's own dominion as also in the neighbouring ones, and take necessary actions.[55]

VI. Prohibition of crimes and maintenance of peace. The spies were required to entice criminals, robbers and adulters by various tricks.[56] They kept watch on the movements of thieves, desperadoes and enemy agents.[57]

Spies were appointed with the clientele on the tavern, the shops of alcoholic drinks, by the king to knew the secrets and information, that might be passed on to interested parties in exchange for money[58] and to check the crimes and any type of dispute among the drinkers. Because criminals used to meet such places and made conspiracy.

Youngmen given to robbery and adultery would also be entrapped by spies enrolling themselves as members of their gang whom they would lead to a village, and into its marked house, by a pre-arranged plan, and to commit there all crimes.

As thieves, they would associate themselves with thieves to have them caught.[59]

Detectives also masquerading as brigands, going among criminals, forest tribes and instigating them to attack caravans or villages stocked beforehand for the purpose with spurious gold and other goods. As the attack took place according to plan, the assailants may be slain by armed forces posted there in advance to lie in wait for them, or they may be arrested while sleeping in intoxication from the effects of drugged food or drinks provided for them.[60]

During curfew, spies were permitted to perform their duties. Curfew was fixed for midnight, secret passages leading from points inside the town to concealed egresses far out in the country, were constructed for spies so that they could go elsewhere to examine the condition and opinion of people as well as to maintain peace.[61]

They were also to find out new arrivals and departures in the villages as well as the movements of harmful persons and enemy agents.[62]

In this connection Manu also refers that spies were employed by the king in his own country to settle the truth in judicial matter. They also used to detect thieves who stole property, who showed themselves openly and those who subsisted by cheating in the sale of various marketable commodities, but the hidden rouges were burglars, robbers, cheaters, gamblers and who took bribes. There seemed to had been a fear of republican uprising in Mauryan period so the people were to be enamoured of the utility of loyalty and its religious sanction too, by the secret agents.[63]

Kautilya mentioned of a class of spies at the pay of various states, for the detection of robbers and others who threatened the security of life and property.

To bring offenders within the clutches of justice, spies (*satrins* etc.) were employed in the villages as well as in the government departments for the detection of enemies. The offenders are said to be of thirteen kinds, though only a few classes are mentioned, such as makers of counterfeit coins, people lowering the quality of gold by mixing alloy with same and trying to pass it off as pure gold, persons agreeing to give false evidence, administrators of justice taking illegal gratification, persons administering poison, and so forth.[64] Spies pretending to have supernatural powers associate with the suspected person such as adulterers and robbers and have them brought to book while ostensibly helping to carrying out their criminal intentions.[65]

For the detection of persons suspected to have committed crimes, persons of the same character, harlots, persons with a persuasive tongue, story tellers, and inn-keepers are employed to watch them and elicit information.[66] Secret agents were also appointed along with police and soldiers to help local officers and military commanders for the suppression of crime.

VII. Counter Measures. Secret agents also used the counter measures[67] against poisons and other acts of sabotage practised by the enemy. Counter measures are the remedial measures for the safety of his own troops and king against the enemy acts. These are similar to the preventive measures taken by modern security services, police and army while bursting teargas shells or using poisonous gases against the agitators or enemy troops. These counter measures were taken with the assistance of secret agents.[68]

'*Mudraraksasa*'[69] also present the similar anti-sabotage techniques used by Chanakya to discover, and later destroy the assassins detailed by *Raksasa* to kill Chandragupta, and who had concealed themselves in the hollowed palace wall. This show the success of efficient spies.

Kautilya suggests the weak king to surrender to a powerful sovereign otherwise he should leave the fort by an underground passage in the guise of heretical monk. He carried out as a corpse by secret agents leaving behind poisoned food and drinks. The enemy should be poisoned by secret agents and destroyed when he is in a place of recreation or resting in a secluded place.[70] A weak king is advised[71] to use every possible secret weapon and strategy. Secret agents earlier infiltrated as door keepers and eunuchs should be used to assassinate the king.

Counter measures suggested by the writers on polity included antidotes against *poison-damsel*, poisons used on war animals and stupefying mixtures.

VIII. To work during the war. When a war is about to take place or is continuing, the spies in company with astrologers and others declare with the object of infusing greater enthusiasm into the minds of soldiers that their operations-will be successful and those of the enemy will be a failure.[72]

Spies were also employed to harass the enemy by setting fire to camps, by communicating to the enemy through envoys who are really secret agents such false-information as the revolt of a section of his subjects in his dominion by inciting the seditious subjects of the enemy into active hostilities towards him, and so forth.[73]

The *Rigveda*[74] speaks of spies, or presumably reconnoitring troops, going forward in an unambiguous context of war, and this is corroborated by another passage. As the opposing armies approach each other, the spies try to find the exact position of the enemy and messenger keep the king informed of the latest happening.[75]

The use of signs and cipher writing and carrier pigeons formed part of military espionage.

The functions of military espionage are to be found in the Epics and the Puranas. When the war was going on the services of spies and diplomatic agents as informers of the enemy's plan, movements and resources were considered essential.[76]

In the Ramayana, Ravana sent his spies in disguise to Rama's Camp to discover the nature, number and disposition of the enemy troops. Ravana himself says that if intelligent kings use spies to inquire about the enemy's troop, they can be easily defeated.[77]

So assuming the form of monkeys, Suka and Sarna, the spies of Ravana, penetrated deep in to the Rama's camp. But Vibhishana, having extraordinary intelligence, discovered Suka and Sarana in disguise. He captured them and brought before Rama and they set free to go. Again Ravana sent other spies to ascertain Rama's day-to-day plans. These spies were headed by Sardula, came to Suvela mountain where Rama stayed accompanied by Lakshmana. Here they were seized with fear to see the vast army of Rama. Again they were detected by Vibhishana, but Rama set them free. Thus these spies were often caught and belaboured, but spared.

Vibhishana also deputed his ministers Anala, Panasa, Sampati and Pramathi to gather information about Ravana's war arrangements. Assuming the forms of birds, they penetrated deep into Ravana's ranks and surveyed the position of Ravana's officers, Prahasta, Mahaparsva, Mahodara, Indrajit, Suka and Sarana with their troops at the different gates of Lanka. On their return they reported to Vibhishana the war arrangements of Ravana and Vibhishana of his turn. Conveyed them to Rama. Accordingly Rama finalized his plan of beseiging Lanka.[78]

IX. To work in relation to economy. Secret agents provided their services in the economic field to a great extent. They were employed by the '*Samaharta*' to gather information regarding the number of fields, houses and families in the villages. They were also required to find out the number of individuals in the villages and their income.[79] So they were to collect certain items of information in connection with the maintenance of statistics required for keeping the census records and the land records uptodate.

The *Nagaraka* was authorised to direct the spies for similar works within the town. The *Samaharta* had also to set the spies on the *Adhyaksas* (heads of departments) to ascertain their honesty.[80]

They were directed to make assessment of the quality of goods produced in the country mines, forests, factories and fields.[81] The spies checked the report about the detailed village records prepared by the *Gopa* or *Sthanika*.[82]

Informers set upon by the king on government employers to detect deflection of government revenue were given guarantee against reprisal by the officers concerned and were rewarded a part of the recovered defalcation amount by the officer concerned.[83]

Spies tried to replenish the government treasury in times of financial difficulties. They collected the donations from citizens stimulating, posing as donors, their desire to surpass one another in the amounts paid by them.

They also played upon the religious credulity or superstitions of the people and realized the sums from them.[84]

Spies worked as a safeguard in the security of state at every step. A State cannot be remain stable and secure still king is not familiar with the internal and external condition of his state. And if it is a vast empire and full of different people of different caste, creed and colour, the matter of security of state becomes more important. In these condition espionage covered many vital fields of state life. Secret agents collected the news, can be drawn in relation to the modern press.[85] They take the essential steps and make aware the king about the condition of state.

(b) Security of King and Royal Dignitaries

"The king and his rule, is the sum total of the constituents of state". The king was the pivot to the working of the entire administrative system appointing, guarding, correcting, strengthening and shaping its destiny. This made him the natural target of attack from the various interested quarters.

The threat to Indian kings was intimate, being built into the atmosphere of intrigue and the rivalry of relatives and nobles.[86] Political thinkers betray enormous concern on the security of kings in view of the politically unsettled conditions and the multiplicity of small states in ancient India. This danger could be engineered by foreign agents, disaffected individuals, feudatories, court officers, queens and princes.

Kautilya advises, "the wise king to guard others from others, and others from his own people, and always guard himself from his own people and from others".

The *Mahabharata*[87] also stress upon the safety of king, saying that, "Nobody is nobody's friend, nobody is nobody's enemy, persons become friends or foes only for reasons of self interest, and therefore, warding of innumerable dangers by hundreds of means the king should always protect his life."

Kamandaka[88] and Sukra reveal the lust for kingdom of the princes that turn the son against his father. Kamandaka makes it obligatory on the king to protect his person with a view to benefiting the people whose protection is his responsibility, and which in turn depends upon the security of the king's own life.

Somadeva supports the view that the state is saved in the protection of the king and he should guard himself against his relations and enemies.

The *Arthasastra* repeats the view, if king is secure, the kingdom and the community is also secure.[89] Regarding these views very effective and careful security measures had been advised for kings in ancient India. Except the security men and secret agents, birds and animals, science and technology based security precautions were made for the security of king.

A king himself should be possessed of such attributes and personality that he could defeat the enemies on the initial stage and could create an impression upon them. Kautilya[90] recommends an elaborate code of conduct, "He (king) should acquire control over the senses, cultivate his intellect by association with older, keep a watchful eye by means of spies, bring about security and well being by (energetic) activity, maintain the observance of their special duties (by the subjects) by carrying out (his own) duties, acquire discipline (by receiving) instructions in sciences. With his senses, thus under control, he should avoid another man's wife, or property as well as causing injury to others. A king should enjoy sensual pleasures without contravening his spiritual good and material well being.

Similar views have been given by other writers on polity. The *Mahabharata*[91] also speaks about the attributes of king as "a king should be obliged to the persons who had assisted him. He must conquer his senses and have simple, liberal and sober nature".

The king's undesirable attitude and behaviour could generate animosity against him amongst his subjects and the bureaucracy. Indian as well as western social and religious traditions desire from a king and his dignitaries to present a ideal character. So that people can follow him. In

Kiratarjuniyanz,[92] a spy reports to the Yudhisthira, that controlling over his six 'vices', Duryodhana is trying to show himself most confidant of subject by employing spies for the safety of his friends and relatives. It is clear with the report of spy that with his attitude, his generosity to his dutiful servants, he had created a security wall around him.

King and members of his family could face the threats of security from the foreign sovereigns and their agents, annoyed subject, members of royal family including queens, royal children or princes, chief of army and senior members of the government.[93]

Kautilya observes, that "A king can protect his kingdom if, he is himself protected from persons near to him and from enemies; first from his wives and sons".[94] So he should always took security measures against the causes that could create damage for him. He further advises, that "the king should appoint the spies on every place and among the enemies, friends, *Madhyama* and *Udasina* kings, his ministers, military chiefs and other eighteen *tirthas*, who are suspicious to him".[95]

The '*Kural*' also mentions, that the spies are to spy on the ministers and then officials the members of the royal family and foes.[96]

A king, at first guard himself against the threats of revolt in the interior and then the outer regions or enemy's because a conspiracy by ministers of interior poses great threats to the security of the king in stead of outer threats.[97]

The *Mahabharata*[98] considers danger from close relations, ministers and dissatisfied soldiers greater than any other threat. *Kamandaka*[99] and *Agnipurana* also shared these views, suggesting that army, anti-social elements, royal favourites, dissatisfied subjects, relations, friends, sons and cupidity of foreign monarchs create the danger for a king.

(a) Security of king against the princess. Protective measures for the king must start from the household which include protection from his sons, wives and the royal retinue. As sons are always ambitious for the throne and Kautilya was aware of the historical examples of the deposition or even murder of kings by their ambitious sons viz. Prasenjita of Kosala and Bimbisara of Magadha. So he gave a particular chapter on it. He holds the opinion, "like a piece of wood eaten by worms, the royal family with its undisciplined princes breaks the moment it is attacked"[100] and like the '*Karkata*' that lives eating his father, princes also desire so. Therefore, precautions should be taken since birth.[101] To check such occurrence, prince should be given anti-natal and post-natal care.

Secret agents were used for ascertaining the attitude of the prince for bringing out his inner sentiments and aspirations. According to Amba Acharya, agent provocateurs were appointed to involve the prince in gambling, wine and women in order to bring out his inner feelings—good or bad and another '*Satri*' protest him to be involve in these bad habits.[102]

But Kautilya neglects this view of Amba Acharya. He says that secret agents should try to divert the mind of prince from gambling, drinking etc. towards good habits.

Later, steps were taken for creating an aversion in him for these vices, and if necessary, secret agents frightened him by certain ingenious methods. As an extreme measure, Kautilya suggests that if a prince is incorrigible, he should be eliminated by secret agents by giving poison or with any weapon.[103]

(b) Security of king against the women of the palace. Women, whether they are mothers or wives, friends or confidants, mistresses or concubines, have been universally considered as a source of danger for royal dignitaries. These have also been exploited for espionage and assassinations.[104]

In the *Mahabharata* women were considered light hearted, whimsical, eccentric, weak and unable to keep secrets.[105] They could be doubtful for their husbands also.

Somadeva observes that they are repositories both of nectar and poison "like the mighty wave of the ocean". A wife, devoted and affectionate, showers nectar whereas those swerving from their path emit poison for their husbands and relations. Kautilya, Manu, Subandu, Kamandaka, etc. polity makers had given a long list of monarchs who lost their lives because of their carelessness in dealing with their queens.

In this connection Kautilya suggests that "the king should visit the queen after she is cleared of suspicion by old woman, who worked as secret agent for king".[106]

Manu[107] also suggested security precautions for the king as to keep away the queens from corrupt women, ascetics, nurses, washer-women, and other female companions who serve as go-betweens. Because these types of persons were used in intelligence operations by the enemy.

Sukra and Somadeva advise very liberal use of secret agents to watch close relations of the kings and keep on eye on their objectives, plans, programmes and movements.

(c) Security of king against the officers. The creation of bureaucracy which was the singular achievement of the pre-Asokan era carried with it the inherent danger of disaffection among the high officials.[108]

Fear of rising was a constant bugbear, and precautions against assassination have been thoroughly dealt with by our authorities. The threat of Indian kings was intimate, being built into the atmosphere of intrigue and rivalry of relatives and nobles.[109]

The desertion of Prasenajita by his minister mentioned in a Buddhist text is indicative of the mood and temper of this class.

Kautilya,[110] therefore, gave emphasis on the activities of disaffected government servants who may pose threat to the security of the king. He observes that king should always be aware of the '*dauvarika*' and '*antarvamsika*'.

In post Gupta period, on account of the growing influence and position of ministers and high officers, they started posing frequent threats to the security of the king and his family.

The *Agnipurana* treats a wicked officer as dangerous as an enemy, fire, poison and snake and advises the king to keep contact and to watch over the officers through a network of spies. He should not believe on the report of a single spy. T.N. Ramaswamy mention that special spies who do security work for the ruler, like carrying his standard, managing throne, his household affairs including his wardrobe should spy on the overt doings of these officers.[111]

(d) Security against poisoned food, clothing and items of personal use. Kautilya was aware of the use of the poison to kill the king. He himself suggested its use against enemy.[112] So he suggested that food should be tasted several times before it was offered to the king.

The 'security service' was responsible to test the food during and after the preparation. There was a special department in espionage in which different techniques were adopted to kill the person by giving poison. '*Satri*', was appointed to give poison in enemy's army by cheating.[113]

The *Mahabharata* suggests appointment of trustworthy persons who may take care of things to be consumed or used by kings, such as eatables, perfumes and clothes.[114]

Manu[115] also suggests that the food must be tasted by devoted servants before it is served to the king.

Security men should test the sincerity and fidelity of kitchen servants. If musical instruments are to be used by king, they should not be allowed to go out of the palace, and even the saddlery of houses, chariots must be kept in protective custody.

Kautilya justifies these arrangements by saying, "as the king keeps a watch over others through secret agents, so should he being self-possessed, guard himself against dangers from others.[116]

So spies were appointed to watch over every thing related to king.

(e) Security on the public places. Like the modern times, in ancient India, security measures had been taken for the king during his visits of public places.

On the occasion of festivals, temples and places of recreation were always fraught with innumerable security hazards. Because Kautilya himself suggests to the spies to murder the king on these places, so spies were always ready to check such happening.

The need to protect the king was not motivated by fancied ideas but was conditioned by the exigencies of existing conditions. The Mauryan kings were adequately protected by armed bodyguards who never left him alone in the public. The murder of the Nanda king was the result of the carelessness of secret agents.

(f) To liberate the hostages. Sometimes during the internecine struggles, kings, princes and queens could be taken prisoners of war or kidnapped. Hostages were also given as a mark of surrender, and for peace keeping. The secret agents were appointed to liberate a prince that has been kept as a hostages in the enemy kingdom.[117] Success in this task was depend upon the ingenuity of the 'secret services'.

The imperative necessity of a detailed briefing on this important diplomatic and military requirement has not escaped Kautilya's penetrating vision.[118] Only military power was not sufficient to release the kidnapped persons. So secret agents were responsible to do this important task.

The ambassadors and secret agents, disguised as artisans or artists in the enemy state, carrying out their work in the vicinity of the prince who is imprisoned were advised to take him away after digging a subterranean tunnel in the night.[119]

The actors, dancers, singers, musicians, reciters of vedas, ministrels, rope-walkers and showmen infiltrated in the enemy territory and gradually reached to the prince and then they make him free under one of their cover.

This operation was carried by prostitutes spies, and other women acting as wives of senior officers.[120]

The secret agents disguised as traders were advised to win over armed guards offering them food and drinks mixed with intoxicants or poison to seduce and immobilise the guards at the time of a royal festival or by selling poisoned articles to them. So that the guards became careless and spies could get free the hostages.[121]

Sometimes spies would set fire in the night to the house of the rich or of the guards and then raise alarm to create confusion for enabling the prince to escape.[122]

In the *Pratigya Yaugandharayana*, Vatsaraja was captured and carried away as a prisoner by Pradyota Mahasena. Then his minister Yaugandharayana, acting as a lunatic and with the help of secret agents succeeded in taking the king away and his beloved Vasavadatta also.[123]

So there are many references when spies liberated the princes, kings, queens etc. from the captivity of enemy by using their talents.

References

1. Aradhana Parmar, Technique of Statecraft—A Study of Kautilya's *Arthasastra*, p. 236.
2. *Atharvaveda*, 4 Kanda, 16 Sukta.
3. *Arthasastra*, B-1, Ch. XI.
4. Kural, Chap. 59, deals with the function of spies in Sangam age.
5. *Arthashastra*, 1. 13-1.
6. S.L. Roy, Diplomacy in Ancient India, Calcutta, p. 186.
7. B.K. Majumdar, War Ideology in Ancient India, p. 80.
8. *Arthasastra*, 13.1.6.
9. सर्वज्ञख्यापनं तु। गहगुह्मप्रवत्तिज्ञानेन प्रत्यादे ाो मुख्यानाम।
   कष्टक ाोधनापसर्पागमेन प्रका ानं राजाद्विष्टकारिणाम।।
   Arthasastra, 13. 1.3-7.
10. दैवतसंयोगख्यापनं तु। सुरगंमुखिनाग्निचैत्यदैवत।।
    प्रतिमाच्छिद्रानुप्रविष्टैरग्निचैत्य दैवतव्यज्जनैः सभाषणं पूजनं च।।
    Ibid., 13.1.9.
11. तेन परपक्षमुत्साहयेद्यथोक्तं पुरस्तात।
    भूयश्र वदयामः। साधारणगर्दभेन दक्षान। २५.२७।
    Arthasastra, 13.1.25-30.
12. I.H.Q. *op. cit.*, p. 636.
13. *Nitivakyamnam*, 20.8-9.
14. भिन्द्याच्चैव तडागानि प्राकारपरि– खास्त्था।
    समवस्कन्दयेच्चैन रात्रौ वित्रासयेलधा।।
    Manusmriti, 7/196.
15. *Arthasastra*, 13.2.1-2,

16. द्रव्यस्त्रीलोलुपमाढयविधवामिर्वा परमरूपयौवनाभिः।
स्त्रीभिर्दायादनिक्षेपार्थमुप नीताभिः सत्रिणः प्रलोभयेयुः।।
13.2.540-5 55.

17. *Arthasastra*, 4.1.2; 12.4.4-6.

18. S.L. Roy, *op. cit.*, p. 192.

19. स्वपतो वा निरूद्धे दे ो गूढ़ाः स्त्रियः सर्परसाग्निधूमा नुपरि मु चेयुः।। 70।
Arthasastra, 1.2/5/70.

20. *Arthasastra*, 14.1.4-34.

21. *Ibid.,* 14.3.88.

22. I.H.Q., Vol. 36, 1960, p. 244.

23. देवप्रश्ननिमित्तवायसाडगविद्यास्वप्नमगपक्षि व्याहारेषु चास्य विजयं ब्रूयुः।
Arthasastra, 13.1.1920,

24. T.N. Ramaswamy, Essentials of Indian Statecraft, 1962, p. 14.

25. Tenth chapter of '*Vinayadikarika*' of *Arthasastra* deals with the functions of spies to test the character of officers.

26. मन्त्रिपुरोहितसखः सामान्येष्वधिकरणेषु
स्थापयित्वामात्यानुपधाभिः ोधयेत।
Arthasastra, 4. 10. 1.

27. स सत्त्रिगिः ापथपूर्वमेकैकम– मात्यमुप–जापयेत।
अधार्मिकोडय राजा साच्पुधार्मिकमन्यमस्य तत्कुलीनमवरूद्धं
कुल्थमेकप्रगहं वा प्रतिपादयामः।।
Arthasastra, 1.10.1.

28. T.N. Ramaswami, *op. cit.*, p. 54.

29. *Arthasastra*, 1.10 7-9.

30. *Ibid.,* 1.10-10-12.

31. असत्वप्रवतो डयं राजा। सहसैनं हत्वान्यं प्रतिपादयामः।
सर्वेषामेतहोचते कयं वा तवेति। प्रतयाख्याने ुचिरिति भयोपधा।।
Arthasastra, 1.10 16-19.

32. N.N. Law, Machinery of Administration in the Kautilya, I.H.Q., Dec. 1929, p. 627.

33. *Arthasastra*, 1.10. 20-25.

34. त्रिवर्गभय सं ाुद्धानमात्यान्स्वेषु कर्मसु।
अधिकुर्याद्यथा ाौचभित्याचार्या व्यवस्थिताः।। २६।
Arthasastra, 1.10.26.

35. *Ibid.,* 1.10.23-25.

36. T.N. Ramaswami, *op. cit.*, p. 55.

37. ाौचा ाौचममात्यांनां राजा मार्गेत सत्स्त्रिभिः।।
Artha., 1.10.30.

38. *Tirthas are—Mantrin, Purohita, Senapati, Yuvaraja, Dauvarika, Antarvamisika, Prasastr, Samahatr, Sannidhatr, Pradestr, Nayaks, Paurav-yavaharika, Karmantika, Man triparisadadhyaksa, Dandapala, Durgapala, Antapala, Atavika.*

39. N.N. Law, I.H.Q., *op. cit.*, Dec. 1929, p. 628.

40. *Arthasastra*, I. Ch. 12.

41. N.N. Law, *op. cit.*, p. 629.

42. S.L. Roy, *op. cit.*, p. 198.

43. *Arthasastra*, 1. Ch. 2.

44. चारांश्र विद्यात प्रहितान परेण भरतर्षभे।
आपणेषु विहारेषु समाजेषु च भिक्षुषु।।
आरामेषु तथोद्याने पण्डितानां समागमे।
दे ोषु चत्वरे चैव सभास्वावसथेषु च।।
The Mahabharata, Shantiparva, 12.69/11-12.

45. A.S. Altekar, State and Government in Ancient India, Motilal Benarasidas, 1977, Delhi, p. 301.

46. P.C. Chakarvorty, The Art of War in Ancient India, pp. 70-71.

47. The Kadambari of Bana, trans, by C.M. Ridding, Calcutta, 1896, p. 112.

48. N. Subrahamaniam, Sangam Polity, Bombay, 1966, p. 102.

49. I.W. Mabbett, (Australia) Truth, Myth and Politics in Ancient India, New Delhi, 1971, p. 48.

50. अतीत दिवसे वत्तं प्र ासिन्त न वा पुनः।
गुप्तै चारैरनुमेतेः पथिवीमनुसारयेत।।
जानीयुयंदि ते वत्तं प्र ासंति नवापुनः।
क चित रोचेज्जन पदेजपजनजपवद कव्यिद राष्ट्र च मे य ाः।।
Mahabharata, Shantiparvan, 89, 15-16.

51. Raghu Vamsa, XIV, 31.

52. H.C. Raychaudhry, Political History of Ancient India, Delhi, 1995, p. 258.

53. T.B. Mookerji, Interstate Relations in Ancient India, Meerut, 1967, p. 178.

54. *Arthasastra*, 1, 13.14.

55. N.N. Law, I.H.Q., *op. cit.*, Dec. 1929.

56. *Arthasastra*, IV, 5.

57. *Ibid.,* 11. 35.4.

58. J. Auboyer, Daily Life in Ancient India, 1961, p. 89.

59. R.K. Mookerji, Chandra G. Maurya and His Times, Delhi, 1943, p. 200.

60. R.K. Mookerji, *op. cit.*, p. 200.

61. J. Auboyer, *op. cit.*, p. 119.

62. *Arthasastra*, 11, 35.10.

63. T.B. Mookerji, *op. cit.*, p. 178.

64. *Arthasastra*, IV. 4 (*Gudhagivinam raksa*).

65. *Ibid.*, IV, 5. (*Siddhavyan janairmanavapraka-rana*).

66. N.N. Law, IHQ, Dec. 1929, *op. cit.*, p. 624.

67. *Arthasastra*, 14.1.11.

68. *Ibid.,* 12.5, 16-20.

69. *Mudraraksasa*, Act-II.

70. *Arthasastra*, 12.5. 37-41.

71. *Ibid.,* 12.5, 47-48.

72. *Ibid.,* Chap. 3.

73. N.N. Law, IHQ, 1929, *op. cit.*, p. 637.

74. *Rigveda*, IV, 4.

75. E.J. Brill, trans. S.D. Singh, 'Ancient Indian Warfare with Special Reference to the Vedic Period, Leiden, 1965, p. 144.

76. B.K. Majumdar, *op. cit.*, p. 93.

77. चारेण विदितः ात्रु पदितैव सुधाधिपैः।
यडे स्वल्येन यत्नेन समासाद्य निरस्थते।।
Valmiki Ramayana, Yudhakanda, 27/22

78. *Ramayana, Yudhakanda*, 25, I.

79. *Arthasastra*, 11. 35. 8-9.

80. N.N. Law, IHQ, *op. cit.*, pp. 631-632.

81. *Arthasastra*, 11, 35. 11.

82. एवं च जनपदचतुर्भाग स्थनिकः चिन्तयेत।
गोपस्थानिकस्थानेषु प्रदेष्टाम कार्यकरणं बलिप्रग्रहं च कुर्युः।।
Arthasastra, 11.3.5.8, 11.35.8A.

83. B. P. Sinha, Reading in Kautilya's *Arthasastra*, Delhi, 1976, p. 59.

84. N.N. Law, IHQ, *op. cit.*, p. 635.

85. T.N. Ramaswami, *op. cit.*, p. 14.

86. I.W. Mabbett, *op. cit.*, p. 47.

87. *Mahabharata, Shantiparvan*, 120 Chapter, (Rajdharmanusharana parvan).

88. M.N. Dutta, *Kamandaka Nitisara*, Calcutta, 1896.

89. *Arthasastra*, 8.1.12-18.

90. वद्धसंयोगेन प्रज्ञां चारेण चक्षुरूथानेन योगक्षेमसाधनं कार्यानु ाासनेन स्वधर्म स्थापनं विनयं विद्योपदे ौन लोकप्रियत्वमर्थसंयोगेन हितेन वत्तिम ।।2।।
Ibid., 1.7. 1-7.

91. *Mahabharata, Shantiparvan*, Chap. 70, 1-13.

92. विधाय रक्षान्परितः परेतरान डिग्ताकारमुपैति ाडिग्तः।
क्रियापवर्गेववनुजीविसात्कताः कतज्ञयामस्य वदन्ति सम्पदः।।
Dr. Krishna Kumar, Kiratarjuniyam, 1975, Chap. 67.

93. V.R.R. Dikshitar, Mauryan Polity, 1932, p. 108.

94. रक्षितों राजा राज्यं रक्षत्यासन्ने यः परेभ्पश्र।।
पूर्व दारेभ्यः पुत्रेभ्यश्र।। 1-21।।
Arthasastra, 1. 17. 1-2.

95. एवं रात्रौ च मित्रे च मध्यमे चावपेच्चरान।
उदासीने च तेषां च तीर्थष्वष्टाद ास्र्वाप।।
Arthasastra, 1. 12.22.

96. N. Subhramaniam, *op. cit.*, p. 101.

97. *Arthasastra*, 8.2.2-3.

98. न यह च्चाच्चं तनुत्राणं रक्षेदात्मानयात्मना।
चार भूमिष्वमिगतान पा ां च पविजयेत।।
Mahabharata, *Shantiparvan*, 120/14.

99. M.N. Dutta, Kamandaka Nitisara, VI, VII, 1896.

100. *Arthasastra*, 1.17. 23-24.

101. जन्मप्रभति राजपुत्रान्नक्षेत।
कर्कटसंघ र्माणो हि जनकभक्षा राजपुत्रा।। (5-6)।
Arthasastra, 1. 17.6.

102. *Arthasastra*, 1. 17. 29-3 1.

103. व्यक्तं गूढ़पुरूषाः ास्त्ररसाभ्यां हन्युः।।
Arthasastra, 1. 19.18.

104. Palmer, *op. cit.*, p. 45.

105. Shakambari Jayal, 'The Status of Women in the Epics, Delhi, 1966, p. 299.

106. अन्तर्गहगतः स्थविरस्त्रीपरि ुद्धा।
Arthasastra, 1.20 21-22

107. *Manu Samhita*, VII, 153.

108. S.D. Trivedi, *op. cit.*, p. 103.

109. I.W. Mabbett, *op. cit.*, p. 47.

110. *Arthasastra*, 9.5.6.

111. T.N. Ramaswamy, *op. cit.*, p. 47.

112. *Arthasastra*, 12.4., 4-6.

113. *Ibid.*, 12.4., 5-10.

114. S.D. Trivedi, *op. cit.*, p. 106.

115. *Manu Samhita*, VII, 217-220.

116. यथा च योग पुरूषैरन्यान्राजाधिति– ष्टिति।
तथायमन्यबाधेभ्यो रक्षेदात्मानमात्मवान।। ४७।।
Arthasastra, 1.21.47.

117. S.L. Roy, *op. cit.*, p. 191.

118. *Arthasastra*, 7.17.

119. *Ibid.*, 7.17, 32.

120. *Ibid.*, 7.17, 122-123, 43-47.

121. *Arthasastra*, 7.17, 53-54.

122. *Ibid.*, 7.17, 55-56.

123. Pratigya Yaugandharayana, IV Part.

4

Techniques of Spies

Secret services have an implicit faith in the fallibility of human nature, and the agents are trained to ascertain the considerations that act as catalysts. This is an important exercise prior to "intelligence approach" and spies are 'desired to study in detail the weaknesses and liabilities of their targets. According to the individual behaviour agents used them by adopting various techniques. As Subhasita mentions, that, "A greedy person should be cultivated by gifts, in cash and kind, a gentleman by bestowing honours, a scholar by intelligent discussion, and a crooked person by thrashing, blackmail and punishment".[1] Many polity thinkers unanimously accepted that in the work of espionage, all methods were admissible—spying, lying, bribing, poisoning, women's wiles and the assassin's knife.[2]

Espionage played an active role in the diplomatic policies. Many shrewd diplomats sought to win their policy by crooked methods and taking recourse to stratagems. In this battle of wits there was extensive use of spies with their techniques.[3]

(a) Dissension and Misinformation. The policy of '*bheda*' or dissension is the policy of 'divide and rule'. A kingdom is apt to be troubled by internal dissension as well as by external aggression. To launch a policy of either aggression or defence, internal peace is essential. To conquer an enemy, it is necessary to create division among his kinsmen or among his subjects and to attack him when they are disunited.[4] It was the duty of the spies to create dissension in enemy camps.[5] In the Ramayana when Vibhishana took shelter of Rama, Ravana become aware of the war occurence immediately so he sent Suka as spy to Sugriva to concitiate him. Suka told Sugriva, "Ravana has not done any harm to you, you are just like a brother to him. He has carried somebody else's wife, and this should not cause any anger to you, so you should go back. Lanka cannot be reached even by the gods". So saying, Suka assumed the form of a bird and rose into the sky. In response Sugriva addressed Suka, thus; Suka, tell Ravana that he is neither our friend nor our benafactor. We are marching to Lanka with our army. Rama will make short work of him along with his brothers, sons, and relatives. So Sugriva remained unaffected by the tactics of Ravana's spy.

Kautilya was a master psychologist when it came to winning over an assorted group of people whether for intelligence use or for disintegrating enemy powers. He advises that, "A king should subjugate the weak by means of conciliation and gifts, the strong by means of dissension and force." The agents were to encourage defection of senior officers and confederates,[6] winning the confidence of enemy king, spies should enter in his state and with the help of his ministers, they should produce the dissension among them.[7]

Brahmans created dissension and dis*Sati*sfaction between the sons of Kunti and those of Madri with the help of spies by the orders of Duryodhana.[8]

Shantiparvan also declare that, "one should never seek to subdue his foes by war. Excited with wrath and bereft of forgiveness, only children seek quarrel...... by employing trusted agents one should render the enemy forces weak through disunion and dissension."[9]

A king should use the policy of dissension at first, against the enemy with the help of spies.[10]

Bhisma advises in this respect, "A king was to apply the art of conciliation backed by force, remonstrance short of war and thus make an opponent come to terms". Secret agents were to be sent to produce dissension among foes and their allies and having produced disunion, peace was to be made with the ally of the foe who was powerful.[11]

Disinformation or misinformation also is a measure that is widely used as an effective technique by modern intelligence services to create disharmony and distrust among friends, ill-will among allies and loss of confidence in the leaders and the government by a calculated circulation or publication of false, forged or motivated information.[12]

Disinformation had also been used by warring groups, monarchs and oligarchies to defeat adversaries by breaking there well knit and cohesive unity.[13]

Kautilya, the *Mahabharata* and the *Ramayana*, highly stressed on the technique of dissension in the battle, in place of military actions to win.[14]

Behind these policies, the polity thinkers suggest some objectives. These were used to create the ill-will against the enemy state and to undermine the political influence of target country. These were to generate or aggravate existing discords among the states. Kautilya had perfected these techniques to strengthen the position of the king. He utilized the 'secret agents' to construct a safe political environment for his country and decried the popularity of the target state. He mentioned such tricks with practical examples, which can change the anti feelings of masses towards king. His propaganda was based on a clever application of mob psychology.[15]

Spies, collecting the people on a public place, opposing one other, tried to know the opinion of people towards king. The virtues of king were eulogized.[16] The loyalists were rewarded with honours and monetary gifts, and the disaffected were won over by conciliation, gifts, dissension or by punishments.[17]

King used '*Kantakasodhans* agents' to propagate his omniscience and divinity in distant lands and to cater information about disloyal elements in the enemy's setup. These agents disguised as astrologers, soothsayers, interpreters of omens, ascetics who tell the supernatural attributes of king and reciters of the *Puranas*, used to win the loyalty of people.[18] They ascertained the nature of rumours spreading among the subjects and restrained the people's participation in activities.

Kautilya marked it the duty of spies to anticipate and prevent hostile combinations by creating dissension and given various techniques for creating dissension between corporate powers, friendly groups, the king and his generals, senior bureaucrats and members of the royal family.[19]

A secret agent by convincing the son of a member of the ruling council who thinks highly of himself, that "you are the son of such and such king but kept here for fear of the enemy" should provide with him funds and troops to fight the other members of oligarchy.[20]

Prostitutes and women spies were also used to create dissension and very skillfully helped in assassination of target. The chief of the ruling council were infatuated by the beautiful women. When they are excited, the women agents decided to meet one head at a particular place, later they started quarrel by creating an impression about their love in one person while going to another or by forcible abduction of youthful domes. Later, the women agents should convey their make-believe lovers that they are being harassed or have been abducted or prevented to go to the latter by another chief. Thus creating enmity among them, the spies can assassinate any chief, with the rumour that other chief of ruling council had killed him.[21]

The spies used to borrow the vehicles or money from members of the oligarchy, but gave it to chief and when other members demanded it back, they blamed the chief as to abduct the money. Thus they produced quarrel among them.[22]

In many ways Kautilya tells the methods for disinformation. He mentioned that, a female mendicant should convey to the chief fond of his wife, such and such a chief conceited by reason of youth sent me to your wife through fear of him, I have brought a letter and ornaments from him, your wife is innocent, steps against him should be taken secretly.[23] Thus condition of war can be created between these two chiefs of councils.

Like this, the agents working as cook or waiter inform the chief about the king's secret instructions for administering poison to the former, and shows the money offered to him for this assignment. Another agent appearing as a trader corroborates the story.[24] Kautilya placed the dissension and disintegration most important methods of secret service, amongst the groups of conspirators to defeat them.[25]

The *Mahabharata*[26] also supports the views of Kautilya and lays down, "the king should afflict the kingdom of the stronger by means of weapons, fire and application of poison. He should cause dissension amongst the counsellors and servants."

There are ample examples to sow dissension, in the Epic. Duryodhana[27] tried to create discord among the Pandavas with the help of Karna's spies, as they inspired the Pandavas to leave the Hastinapur and to settle in Drupada's dominion. The spies were asked to sow the seeds of dissension among the Pandavas to make them jealous of one another in case of Draupadi. Besides it they want to create misunderstanding against Krishna, in this way he will be dissatisfied with them.

Bhisma[28] tells Yudhisthira, that towards the strong foe, the policy of conciliation and chastisement by the secret means should be adopted.

He questioned Yudhisthira, "Have you maintained a strong army ? Have you caused disunion among the foes and setting them against one another ? Thou shall try to know the weakness of king through the agents and make them available the beautiful women and clothes, beds and seats, vehicles, and all of very costly kinds, juices and perfumes and fruits, so that the foe may be ruined himself."

Narada, the indomitable wandering minstrel, may be called the first Indian disinformation agent, who had an uncanny habit of being present at every spot of impending trouble, who advised kings, queens, sages and commoners alike in their hours of distress, who stored out disputes and tangled issues and created strifes and wars at the same time.[29]

In *Puranas*, there are reference of more than seven births of Narada, indicating possibly that "Narada" name had come to be associated with the various masters of the art of disinformation. In a very interesting dialogue with Indra on the occasion of Damayanti's marriage, Narada laments that kings on the earth don't wage war against each other. He considers it necessary to go down to the earth and involve the mortals in deadly wars. He said that..... "discontented with this, he has come to heaven to see thee, in order to have the pleasure of seeing a war."[30] Manu also favoured this policy. He said that, a king, willing to fight should act among the matyas of enemy and controlling them, should know the activities of enemy king. Though Manu does not attach much importance to this policy.

This art of disinformation was very effectively practiced by modern intelligence services on a massive scale during the first and second World Wars to create disharmony and distrust between friends. They created such condition that could demoralize the fighting troops of hostile nations and they could loose the confidence in the state leadership.

So the Epics, the *Arthasastra*, *Smritis*, *Puranas* favoured the policy of dissension and disinformation used by secret agents in place of waging the wars.

(b) Motivation and Temptation. Human activity is proportionately commensurate to impelling factors, and according to an old adage, "even a fool does not act without self interest."

Secret agents were trained as talent spotters with a view to identifying the consideration which motivate a person into extending "co-operation".

Kautilya[31] suggests various tricks to motivate the people to tell the secrets. The agents instigate the burning desires of revenge of the sources and excite them for sex and money. They make them ambitious for authority. Thus exploiting the weakness, the spies make full advantage for their side.

While recruiting the secret agents, some precautionary measures were taken. They were already examined by giving temptations.

Spies were provided with enough money and attractive gifts. Farmers, traders, hermits were given land, trading facilities and honour respectively for the secret operations.[32]

Kautilya studied the psychology of people and gave many methods for spies to disintegrate the enemy and to motivate the sources to tell the secrets.

"The agents should conciliate a pious king by extolling his birth, family, learning and conduct, or by rendering service and refraining from causing injury."

Secret agents should find out defects and weaknesses of target persons, occasions for mutual hatred, enmity or strife among members of oligarchy and should convey to each one individually and motivate them that, "So and so is slandering you" when tempers are frayed, agents working as teachers should encourage them by starting quarrel.[33]

Seditious ministers were to be agitated into taking an unwise move against the king and then on that charge assassinated. The method was to work in the manner of the wolf of Aesop's fables, who accused the lamb of drinking his water in the stream. In the end, the seditious minister was to be killed in one way or another.[34]

Criminals should be won over by paying money and showing other consideration. These can be used against an enemy for causing death by weapon, fire or poison.

Kautilya in a subtle manner and with an intimate knowledge of human psychology selected his targets in foreign lands depending on their weakness and motivation. People generally go against their master for money, sex, ideological considerations, for satisfying their vanity avenging a personal grudge or for reasons of blackmail. Secret agents must ascertain the motivation before an intelligence assault is mounted.

There is a long list of persons who can be easily motivated to go against their king. The *Arthasastra* gave them some names such as "*Kruddhavarga*"[35] or 'enraged' or 'discontented persons'. They were dissatisfied with their king or had been humiliated, exiled, wrongly imprisoned and fined, or deprived of their rightful inheritance to office or whose women had been molested by force. Another group was those of '*Bhitavarga*'[36] or 'frightened people'. They have committed a sinful act and got defamation among the public, or always frightened by punishment meted out to another for a similar offence, who have seized someone's land, who are subdued by force.

Lubdhavarga,[37] 'the group of greedy', these people were impoverished, their property was snatched away by another, a miser and the person who was in calamity and indulged in vices.

One more group was those of proud or called '*Manivarga*'.[38] These people were over-ambitious, jealous of their prosperous colleagues, violating and were dissatisfied with their emoluments.

Agnipurana also give some directions to secret agents as to motivate the people and to win their favour. It suggests that a spy should speak sweetly to his target that would melt his heart. He should motivate and made temptations for those persons who had been invited and insulted by their master and were displeased with their sovereign and for the shake of money they would sell their secrets.

The spies were directed to operate among these groups adopting a technique suitable to the situation, and after analysing the weaknesses of targets, should play up to them accordingly.[39]

They must be instigated, and provoked by agents operating under 'cover'. Each of the targets was to be individually approached.[40]

The '*kruddhavarga*' category should be provoked by saying, "just as an elephant blinded by intoxication and being driven by an intoxicated person, crushes whatever comes in the way so this king, not possessed of the eye of science, and hence blind, has risen to destroy the citizens and the country people; it is possible to do him harm by inciting a rival elephant (Prince) against him; show your resentment."[41] Giving such fury statements, the secret agents motivate the people to go against their king.

Those of the 'frightened' group was made fearful and conscious about their lives. Kautilya says, "that the agents should create fear among these people, saying that, "like a serpent, lying in hiding, emits poison at the place from which it expects danger, so this king is apprehensive of harm from you, he will emit the poison of anger at you; so to save your life, you should left this place."[42]

In the *Ramayana*, the technique to create fear is also practiced. Rama directed to the both spies of Ravana that, "tomorrow, I will destroy your Lanka with its fortification and will kill to the *Raksasa* by arrows," such harsh message was to create fear in the enemy.[43]

In case of 'greedy', the principal officers among the chiefs of the army should be tempted with land or money. Then the secret agents should make them ready to fight their own people by conveying to them highly exaggerated threats from the king.[44]

The spies unleashed a whispering campaign against enemy kings by giving currency to their failings and frailities real and fancied, while publishing the invincibility and virtuous conduct of their own sovereign.

The people in the group of proud (manivarga) have to be played with feelings by saying, "just as the well of the *Chandalas* is of use only for the *Chandalas*, not to others, so this king, being low, is of benefit only to low persons, not to Aryas such as you; that other king knows how to appreciate persons of distinction (like you) go to him."[45]

Ambitious princes or the people of desirous of superior stature should be played up with their aspirations. A secret agent should instigate the son of a member of the council staying near or in a fort, saying, that, "you as a son possessed of greater personal excellence, yet you have been set aside; why are you indifferent? Fight and seize the kingdom otherwise the crown prince will soon destroy you."[46]

The spies used the technique of temptations to test the character of probationers for posts in any of the government departments. The nature of the temptations (*upadha*) varied according to the qualifications needed for discharging the duties of the post for which a particular probationer was a candidate. These tests were (a) *Dharmopadha* (b) *Arthopadha* (c) *Kamopadha* and (d) *Bhayopadha*, relating to religion, wealth, love, and fear, respectively.[47]

Such seducible or vulnerable parties in the enemy kingdom should be then given money and gifts.

(c) Blackmailing and cheating. When normal intelligence approach fails to achieve the desired result, Kautilya does not easily give up efforts at targeting and suggests that they may even be blackmailed for cultivation.[48]

Dr. V.A. Smith seems to believe that, "intrigue spies, winning over the enemy's people seize and assault, had much to do with the creation of the Mauryan empire and the theory of politics expounded in the *Arthasastra* is substantially identical with that of 'the Prince'. In plain words it was the Machiavellian.[49]

Spies used to cheat the people for their purposes. The cheating and even murdering of the seditious and the wicked through spies, and the appropriation of the properties thus acquired.[50]

A spy in the guise of a tradesman becomes the partner of a rich trader. As soon as a large sum of money is to hand from the sale-proceeds, deposits etc. he causes himself to be robbed of same. That the consequence of these measures might, when misapplied, prove ruinous to the king himself was realized, and hence a warning has been given that they should in no case be applied to people other than the wicked and the seditious.[51]

Thus cheating to the rich people, the spies replenish of the government treasury in times of financial difficulties.

The agent also used to kill the enemy king by cheating. The spy in disguise of horse trader called the king as to see horse to sell them, when king will be busy to check them and surrounded with the horses, the spy should kill him and attack on his palace with these horses.[52]

Kautilya suggests many tricks to kill the enemy king by cheat. He said that, "assassins should kill the king by fire when he is in a narrow place, by smoke when he is in a desert, by poison if he is in his residence, by frightful crocodiles or persons moving in water, if he is bathing in river water or kill him as he is coming out of his apartment which has been set on fire." So secret agents were permitted to do such crimes, which were considered illegal in actual.

The secret agents could sell cooked poisoned meat and rice to enemy troops by offering it cheaper than the other dealers and thus they were easily successful to kill the soldiers of enemy's army. Like this the secret agents took away the king by misguiding him on a solitary place or in a cave or jungle and when king was fully under their confidence they killed him.

(d) Double Agent operation. *Ubhayavetana* : A 'double Agent' or '*Ubhayavetana*'[53] is a distinctive feature of the Kautilya's machinery of administration. A 'double agent' is a spy who works for the opposition while pretending loyalty to those who employ him. This technique is an absolutely necessary facet of agent running, and was extensively practiced in ancient India.

Kautilya suggests that for intelligence abroad the '*Ubhayavetanas*' (special agents), who are "in the pay-roll of both countries" should be employed. These agents manage to security service with the ruler or some high official in a foreign state. When they have won the confidence of the latter, they are in a position to collect and pass on valuable information secretly to their native state and thus render a useful service to it.[54]

A 'double agent' operation could be organized either by deliberately floating agents or by winning over hostile sources.[55]

It is a professional phenomenon to change the sides by agents and both the parties benefited with this. It is also suggested that spies should take the money as their payment from the target for their working with them as employees. So the '*Ubhayavetanas*' were paid by two parties. They could cross over to the enemy while still working for the original master.[56]

The king was advised to examine the loyalty of these agents through spies of their type, before they were employed. If they were failed in their mission in enemy state, they were silently punished, more ever, the king should hold their wives and children as hostages.[57] Thus, to advance the interest of the king, Kautilya does not hesitate to prescribe measures which are apparently callous and even immoral.[58]

The services of 'double agents' were utilized in efforts to cause a split in the combination of several kings against one.[59]

They were also used for creating dissension and confusion among the confederates of the enemy, his army and cavalry chiefs. They helped in demoralizing and disintegrating the enemy power.[60]

These agents spread the rumours, floated false documents, got them seized from the possession of army chiefs, and thus weakened the enemy.[61]

'Double agents' worked also as the regular spies and collected the information of foreign kings and states and suppressed the criminals. These agents were sent in the enemy territory to seek the employment so that they can get secret of enemy king. Sometimes the king or senior *amatyas* dismissed the officers and they were given shelter by enemy kings. There they were directed to gain their favour and confidence. All this carried on in a pre-planned way. These 'double agents' worked for enemy king but being devoted to their master. And as soon as got opportunity, they killed the adopted master or used to poisoned their ears against their own staff, or led them to a life of vices and degeneration.[62]

The technique of 'double agent' operation continued throughout the ancient period. *Kamandaka* also suggest for this technique he suggests that such agents should be deployed for the collection of intelligence and winning over sensitive targets in other countries.[63]

The *Mudraraksasa* vividly dealt with this technique. Chanakya dismissed many officers from Mauryan administration to create dissension in enemy kingdom, pretending as terrified with Chandra Gupta Maurya, they joined '*Malayaketu*' who failed to get the real motive behind these defections. One of the agents of Chanakya succeeded in getting employment with *Raksasa* himself.[64] Thus he served the *Malayketu* as well as his real master and spied on the enemy, Act V of Mudraraksasa mentions one Jivasiddhi who was known as a friend of Raksasa but was in reality a spy of Chanakya. Magha, in post Gupta period, also refers to the '*Ubhayavetanas*' as a special class of spies, who would enter the service of other kings under disguise. They won the confidence of the principal officers there and estranged them from their kings at opportune moments by producing documentary evidence.[65]

The 'double agents' were used to win over the confidence of their adopted masters by sacrificing a few exposed, treacherous or disaffected spies; those who were inefficient or the robbers and disaffected forest chiefs harassing the two states.

This technique is still playing an important role in intelligence services and secret agents are encouraged to seek employment with the targets.

(e) Counter Espionage and Counter Intelligence. These are two operations handled by the secret agents against the enemy of foreign land. 'Counter intelligence' and 'counter espionage' are sometimes taken as interchangeable terms and confused.

Espionage and measures to counter the same, both, within the state and without it, must have been deep rooted in the Indian society of the Chanakya's time. An extensive treatise has been written by him on this subject.[66]

Counter intelligence operation is directed at discovering the identities and methods of spies and intelligence officers working for the opposition.[67]

All the types of spies, operating against the enemy spies were entrusted in counter intelligence.[68]

While a 'counter espionage' operation is aimed at penetrating the opposition's intelligence service and operations. The objective in both these operations is to defeat the aggressive designs of the hostile secret service.[69]

With the help of these operations, secret agents locate the foreign spies and the officers from the enemy group and liquidate them.[70]

Astrologers, palmists, prophecy makers, etc., disguised spies, having influence among the masses, successfully ascertained the contacts between the local people and foreign agents and go through the information.[71]

The unconventional trade routes on the frontiers, were covered by the smugglers, and merchant spies, as these routes were extensively used by foreign agents entering the country. Along with this, these routes were considered as the most important means of over reaching the enemy. Troops and spies used to go into the enemy territory and purchased of weapons, carriages and vehicles from foreign lands, since the ancient times to modern period.[72]

Both the 'stationary and roving sources' assuming appropriate 'covers' were advised to discover the enemy agents and to watch enemy movements during the march of the enemy on a special operational requirement.[73]

The counter espionage staff was deputed during the army march in the day and night to discover enemy infiltrants.

The 'counter espionage' agents posted in the frontier should be non-seducible, while they should pretend as if they are motivated and tempted by them. This was an intelligence use of lure hostile agents into making intelligence approach against officers in the border region which may eventually lead to their arrest.[74]

Still this 'coat-trailing operation' is frequently used by modern intelligence services for exposing their targets.

These secret agents were also appointed at the places of entertainment, conclaves of people, among beggars, in gardens and public places and the areas which a king expected to visit, to discover the foreign spies.[75]

The *Ramayana*[76] makes vivid references to counter espionage. The spies of this operation, observed the *Vibhisana* for a long time, in a systematic deployment and arrested him and presented him to Rama. Before capturing him, they watched his behaviour and movements over a considerable period to confirm whether he was a secret agent or an envoy.

Rama was advised to depute agents in Lanka to collect background information about Vibhisana, when his story was doubted.[77]

In modern times also, before arrival of any diplomatic envoy, many precautionary steps are taken about his background, character and his intentions.

The agents of Ravana detailed to observe the troops of Rama, were captured by latter's watchful agents' eyes and brought before Rama. They gave up all hopes of their life. Thus baffled, Ravana once again sent spies into the invading army. Once again they were discovered, maltreated, belaboured, but ultimately set free.[78]

This proves the efficiency of the "counter espionage" staff of Rama, especially as Ravana's agents were disguised as "Vanaras" making their identification difficult. Shuk and Sarana were the agents of Ravana while trying to know the strength of Rama's army, were captured but granted apology and warned for future.[79]

Ravana's intelligence staff also quickly discovered the Hanumana's presence in Lanka while disguised. Vibhisana deployed agents viz. Anala, Sarbha, Sampati, and Pradhasa to collect information on the strength of Ravana's troops, army movements and plans under the counter espionage.[80]

The *Mahabharata* accepts the idea of *Arthasastra* and the *Ramayana* on the deployment of counter-intelligence agents. It advises that, "to know the spies of your enemy by detailing spies in shops and places of amusement, amid concourses of people, among beggars, in gardens and parks, in the courts, in public places, in places where the king holds his court, and in the houses of the citizens. The king possessed of intelligence may then discover the spies dispatched by his foes."[81]

Kamandaka[82] advises in the Nitisastra to be careful of foreign spies. It lays down that, "kings should remain constantly watchful of their role and should deploy able agents to locate and liquidate foreign spies."

Bharvi also give reference of counter-espionage. He suggests, "let, therefore, counter measures be taken at once against him who is ready with operational facilities to harm you."

"Counter espionage" in its practical form has been handled with its technique in the '*Mudraraksasa*'[83] where Chanakya and *Raksasa* confront each other with ingenious operational technique.

In Chanakya's view, counter espionage was to be countered by placing spies over spies. Although war had to be fought by the armed forces but to Chanakya, it was the enemy commander's mind, and morale, which had to be attacked and defeated by various stratagems much before the two armies met. Then everything else being formed, the army was to deliver the final blow, this strategy formed the basis of Chenghis Khan's operations as even, on a small scale the Chinese 1962 operations against us.[84]

(f) Secret Codes. Proper and swift communication of intelligence is very essential for further proceedings, unless it looses its value and validity. So the writers on polity had devised the technique of secret codes and messages.

The disadvantage of the lack of efficient means of communication and transportation was overcome to a great extent by spies with the means of secret codes or sign-alphabets.[85] It is stated that the officers in the institute of espionage should not call the working spies, but should give written directions.

So the cipher writing or "*Gudhalekha*"[86] was to be used by the spies, and carrier pigeons were to carry secret intelligence. The idea is that even if the message falls in the hands of ordinary citizens or foreign spies they cannot make out its contents.[87]

During Mauryan period, the movements of foreigners were closely watched and the CID efficiently used the secret codes. Even spies in employment did not know the meaning of several of them.[88]

While the secret agents could not enter the houses of senior officers and ministers to spy upon them, they enter disguised as the parents of servants in the houses or posing as female artists, singers or menial workers and collected the information and writings concealed in musical instruments.[89]

For long distances, the information was sent by a relay system. Secret agents used to produce identifiable sounds by blowing conches or beating drums.[90]

The use of signs and cipher writing and carrier pigeons formed part of military espionage also.[91] During war, these were used to convey message from distance. War music rousing the spirit of combatants, invoking God's gifts and wishing victories and striking terror played an important part.[92]

The *Mahabharata* mentions the techniques of coded language and signal for secret communication.[93] Pandavas used the predetermined coded language termed as '*Mlechha Bhasha*'.

The *Ramayana* also mentions the use of coded message, identification signals and signs.

Mudraraksasa is a fine example for the use of secret codes. So with the help of secret languages, and signals the secret agents sent the message as well as receive them, in the absence of proper means of communication and transport and spied upon the target.[94] This is the technique which was widely adopted by the modern intelligence system during the World Wars.

The king is advised to adopt all means during the spying. Spies under the guise of disciple, a recluse, a house holder, a merchant, a mendicant woman should consider the weakness of their targets and should try to win those people who are greedy, fearful, enraged or proud. The people, whom the king had categorised into haughty and provocative were more likely to be exploited by own spies through several ways and create nucleus of these functions.[95]

But Kautilya is called Machiavellian due to his policies. The learned historian Bana quotes to prove how detestable the Kautilyan principle. He described the science of Kautilya as merciless in its precepts and rich in cruelty.[96]

But A.L. Basham did not consider it mere Machiavellian instrument or maintaining power but an integral part of the state machinery.

References

1. लुब्धामर्थेण ग्रहणीयात साधुमंजलि कर्मणा।
   दुष्ट दण्डानुरोधोन तत्वार्थेन च पण्डितम।।
   Subhasita.
2. B.K. Majumdar, Role of Secret Services in Ancient India, I.H.C., Vol. 19, 1956.
3. T.B. Mookerji, *op. cit.*, p. 141.
4. S.P. Chhangani, Interstate Relations in Ancient India, S.K. Pub., New Delhi, 1986, p. 32.
5. *Ramayana, Yudhakanda*, xxv, 21.
6. *Arthasastra*, 1.11.9-13.
7. भेदं वास्य स्ववर्गेभ्यः कुर्युः। 50।
   Arthasastra, 3.13.50.
8. *Mahabharata, Adiparvan*, 192.
9. भेदेनोपप्रदानेन संसजेदौषधौस्तथा।
   न तवेवं खलु संसर्ग रोचयेदरिभिः सह।। 17
   Mahabharata, Shantiparvan, Chap. 103.17.
10. भेदं च प्रथमं चुय्जयात तूष्णीं दण्डं तर्थेवचि।
    Mahabharata.
11. T.B. Mookerji, *op. cit.*, p. 70.
12. दुर्ग दग्धां हृतं वा ते कोपः कुल्यः समुत्थितः।
    ात्रु राटबिको वेति परस्योद्रेग माचरेत।।54
    Arthasastra, 10/6/54.
13. S.D. Trivedi, *op. cit.*, p. 66.

14. Beni Prasad, The Theory of Government, Allahabad, 1926, pp. 344, 368.
15. *Arthasastra*, 1. 13. 2-10.
16. कतमहामात्रापसर्पः पौरजानपदान–पसर्पयेत।
    सात्त्रिणोद्वंद्विनस्तीर्थसभा ाला पूगजनसमवायेषु विवादं कुर्युः।।12
    Arthasastra, 1.13.2.
17. *Ibid.,* 2. 10.47.
18. *Arthasastra*, 1. 13. 14.
19. *Arthasastra*, 1. 16.3-4.
20. *Arthasastra*, 11.1.36-39.
21. *Ibid.,* 11.1.44-46.
22. संघाना वा वाहनहिरण्ये कालिके
    गहीत्वा संघभुरण्याय प्रख्यातं द्रव्यं प्रयच्छेत।।
    तदेषां याचिते दत्तमनुष्मै मुख्यायेतिब्रूयात।33-34
    Ibid., 11.1.33-34.
23. बन्धकीपोषकाः प्लवकनटनर्तकसौभिका वा प्रणिहिताः स्त्रीभिः।
    परमरूप यौवनाभिः संघमुख्यनुन्मादयेषुः।। 40।।
    Arthasastra, 11.1.40.
24. *Arthasastra*, 12.2.22-23.
25. S. p. Chhangani, *op. cit.*, pp. 32-33.
26. *Mahabharata, Shantiparvan.*
27. *Ibid.,* LXXXXIX.
28. *Shantiparvan*, LX I X.
29. Devibhagvata, 1, X Vettam, p. 526.
30. उपजप्यानुजभेद बुध्येतैव च तत्कतम।
    Manusmiriti 7/197.
31. *Arthasastra*, 1.1.12.2.8.
32. *Ibid.,* 1. 11.9-13,1.1.21, 1.13.17.
33. *Arthasastra*, 11.1.6-8.
34. J.W. Spellmen, Political Theory of Ancient India, Oxford, 1964, p. 140.

35. *Arthasastra*, 1. 14.2.
36. *Arthasastra*, 1. 14.4.
37. परिक्षीणो अत्यात्तस्वः कदर्यो व्यसच्यत्चाहित व्यवहार चेति लुब्धवर्गः । 5 । *Ibid.*, 4. 14.5.
38. आत्मसंभावितो मानकामः ुत्रपूजामर्षितो नीचैरूपहितस्तीक्ष्णः साहसिको भोगेनासंतुष्ट इति मनिवर्गः । । 6 *Ibid.*, 1.14.6.
39. S.D. Trivedi, *op. cit.*, p. 63.
40. *Arthasastra*, 1. 14 . 7.
41. यथा मदान्धोहस्ती मत्तेनाधिनिष्ठतो यद्यदाससदयति तत्सर्व प्रमद्वात्येव मयम ास्त्र च क्षुरन्धो राजा पौरजानपदववधा– याम्युत्थितः । ।8 । । *Arthasastra*, 1. 14. 8.
42. *Arthasastra*, 1. 14. 10.
43. *Ramayana, Aryana Parva*, Ch. 267.
44. *Arthasastra*, 1.14.11-12.
45. *Arthasastra*, 1.14.13.
46. *Ibid.*, 11.1.9.
47. N.N. Law, Machinery of Administration in the Kautilya, I.H.Q., Dec. 1929, p. 627.
48. *Arthasastra*, 1. 14. 12.
49. B.K. Majumdar, Role of Secret Services in Ancient India, I.H.Q., Vol. 19, 1956, p. 121.
50. N.N Law, I.H.Q., *op. cit.*, p. 635.
51. *Arthasastra*, (*Kosabhisambharana*).
52. अ वपण्योपयाता वैदेहकव्य तजनाः पाण्योपयाननिमित्त माहूय राजानं पण्यपरीक्षायांमासक्तमश्रतिकीर्ण वा हन्युर वैश्र प्रहरेयुः ।30 *Arthasastra*, 13,2,30,
53. कण्टक ाेधानोक्ताश्रापरूर्ष परेषु कतवेतना वसेयुः सपातनिश्रारर्थम त उभयभेतनाः । । 19-20. *Arthasastra*, 1, 12,19-20.
54. Aradhana Parmar, Technique of Statecraft : A Study of Kautilya's *Arthasastra*, pp. 238-239.

55. S.D. Trivedi, *op. cit.*, p. 45.
56. *Arthasastra*, 1. 12. 19.
57. गहीत प दारांश्र कुर्या दुभयवेतनान।
    ताश्ररिप्रहितान्र्वद्यात्तेषां गोचं च तद्विधौः।।21
    Arthasastra, 1.12.21.
58. Aradhana Parmar, *op. cit.*, p. 239.
59. N.N. Law, I.H.Q., Dec. 1927, *op. cit.*, p. 636.
60. *Arthashastra*, 4. 4. 3-5, 4. 5. 1, 7.14. 5-9.
61. *Ibid.,* 9. 6. 34- 41, 9.6. 46-48.
62. *Arthasastra*, 12,3.1-6, 8-14.
63. *Kamandaka*, xiii / 26.
64. *Mudraraksasa*, H.L. *Sukla*, *Mudraraksasa Ka Sanskritic Anusheelan*, Nagpur, 1976.
65. D.K. Ganguly, Aspects of Ancient Indian Administration, New Delhi, p. 295.
66. H.S. Bhatia, ed. Political, Legal and Military History of India, Vol. ii., N. Delhi, p. 347.
67. *Arthasastra*, Ch. xii.
68. S.K. Bhakari, Indian Warfare, New Delhi, 1981, p. 87.
69. Palmer, *op. cit.*, p. 100.
70. *Arthasastra*, 1-12-24.
71. *Ibid.,* 1, 12 10, 25 10.1.14.
72. *Arthasastra*, 2.21.22-27.
73. *Ibid.,* 10. 11. 11-14.
74. अकत्यान्कत्यपक्षीयै दर्गितान्कार्यहेतुभिः।
    परासर्पज्ञानार्थ मुख्यानन्तेषु वासयेत।।27
    Arthasastra, 1. 12.27.
75. *Ibid.,* 13. 1. 1.
76. *Ramayana*, *Yudhakanda*, 17.22-28.
77. *Ibid.,* 17.43.44.

78. P.C. Chakravarti, The Art of War in Ancient India, p. 74.
79. अव यं चापि विज्ञेयै तन्मया वानरं बलस।
Yudhakanda, 25.3.
80. Prabhakar Dikshit, *Valmiki Ramayan main Rajnitik Vichar*, p. 157.
81. *Mahabharata, Shantiparvan*, Ch. 69.11-12.
82. M.N. Dutta, *Kantandaka Nitisara.*
83. M.R. Kale, *Mudraraksasa* (trans.), Varanasi, 1965.
84. H.S. Bhatia, Ed., *op. cit.*, p. 348.
85. Aradhana Parmar, *op. cit.*, p. 236.
86. *Arthasastra*, 1. 11. 12.
87. S.L. Roy, Diplomacy in Ancient India, p. 187.
88. T.L. Shah, Ancient India (BC 900-AD 100), Vol. 2, 1938, p. 200.
89. *Arthasastra*, 1.12.11.14.
90. *Ibid.,* 10. 1. 11.
91. B.K. Majumdar, The Military System in Ancient India, 1955, p. 73.
92. *Ibid.,* p. 37.
93. *Mahabharata, Virataparvan* and *Adiparvan.*
94. *Mudraraksasa* (trans.), M.R. Kale, Varanasi, 1965.
95. H.S. Bhatia, *op. cit.*, p. 348.
96. B.K. Majumdar, I.H.Q., Vol. 19, 1956, p. 121.

5

Various Covers of Spies

Espionage requires utmost secrecy working under disguise and creation of various covers by spies is the essential part of spy system. It was the distinguished feature of spies to work concealing their identity by changing different faces. Kautilya gives various covers to be adopted by spies.[1]

Manu[2] points out that the wind moves everywhere and penetrates all created beings. Just so should the king penetrate everywhere by the means of his unidentified agents".[3]

The success of the work of the spies depended very much upon the secrecy with which they could carry it out, and the way in which they could clothe it in a grab of superficial sincerity and naturalness.[4]

There is no limit to the disguises under which the spies have to work. Throughout his work, Kautilya displays an abnormal anxiety to enlist religion in the service of espionage. He didn't consider appropriate to any means used for the security and welfare of the state.[5]

A spy may be disguised as hump-backed, deaf, dumb, dwarfish and blind or a dancer, a singer or a performer on musical instruments.[6]

Intelligence officers on field assignments invariably work under some kind of 'cover'. "Because their work is secret and that secrecy must be preserved, secret agents must appear to be other than what they actually are".[7]

'*Kural*' also mentions that spies should go about in strange disguises and even if detected are never to lose courage and never to blurt out any information they had gathered.[8]

It gives the names of covers of spies in which they are to disguise themselves as Brahmins, ascetics, pilgrims etc. that they may have access to places normally unapproachable.[9]

In order to gather the necessary information they moved in disguise of different persons in the native and enemy's country and visited the places for recreation, places for drinking water, wine houses, gateways of the cities and public halls and tried to gather secret information.[10]

Disguised as Professional Workers

Secret services were generally organised by the state. These were not used as private practice in ancient India. The *Vedas*, the *Ramayana* and the *Mahabharata* present a complete picture of espionage department organised by state. 'A kingdom', declares the Shantiparvan, "is to have its roots in spies and secret agents".[11] In Mauryan and Gupta period had its separate central department.

Secret services were used mainly for the security of the state and to maintain peace in the country. So spies were appointed by state on a decided salary. Rewards were also given them as a salary and as to promote them to work with great zeal.[12]

They were granted aid time to time and sometimes they were supported and rehabilitated by the state, if they were fallen from their profession.[13]

Like modern times espionage was existed as a profession in ancient India. The spies worked professional workers on the payment basis. To work secretively and without identifying themselves they had to use different covers.

Merchant spy (*Vaidehaka*) : The 'Merchant spies' lived inside the forts and cities to ascertain the manoeuvres of enemies.[14]

A merchant is to carry on with his trading and other business, although his primary task is to spy on manufacture of merchandise. As merchants, spies might sell poisoned food or kill whilst their client was examining the merchandise."[15]

To qualify for the post of merchant spy, he had to be traders with a foresight but become poor in his profession. He was to produce merchandise in the land allotted to him and look-after the needs of a few spies.[16] They were to use any religious beliefs to their own advantage."[17]

Ascetic spy : Normally Brahmin, pilgrim and ascetic have privilege to go every places without any strict inquiry.[18] So spies used to be disguised as ascetics.

A man with shaved hair or one with braided hair desirous of earning a living was to be an ascetic spy. Thus a Buddhist monk or a Saiva was to be appointed.[19]

Kautilya advises a ruler to appoint not ordinary man as an ascetic spy but to make the disguise better and effective. He wanted the ruler to appoint as spies men who really were in that line or profession.[20]

In *Mudraraksasa*, there is mention of a spy, employed by Kautilya, Nipunaka by name who moved through the city of Pataliputra under the guise of a mendicant and related afterwards to his master.

An ascetic should be provided with money, land and followers and under the disguise of carrying out his occupational pursuits, he should instruct his followers to report to him various crimes being committed against the interest of the king.[21]

Merchant spies were to become the disciples of the ascetic and pronounce him to be a man possessed of supernatural powers[22] to make his drama successful.

Physician spy : The '*Agnipurana*', Kautilya etc. mention the cover of physician as one of the common disguises of spy.

A spy may, as a physician, undertake to cure a seditious person, who may be made to believe that the illness from which he is suffering is likely to be fatal and put him to death by poisoning him through medicines and diet.[23]

The writers on polity had not given such a direction that the 'cover' of secret agents always be fictitious. It may be their true occupation in nearly all cases, those spies following specialized occupations are supposed to be persons who have fallen from their particular vocation.[24]

Kautilya had specially emphasised on this fact that some agents use their real lives to provide cover for their specific activities.[25]

In ancient India physicians were better used for spying. Kautilya exploited the persons, engaged in the welfare of mankind and the quacks and physicians for a variety of secret operations. Physician spies tried to declare the prevailing conspiracy in the palace. They could be used to determine a person of seditious character as well and could contrive to poison him while treatment. These spies were also sent to the foreign countries, where they used to poison the enemy king.[26]

Palmist or Fortune-teller as spy : Disguising as palmists, the spies should rouse the ambition of becoming a king in the chief and high officers of the state, thereby making them unloyal towards the king.[27]

This type of palmistry must have been rather unfortunate for the client whose palm indicated execution. The power of such spies must have been very considerable, especially since Kautilya tells the king's minister to direct his affairs in accordance with the ascetic's prophecy.[28]

Orphans, who were maintained by the state, were well versed in palmistry, were utilized as palmist spy.[29]

Astrologer spy : Astrologer spies to create fear in the persons who believed in God and foretell future events to people. During war time, when the war was about to commence or was already in progress, the spies in the grab of astrologers, forecast the victory of own forces and failure of the enemy plans. This was done to boost the morale of armed forces and of the civilian population.[30]

Cultivator spy : The cultivator spies lived in villages. They were to be honest cultivator in bad days, were allotted land to till and supported number spies like the recluse.[31]

***Udasin* spy**: *Udasin* was one, who had left the four orders of life and had become *Sanyasi* but who had subsequently returned to household duties after completion of his term in monastery. Such a man, with intelligence and purity, was to be an *Udasina* Spy.[32] This man was to be allotted land for agriculture, and cattle rearing and from the produce he was to maintain disciples and help all kinds of hermits. The *Udasina* spy was to employ these hermits as spies by repeated requests and insistence. Sometimes monks also protect the nuns in the covers of nuns. If a young nun was tormented by mischievous persons, it was the duty of some young monk who was well versed in the art of lighting, to meet the tormentor in the disguise of a nun and punish him.[33]

These hermits under the guise of a Buddhist monk or a *Shaiva*, etc., working for the welfare of his own ruler, was to ascertain the financial stability of another kingdom, by being present at the time of payment of wages (in that foreign state).

Criminal Spy : For crimes that are more difficult to detect, a spy may even apprentice himself to the criminal so as to be able eventually to prosecute.[34] A spy, for example, might pretend to have been charged with a criminal offence. After promising large sums of money to persons who agreed to falsely in his behalf, he might arrest them as false witnesses and have them banished.[35]

Musical performer as spy : The spies in the cover of music performer generally were used to communicate the secret messages in coded language. They entered in the palace in guise of bard or singer, and sent the message through songs, recitations and writing concealed in musical instruments.[36] Sometimes they used to agitate the people to get the secret among the crowd by reciting the songs.

Deaf, Dumb, Blind as Spy : Bhisma said to employ such persons as spies, who lived as blind, dumb and deaf.[37] Bhisma sent these spies in the kingdom of Drupada and they informed him that Shikandi was hermaphrodite.[38]

As a Joker and Fool : The *Mahabharata* mentions that the outward physical appearance of spies should be like those of fools. They should pretend as jokers, to amuse the people. But they should be very wise by nature.[39]

The *Ramayana* suggests that man who can act as idiot, blind and deaf cannot be easily recognised or identified should be appointed as 'spy'.[40] In the *Mahabharata*, '*Chara*' is called '*Vividhopays*' indicating that he could assume different 'covers' to collect intelligence about the enemy or any assigned target.[41]

Snake Charmer. The cover of snake charmer was imaginative as he gets easy entrance into the crowed places and colonies inhabited by elitist elements. He is welcome among the children and women.

Besides these covers, other most common disguises were those of mendicant, artisan, cook and confectioner, wondering minstrel, artist, barber and shampooer, bath and toilet attendants, food server, flower and perfume attendant, groom, driver and animal trainer. They used these covers to watch the activities of government servants and ministers at their residents, officers or place of work.[42]

The expertise in developing covers of the most ingenious type seems to be embedded in Indian culture. It is doubtful if the mythological tradition of any other country could claim of such an expertise in assuming 'covers' and taking disguises as those of India. Not only the ordinary run of gods and goddesses, but the Great Trinity could be frequently observed taking, a variety of 'covers' to help the faithful in eliminating undesirable or achieving favourable results.[43]

Vishnu disguised as the beautiful damsel of pristine grace and charm to entice the danavas fighting for the nectar pot, and that of the 'ascetic' taken by Siva to test the love and devotion of his eternal consort.

Historically, the most interesting incident which changed the passage of Indian history in the early centuries of the Christian era is that of Chandra Gupta Vikramaditya killing the Saka king while disguised as a lady for the sake of dignity of Gupta empire.[44]

There also desperate agents who worked as bearers of umbrella, water vessel, fan, shoes, seat, carriage and riding animals, deserved the outdoor activities of government servants.[45] They had to communicate the collected information to the '*Samstha*'.

Kautilya organised the department of espionage in the most thorough going manner and would justify all means if they help in achieving the well-being of the people and the state.[46]

It was advised to king to consider the feasibility as regards the country, dress, profession, language and the emotional and physical background of the agent, while deciding on a 'cover'.[47]

A 'cover' although very much dexterious in his profession, still there are chances of disclose of secret sooner or later'[48] so the spy should be alert for the safety of his 'cover' and he should maintain the closest proximity of his target by assuming a 'cover' that should justify his presence.[49]

Arthasastra describes that as artists, the spies are to pretend to take sides in public debate about the government's virtues, inducing other people to reveal their views; through drama.[50]

Different categories of agents were detailed in different places enabling them to carry out their tasks. The 'merchant-spies' lived inside the forts and cities whereas, the mendicants' moved in sub-urban areas.[51] The 'cultivator spies' stayed in villages and the cattle traders and herdsmen on the outskirts of town; foresters, hunters and recluses living in forest tracts and wild tribes acted as 'observer sources', while ostensibly engaged in their respective professions.[52]

Others disguised as servants and professional workers sought employment with their targets. The spies meet at the residences of the main secret agents at odd hours.[53]

The *Agnipurana* lays down that the spies are the 'eyes of the king' who are disguised as merchants, physicians, astrologers etc. while under 'cover' they watch the doings of all concerned and the strength of the foreign powers.[54]

Woman as spy : Women are universally employed in secret services as the most effective tool of espionage. Women were engaged in prostitution. The fascinating smile, sharp features, sexual and attractive activities of these women are always appealing towards the men. So polity makers took advantage of this natural weakness of men and used the beautiful and talented women in secret services. Not only the women but men engaged in prostitution[55] have unobstructed access everywhere, and do not arouse suspicion. Their presence in the places usually frequented by unidentified men and women is readily accepted.

The '*Sarama*' in Vedic period was the spy of Varuna. She goes around in search of criminals. *Panisukta* of Rigveda mentioned the lady Sarama who participated in the politics.[56]

Elsewhere *Sarama* was sent as an ambassador to Pani with an ultimatum for war. The character of Sarama shows the high moral quality of the then ambassador. *Sarama* was a lady and though Pani tried to win her over by bribes, she refused to join the enemy. She was an embodiment of honesty, sincerity and truthfulness.[57]

In epic period women were not considered to be confidant enough to rely upon them. They were considered light hearted, whimsical, eccentric, weak and unable to keep secrets. No secret councils of the state were to be held in women's presence. It has been stated that success in all those matters which rests on the initiative and performance of women will always be doubtful.[58]

Women were not regarded even worthy of being entrusted with state secrets. Generally they were not taken in confidence into the transaction of state business and treated as incapable of shouldering the burden of difficult and taxing duties of administration.[59]

So it is doubtful that women were used as spies in epic period.

Mahabharata also says, "there should be no dwarf, no humpbacked person, no dean man; no lean man and blind man, no idiot, no woman at the spot where the king holds consultation.[60] These references show that women were not considered worthy for the secret services. But in the Ramayana, there is a reference of a lady Sarama other than the spy bitch of Varuna in Vedic period. Who according to commentators, was the wife of Vibhishana she was appointed by Ravana to look after Sita. Very soon she became the friend of Sita. At that time being a friend, she worked for her as a spy to informed Ravana's war preparations as his might and cruelty created apprehension in her mind about Rama's safety. Sarama, went to the palace where Rakshasas were discussing war strategy. She heard their decision and reported to her.

Kautilya used all types of men and women for espionage whether they were *rupajiva*, *vaisya*, *dasi*, *parivrajkas*, *panchali*, *silpakarika*, *vrishalis*, *kausikastri*, *bandhaki* and *munda*.[61] The prostitute spies were more successful, although they were not allowed to mix with high born ladies. But they were permitted to go in royal palaces without any interruption.

Strabo evidently refers the class of '*Vrishalis*'. A '*Vrishali*' is taken to mean a ganika or courtesan by the author of the '*Bhagavadajjukiyam*'. *Pumschali vesya*, *rupajiva* were given the status of courtesan spies in *Arthasastra*.[62]

Kautilya has used several expressions for prostitute and each one of the category is used for a specialised purpose in spying.[63]

0They could also, if necessary, be called upon to act as spies for the state, Megasthenes hold this fact.[64]

He used prostitute agents as thieves as they could mix conveniently with criminals and persons of low character. They used the covers those of ascetics (*Siddha tapsa, Parivrajita, Chabrachara*), of bards (*Charana, Kuhaka, Kusilava*), of foretellers (*naimittika, mauhurtika*), of cripples (*unmatta, muka, vadhira, jada, andha*), of workers (*Karu, Silpin, Vaidehaka*), of those who prepared food and drinks, (*Soundika, anupika, pakva, mansika, audanika*).[65]

Prostitute spies were used to excite love among the undesirable men, make appointment with them at predetermined rendezvous where they were either done to death by 'fiery spies' or were arrested. The procurers were used to collect taxes, and worked as king's servants.[66]

In Gupta period also '*Ganikas*' and maid servants worked as spies. They were used to attract the enemy and to examine the truthfulness of soldiers. Foreigner maid servants didn't know the language so they talk in signs, and worked as spies.[67]

The prostitutes were also used to spy on defence personnel, and for kidnapping princes. The women spies were detailed as wives of prince when an operation to kidnap the prince was launched, and worked with the other agents who had earlier taken up 'cover' jobs i.e., carpenters, artisans, dancers, actors, etc.

Prostitutes had to attend court and were regularly employed in the royal household on high salary. They were also employed in the store house, kitchen, bathroom, in the harem of king.[68] They were also employed in the city by the city superintendent along with liquor dealers and those who dealt in cooked meat or food. They collected intelligence on habitual offenders. The device of employing harlots for espionage was continued throughout the subsequent Hindu period.[69] The *Arthasastra* remarked that brothels were excellent places for spies to collect information.

In wartime the women spy used to distribute wine or liquor, mixed with poison among the important military officers.[70] We also come across woman dressed in man's attire, putting on armour, equipped with weapons, arms, shields, bows and arrows. We hear of a certain queen who fought a battle in the disguise of her lord.[71]

Jain Sanskrit epics also mention to appoint the women in secret services.[72] Prostitutes could be used as spies.[73]

Woman working as *Bhiksuki* spy said to the wife of *Mahamatra* that she knows the treatment of hypnotise you give this medicine to your husband and thus giving the poison in place of medicine, minister was put to death by his wife.[74]

Disguising as bards the women spy entered the palace and sent the information through songs, and concealing the message in musical instruments.[75]

Foreign spies were to be seduced by female spies and then murdered.[76] Female spies were sent to visit the families of officers. They excited love among them. When more than one officers were engaged in a lady then fiery spies create the quarrel among them and murdered them, declaring that these were killed by another lover as the result of external triangle.[77]

Rich widow woman, *Gudhajiva* (widow), *Aditi* woman (who shows the pictures of God and Goddess to earn livelihood). *Kaushika* women (wives of snake charmers) also worked as spies.

Strabo speaks that women followed the post of inspectors (spies) of the camp. The employment of women of easy virtue as spies, is alluded to by the Kautilya's *Arthasastra*.[78]

King as spy : The success of an espionage system depends on the king. A king also should be dexterous in secrecy along with his secret agents. The *Ramayana* mentions that to follow the secret policy is the attribute of a king. Although a king is called 'thousand eyed' due to his spies but he should also himself investigate the truth in the society. He should be farsighted like a vulture, cunning like a crane, vigilant like a dog, violent like a lion, fearful like a cow.

In Mauryan period kings used to wonder in disguise of an old person, a customer, watchman at night to see the real condition of people and to get the public opinion about himself and other officers.

Puranas also mentions, even enemy kings were said to move about in disguise to know the affairs in other states and so a king was to be particular in choosing a minister.[79]

Sukra also, while recommending tours of inspection, observes, that the king or the higher officers should inspect the villages and towns in order to have a first information about the real condition and feelings of their residents. The solitary reference, to the inspection agency in epigraphs may be accidental. Administration is hardly possible without an efficient inspecting machinery.[80]

Shantiparvan mentions that king himself should make a supervision of the city to know the internal condition.[81]

Duta as spy. A duta or ambassador was regarded as a glorified spy.[82] Success of a state in its relations with others depended to a large extent on diplomacy. The services of a tactful ambassador were needed for diplomatic success.[83]

The main duty of an ambassador was the maintenance of the peaceful diplomatic relations between different states. Alongwith an embassy was to be control-centre of the espionage in another state. An ambassador had to remain there, to supervise the work of the spies, to win over discordant elements, help fifth columns and thus impair the internal security of that state.[84] He was empowered to employ spies for eliciting secret information about the enemy's strong and weak points.[85]

The Ambassador himself was certainly the most dignified spy in ancient India whose charter of duties in foreign countries has been enumerated by political thinkers.[86] Altekar mentions[87] that in ancient as in modern times, the ambassador was a licensed and open spy; during his stay at the foreign court, he was to cultivate friendly relations will the officials with a view to get a clue to the real policy of the government. He was also to see that the terms of earlier treaties were observed by the king to whose court he was accredited and also to impress upon him how his own king was very strong and rich resources. He was to gauge the general situation, estimate the state's resources in men and money and get a first hand information from his own spies about the condition of the defenses and forts of the country. He was to send his reports in a cipher code (gudhalekha).

It is however, really curious, how the work of an ambassador as almost a spy could be termed as his duty.[88] Kautilya describes how an ambassador work as a spy ? He was expected to travel widely in enemies territory to gather information about its defences, and sources of power both military and financial, and its possible defects and weak points.

He was also to know the possible division and, factors in a country, that they might be utilized as centres of fifth column activities in times of war.

He was to gather these facts by conver*Sati*on with men from various walks of life as well as from paintings and secret writings.[89]

Failing to elicit information from them, he was to know the facts from beggars or intoxicated persons. He was to be very alert and try to do his job whenever he got an opportunity.

He was advised to study the signs made in temples or to decipher secret scripts. This advise might have been also for an attempt to decipher the secret codes of an enemy, which might help immensely in times of war.[90]

Defining the other functions of *duta* Kautilya says that he should win the friends, carry on intrigues in the enemy's territory, show dissension among the friends of enemy, empulse of the enemy's secret agents and armymen and he should find out about the investigation of seducible parties, the employment of secret agents non-seducible parties, the loyalty or disaffection towards their master and weak points in the constituent elements (of the enemy's realm) through spies.[91]

The *Ayodhyakanda* also insists on the employment of such ambassadors as were citizens of the kingdom, capable of guessing the motives of others.[92]

Kalidasa, in the age of Gupta's does not mention ambassadors at all in his works. This has given rise to the speculation that 'probably the work of these costly and comparatively useless and ornamental figureheads was more efficiently done by clever spies who were deputed to watch the activities of enemies in foreign territories.[93]

Likewise in Tamil literature, though the spies were a different category of official from *dutas*, the functions assigned to those two varieties of officials seem to overlap. But the distinction between the *Dutas* and '*orrar*' does not seem to have been fully excepted in practice for it is clear that often times *Dutas* were also employed as *orrar*.[94]

The *Kural*, also observes that 'an ambassador may be a spy in some circumstances'.[95] So usually it is to ignore the distinction between *Dutas* and *Orrar* and the same officials performed the functions of an envoy as well as spy, and that normally they were spies and on extraordinary occasions when open contact with foreign courts was desired, they became '*duta*'.[96]

Kamandaka also accepted '*duta*' as a spy and called him '*Prakasacara*'.[97] They should visit the capital and the court of the enemy at opportune moments and gathered all sorts of information in regard to the strength and equipment of forests, official secrets, vulnerable points and financial as well as military resources.[98]

In the times of war, *duta* should befriend the frontier as well as the frontier tribes and should find out the inland and navigable communications and easy routes, all for facilitating the unimpeded progress and march of his army.[99]

Thus, occasionally the *duta* also performed the duty of spy in indirect way. Many polity makers called the '*duta*' 'an open spy'.

Difference between duta and spy : The terms like Cara, etc. are used in Indian literature to denote a spy in contrast with the word *duta* which is generally employed in the sense of an envoy.[100] A broad distinction between them as '*Dutas*', 'open spies', that is, envoys and caras or secret spies 'real spies'.[101]

The Sangam literature distinguishes '*duta*' from a 'spy' on the pattern of the Sanskrit words. It called the '*duta*' an 'open spy'. But sometimes, the distinction was overlapping and the functions assigned to these two categories were indistinguishable.

Theoretically the distinction was recognised for, the *Kural* has separate chapters on '*Orrar*' and '*Dutas*' and describes their functions and qualifications with great precision.[102]

Officially the '*Dutas*' were considered superior to the '*orrar*' and that while the king looked upon Dutas as part of his court (on a footing of equality with the ministers), he considered the Orrar as part of his personal guards and information service.[103]

It is perfectly clear that the '*Kural*' doesn't include the *orrar* among the ministerial category because the chapter on '*orru*' is in '*Arasiyal*' and is not in the '*Arrgaviyal*'.

The spies had no official status in foreign courts while ambassadors or envoys enjoy this position. The ambassadors were public servants and were to be located honourably, the spies performed secret service and were not given such respect.[104] The *Mahabharata*[105] evidences that the '*dutas*' occupied a very high and enviable position befitting their status and functions.

Furthermore, '*Dutas*' were granted lands[106] which were not transferable through sale or mortgage and they were also exempted from paying tolls while crossing rivers.[107]

Kangle, thinks that *Dutas* were entitled to their regular salary also.[108] While spies were not provided with any other privileges except salary.

An ambassador enjoyed diplomatic immunity. He could not be slain. It is said that a king should never sentence an ambassador to capital punishment. If he does so, he sinks into oblivion and is subject to torture of the hell together with his retinue of responsible officers.[109]

The *Ramayana* also prohibits the murder of an ambassador who is simply the mouth piece of his master.[110] While spies were not given opportunity of this immunity. They had always the danger of their lives, if they were recognised or caught by enemy.

A mythological instances makes clear it when a *duta* named 'Suka' in Lankakanda, being dispatched by Ravana to Sugriva but he was arrested or being suspected to be a spy,[111] who had come to count their forces. He was subsequently released by Rama on the ground that he was really a Duta and not a spy.[112] So the Ramayana gives a clear difference as spies did not enjoy any diplomatic immunity while a 'duta' was always respected and apolised.

It is worth noting that even in modern times spies are not granted any diplomatic immunity and every state punishes them severely if they are caught committing an act which is a crime by the law of the land or expels them if they can't be punished.[113]

Generally, Brahmanas were appointed for the posts of ambassadors and thus their persons were doubly inviolable.

Side by side with this emphasis on the immunity of an envoy, the *Mahabharata* as well as the *Ramayana* allow to punish or even to murder an ambassador, who is unfaithful or undutiful and if he does not convey the message properly.[114]

While distinguishing an ambassador from a spy, the Kural observes, 'An ambassador may be a spy in some circumstances, but a spy cannot be an ambassador who must be of high birth, good manners and loving nature.[115]

References

1. T.B. Mookerji, Interstate Relations in Ancient India, Meerut, p. 177.
2. Manu Samhita, IX, 306, G.N. Jha.
3. J.W. Spellmen, Political Theory of Ancient India, Oxford, 1964, p. 137.
4. N.N. Law, IHQ, The Machinery of Administration in the Kautilya, Dec. 1929, p. 32.
5. Beni Prasad, Theory of State in Ancient India, Allahabad, 1968.

6. N.N. Law, Machinery of Administration in the Kautilya, IHQ, Dec. 1929, p. 626.
7. Palmer, *op. cit.*, p. 64.
8. N. Subrahmaniam, Sangam Polity, Bombay, 1966, p. 101.
9. Kural, 596, quoted from 'Sangam Polity'.
10. Brajdeo Prasad Roy, Political Ideas and Institutions in the Mahabharata, Calcutta, 1975, p. 366.
11. Mahabharata, Shantiparvan, 83.50.
12. Brajdeo Prasad Roy, *op. cit.*, p. 365.
13. D.K. Ganguly, Aspects of Ancient Indian Administration, New Delhi, 1979, p. 211.
14. T.B. Mookerji, *op. cit.*, p. 178.
15. J.W. Spellmen, *op. cit.*, pp. 139-140.
16. Major, S.K. Bhakari, Indian Warfare, New Delhi, 1981, p. 87.
17. J.W. Spellmen, *op. cit.*, p. 149.
18. N. Subrahamaniyam, *op. cit.*, p. 101.
19. T.B. Mookerji, *op. cit.*, p. 178.
20. *Arthasastra*, *Ibid.*, p. 177.
21. J.W. Spellmen, *op. cit.*, p. 138.
22. Major S.K. Bhabri, *op. cit.*, p. 87.
23. N.N. Law, IHQ, Dec. 1929, *op. cit.*, p. 621.
24. J.W. Spellmen, *op. cit.*, p. 138.
25. Palmer, *op. cit.*, p. 69.
26. S.L. Sternback, Juridical Studies in Ancient Indian Law, Delhi, 1965, pp. 298-299.
27. Manorama Jauhari, Politics and Ethics in Ancient India, Varanasi, 1968, p. 226.
28. I.W. Spellmen, *op. cit.*, p. 139.
29. T.B. Mookerji, *op. cit.*, p. 178.
30. Major S.K. Bhakari, *op. cit.*, p. 88.

31. *Ibid.,* p. 87.
32. T.B. Mookerji, *op. cit.*, p. 177.
33. J.C. Jain, Life in Ancient India, As depicted in Jain Canons, New Book Company, Bombay, 1947, pp. 59-60.
34. J.W. Spellmen, Political Theory of Ancient India, Oxford, 1964.
35. *Arthasastra*, IV, IV 2 11.
36. *Arthasastra*, 1.12, 11-14.
37. "प्रणिधींश्रा ततः कर्याज्जडान्धअबधिराकतीन।
    पुंसः परीक्षितान प्राज्ञान क्षुत्पिपासाश्रमसमान।।" 69/8
    Mahabharata, Shantiparavan.
38. Manorama Jauhari, *op. cit.*, p. 225.
39. Brajdeo Prasad Roy, *op. cit.*, p. 365.
40. *Ramayana, Yudhakanda*, 20. 1.
41. *Mahabharata, Shantiparavan*, 5 8. 1.
42. *Arthasastra*, 1.12, 9-10.
43. S.D. Trivedi, *op. cit.*, p. 55.
44. D.R. Bhandarkar, New light on the Early Gupta History, Malaviya Commemoration, 1932, p. 189.
45. *Arthasastra*, 1. 12.7.
46. Beni Prasad, *op. cit.*, p. 276.
47. *Arthasastra*, 1. 12.6.
48. Palmer, *op. cit.*, p. 74.
49. *Arthasastra*, 14.1.2.
50. I.W. Mabbett, Truth, Myth and Politics in Ancient India, 1971, p. 48.
51. Major S.K. Bhakari, Indian Warfare, New Delhi, 1981, p. 87.
52. T.B. Mookerji, *op. cit.*, p. 178.
53. *Arthasastra*, 1. 11. 4.
54. *Agnipurana*, CCXLI, 241.

55. Vijay K. Thakur, Facets of Prostitutes, JBORS, Vol. LIX, 1973, p. 241.
56. *Rigveda, Panisukta*, 10108.
57. T.B. Mookerji, *op. cit.*, p. 23.
58. Dr. Shakambari Jayal, The Status of Women in the Epics, Delhi 1966, p. 299.
59. Prof Indra, The Status of Women in Ancient India, Banaras, 1955, p. 148.
60. *Mahabharata, Shantiparvan*, 73-55.
61. L. Sternback, Juridical Studies in Ancient Indian Law, Delhi, 1965, pp. 258-262.
62. H.C. Roy Chaudhry, Political History of Ancient India, Delhi, 1995, p. 259.
63. *Arthasastra*.
64. Vijay Kumar Thakur, JBORS, Vol. LIX(52), 1973, p. 241.
65. Sternback, L.; Juridical Studies in Ancient Indian Law, Delhi, 1965, pp. 298-99.
66. S.D. Trivedi, *op. cit.*, p. 58.
67. Anvita-Annand, *Guptakal mei Nariyo Ki Isthiti*, Delhi, 1992, p. 46.
68. Vijay Kumar Thakur, *op. cit.*, p. 241.
69. Benjamim Walker, Hindu World, An Encylopedic Survey of Hinduism, Vol. II, p. 248.
70. Manorama Jauhari, Politics and Ethics in Ancient India, 'A study based on the Mahabharata', Varanasi, 1968, p. 227.
71. Vya Bha. I, p. 100.
72. Dr. Mohan Chandra, *Jain Sanskrit Mahakavya Mei Bhartiya Samaj*, Delhi, 1989, p. 463.
73. एव माज्ञापयामास वे या यातर्य ग़ालिनीः ।
    मनिवेषेण गत्वाडगस्परौन्विनवोक्तिभिः ।।
    Parisista Parvan, 1.42.43.

74. S.D. Trivedi, *op. cit.*, p. 57.
75. *Arthasastra*, 1.12, 11-14.
76. J. Spellmen, *op. cit.*, p. 140.
77. *Arthasastra*, 11, 1. 36-52.
78. H.C. Raychaudhry, *op. cit.*, p. 259.
79. T.B. Mookerji, *op. cit.*, p. 114.
80. Padama B. Udgaonkar, The Political Institution and Administration, Delhi, 1969, pp. 108-109.
81. उपजापश्रा भव्यानामात्मनः बुरद निम।
अवि वासः स्वयं चैव परस्याश्रवासनं तथा।। 11/58।।
Mahabharata, Shantiparvan.
82. I.W. Mabbett, Truth, Myth and Politics in Ancient India, N. Delhi, 1971, p. 49.
83. T.B. Mookerji, *op. cit.*, p. 49.
84. *Ibid.,* p. 175.
85. D. K. Ganguly, p. 211.
86. *Arthasastra*, 1, 16.33; 13, 1.11.
87. A.S. Altekar, State and Government in Ancient India, p. 301.
88. T.B. Mookerji, *op. cit.*, p. 175.
89. D.K. Ganguly, *op. cit.*, p. 211.
90. T.B. Mookerji, *op. cit.*, p. 175.
91. D.K. Ganguly, *op. cit.*, pp. 210-211.
92. Ramayana, Ayodhyakanda, 100, 36.
93. S.A. Sabnis, Kalidasa, His Style and His Times, Bombay, 1966.
94. N. Subrahmaniyam, *op. cit.*, p. 102.
95. D.K. Ganguly, *op. cit.*, p. 217.
96. N. Subrahamaniyan, Sangam Polity, Bombay, 1966, p. 102.
97. S.P. Ghannagani, p. 63.

98. D.K. Ganguly, *op. cit.*, p. 219.
99. T.B. Mookerji, *op. cit.*, p. 176.
100. D.K. Ganguly, *op. cit.*, p. 282.
101. Beni Prasad, Theory of Govt. in Ancient India, Allahabad, 1968, p. 366.
102. N. Subramaniyam, *op. cit.*, p. 103.
103. K.A. Nilakanta Shastri, 'The Cholas', Madras, 1955, p. 63.
104. N. Subramaniyam, *op. cit.*, p. 102.
105. *Mahabharata, Shantiparvan*, 85. 26-28.
106. R. Shamasastry, *Arthasastra*, Book II, p. 46.
107. D.K. Ganguly, *op. cit.*, p. 212.
108. R.P. Kangle, 'Kautilya *Arthasastra*', p. 212.
109. Shantiparvan, 26/85.
110. The Ramayana Sundarakanda, 52, 51.
111. H.P. Shastri, The Ramayana of Valmiki, London 1959, 111, pp. 20, 29.
112. *Ibid.*, pp. 20, 34.
113. L. Oppenheim, International Relations, I, p. 862.
114. Manorama Jauhari, *op. cit.*, p. 219.
115. D.K. Ganguly, *op. cit.*, p. 217.

6

Visakanya : The Poisonous Beauty

Secret services in ancient India had adopted various techniques to fulfil the requirements of the king. They not only used the nascent technological advancement available to them, but also exploited human weakness for sex to achieve royal objectives. Visakanya, is a unique feature of the Indian genius. References to Visakanya are scantily scattered in ancient Indian folk-lore and literature from where the conception evidently travelled west.

No less important was an understanding of the poisons generated from the embraces of the so called poison-maidens. According to popular legend these girls, specially chosen for their beauty, were fed from infancy on the flesh of venomous reptiles and insects, and on toxic herbs and plants, so that they became immunised to these effects and their body became saturated with poison.[1] The *'Astang Sanghra'*, shows that these Visakanyas become so poisonous that flowers, decorated on their body were withered, jewelleries became fade and shineless with touch their body. It is said in an ancient work[2] that their sweat, hair, nails become poisonous by use of the poison. They can faint a person by their respiration. If someone makes physical contact with her, she can be the cause of instantaneous or slow death of that person.

The idea behind the technique of using Visakanya was to trap the enemy by exploiting the human weakness for sex and to achieve the royal objectives. These venomous beauties can be put into various categories. Such as a damsel, whose body is saturated with gradual doses of poison, she transmits the poison from her body to another person coming in contact with her.

Sometimes a woman treacherously captivates the heart of a person, and then mixes poison in his food or drink, likewise, a woman suffering from venereal disease is a Visakanya of this kind. Being infected with disease or poisoned, she is likely to convey it into the person coming in contact with her. Another type of Visakanya are those girls who are born under an inauspicious configuration of planets, and who causes the death of her husband.

Visakanyas are, however, only of two kinds, viz. one born under an inauspicious configuration of planets, and the other who being systematically fed on small doses of poison and becomes poisonous.

Vishakadutta had mentioned the use of Visakanya in his play *Mudraraksasa.*[3] She was prepared by regular doses of Virulent poison adminsitered to her.

She is called "*the messenger of certain death*" by Raksasa, who had prepared the poison-damsel for Chandragupta's undoing. Drama starts with the accession of Chandra Gupta Maurya. Chanakya played an unforgetful role in his success and he made his his chief minister, and it is at this point that the Mudraraksasa commences. Chanakya involved in a maze of political intrigue, employing every form of cunning and strategy imaginable. He uses all possible intelligence techniques to win over Rakshasa, the minister of Nanda, who ensure the uninterrupted rule of Mauryas. Chanakaya, saved the life of Chandragupta many times. At last Raksasa prepared the Visakanya for Chandragupta's death but the plot was discovered by the ever-watchful Chanakya, who instead of killing or returning the girl, passed her on Parvataka, who, although former ally of Chandragupta, was thought best out of the way.

At that time, Raksasa laments[4]

"Tis ever thus-fortune in all befriends

The cruel Chandragupta-When I send

A messenger of certain death to slay him.

She wields the instrument against his rival

who should have spoiled him of one half of his kingdom

And arms and drugs, and stratagems were turned

In his behalf, against my friends and servants,

So that whatever I plot against his power

Serves but to yield him unexpected profit".

This incident may be considered the first historical mention of playing back a spy.

The Visakanya that was used against enemy (Parvataka), was prepared by regular dose of virulent poison administered to her and that can be used only once. It appears that such Visakanya, like a deadly snake could poison only once, and would be of little danger, when she pours out her poison in her first contact. Kautilya, perhaps was aware of this type of Visakanya, while he suggests the king for being very careful about the limbs of women as well as the articles of an army, that should be washed in tepid water prepared from the concoction of several herbs and animals, it removes the bad effects of poison.

While Rekasasa was failed in his conspiracy, he remembers the famous incident in *Mahabharata*. When Karna was intended to kill Arjuna by a strong lance capable of destroying only one person once and for all, but as the lance, to the great advantage of Krishna, killed the son of Hidimba and the life of Arjuna was saved likewise he also kept a vigorous poisonous maid to kill Chandragupta but due to the prudency of his minister Chanakya, she killed the lord of mountains (Parvataka) and Chandragupta was saved.

The Jain titlerary source *'Parisistaparvan'* also gives reference of *Visakanya* in a slightly difference in the story of *'Mudraraksasa'*. Here king Nanda himself prepared a maiden of his palace, in the form of Visakanya, who was fed on poison form the time of her birth. His minister Raksasa did not play any role in it. The plot is written like this, 'when Chandragupta and Parvataka entered Nanda's palace, Parvataka attracted to words that beautiful maiden, Chanakya, however knew the conspiracy behind this plan, but he let him go to that lady, now her poison transferred to king through perspiration that caused Parvataka great agony, all his limbs relaxed, and he was about to die. But neither Chanakya nor Chandragupta helped him and let him die.

References of poison damsels are found in Europe on *preudo Aristotelian* work called *'secretum secretorum'*.[5] It is a collection of the most important and secret communications sent by Aristotle to Alexander the Great on his campaign when he was too aged to attend his pupil in person.

As Chandragupta, was benefited by the advice of his minister Chanakya, in the same way, Aristotle was credited with the wise teachings and prudent counsels which helped him in his Eastern campaigns and prevented him from losing his life at the hands of poison damsels. So both kings were saved from deadly results of a poison-damsel by their equally clever ministers. Aristotle draw the attention of Alexander on the precautions, he should take while travelling through the ancient Orient, where people can easily cheat a person, and he should be careful in maintaining relation with unidentified women and their poisonous effects which had taken life of many kings earlier. Alexander was warned to be conscious in case of any type of treatment by a single physician. He should take consult of different doctors. As Aristotle was aware of the technique of using poison damsels against kings in India, he made remembered to Alexander incident when the king of India, sent rich gifts and beautiful maiden who were poisonous like a deadly snake, whose embrace and perspiration could be able to kill him surely. So idea of using poison damsels was so prominent in ancient India that Europeans were also aware of this.

Varahamihira also gave some different references of poisonous ladies. Queen of king Viduratha, murdered him with a weapon concealed in her tresses. Likewise, king of Kashi was killed by his queen by means of her anklets smeared with poison. So he mentioned such women who used most heinous methods to kill the royal dignitaries. He advised nobility to take some security measures during physical relationship with ambiguous women. He told some symptoms which can be helpful to detect the women who are inauspicious or unfit for the royal persons; a woman whose forehead is hanging over kill her husband's brother; if the belly is hanging over, she will kill her father-in-law, if the buttocks, her own husband. A women who is too tall and whose upper lip is hairy, she is unlucky for her husband.[6]

Kamsutra of Vatsyayana[7] also throw light on such women who could be harmful to the men. He forbids intercourse with certain types of women considering physical relationship with them as fatal or injurious to health.

The poison damsel finds mention in *Suvabahutta rikatha*. The King Dharmadatta prepared poisonous matter for the daughter of king Kamasundara. But his minister

Siddhartha falsely informed him that the princess is a poison-damsel, and thus created fear in him. So whether she was poison damsel or not, what is more important behind the story is that the idea of Visakanya was also prevailing in that time.

Susruta samhita[8] a well known medical work of Vagabhatta, dating from about the beginning of the Christian era, suggests that a girl can become poisonous through regular doses of poison and even her touch, sweat and breadth become fatal. *Kathasarit Sagara* of Samadeve also refer to Visakanya in his 'The ocean of story', Vol. II. Here he mentioned the methods employed by Yogakarandakasa the minister of Brahmadatta, against the king of Vatsa.[9] He tainted, by means of poison and other detecterious substances the trees, flowering creepers, water and grass all along the line of march. And he sent poison damsels as dancing-girls among the enemy's host and he also dispatched nocturnal assassins into their midst.[10] So the reference of poison damsels is a very interesting aspect of Samadera stories collection, that was much more uncommon.

Although the technique of using Visakanya against the enemy was institutionalised in the centuries around the Christian era, but these were perhaps known during the earlier period also. First reference of Visakanya is found in Srimad Bhagavata Mahapurana[11] in a different form. Putana, the demoness detailed by Kamsa to kill Krishna, she pasted poison on her breasts. As she was accustomed to killing infants in towns, villages, cowherd sheds etc. She make up as a beautiful lady and reached Gokul and entered Nand's home. She took sleeping Krishna in her lap and put into the baby's mouth her breast smeared with deadly poison. But Krishna was aware of this trick. He squeezed it hard and sucked the poison along with her life. She cried to leave her. Putana fall down on land. The *Mahabharata*, the Vishnu Purana and the Agni Purana also mention about this story.[12]

Wendy Doniger also indicates about the incident of Putana and practice of using ambivalent milk. He illustrates that the symbolism of ambivalent milk is enhanced by the belief that, since milk is good, an evil woman has either no milk or else poison in her breasts, like Putana. He further talk about the nature of poison that, "the poison as the inverse of Soma appears through out the mythology; a fierly poison is said to devour the world-like the dooms day fire-in contrast with Soma or milk, that is itself devoured." Poison is also thought to recide in the genitals of the destructive erotic woman, the poison damsel.[13]

A Bengali work, the *'Manasa Mangal'* points out the snake damsel (often symbolizing woman). Here Lakhindara is fated to die on his wedding night (the recurrent myth of fatal sexuality); when he flies in the face of the prophecy, he is bitten by the snake damsel and dies of her poison. Snakes perform an alchemy in which milk is transmuted into poison, the inverse of that alchemy that woman perform by turning blood into milk.[14]

The fiction in later century the *'Chandrakanta santati'* of Devaki Nandan Khatri presents many illustrations of 'Visakanya' as well as 'Visapursha' They were given slow poison since birth.

Acharya Chatursen has mentioned Visakanya of Magadha named 'Kupadeni' in his book, 'Vaishali ki Nagarvadhu'. Who killed the king of Champa Dadhichahan by her poisonous embrace. Likewise the poison damsel Mallika killed king Aammi. Albaruni also mentioned the use of Visakanya in his book 'Tehkikat-i-Hind'. According to him, king of Peshawar sent a beautiful Visakanya of Muttan to kill a Sipah-Salar named Gaji Masood. But the secret agents of Gaji Masood caught the plan and they killed that poisonous beauty. Raiput frequently used the Visakanya for spying and killing the enemies in Sultanate and Mughal period. Colonel Tod had mentioned, (in his well-known work 'Annals and Antiquities of Rajasthan'), about those Rajput girls who used poisonous weapons, jewellery and cloths for their protection. They were also adapt in alchemy. According to him the poisoned robe or shirt was firmly believed in by the Rajputs and he gives several examples of its use. First, there was the case of the queen of Ganor, who gave a poisoned weeding robe to the Khan whom she had been forced to marry; then there was the Raja Bakhta who died after donning a role given him by his niece at the instigation of Isari Singh, Maharaja of Jaipur. Another one, princess, Sardar bai, the daughter of the king Khemraj of Ranipur, used strong poison against Rehmat Khan for the safety of her virginity and finally, there was the case of Aurangzeb, who jealous of the possible power of Prithi Singh, presented him with a dress of honour, which proved to be so full of poison that the victim expired in great torture soon afterwards.

Another story about the Emperor Aurangzeb (1659-1707), to be found in the Travels of Alexander Hamilton,[15] and concerns the method by which he sought to be revenged on his son, the prince Akbar. He had planned to capture the Raja Shivaji as he was leaving his camp, but Akbar warned him of his father's treachery. Whereupon Aurangzeb's anger was turned against his own son, feigning kindness, he sent him a richly comparisoned horse and a very beautiful vest, which was poisoned by a perfumed powder. His son, however, 'Smelt a rat' and ordered it to be put on a slave who died a day or two after he had put it on.[16] So practice of shirt poisonings along with poisonous women was also going on in past India. In India the most deadly poison is undoubtedly the variety of aconite found in the Himalayan districts. This is so called "Nepal aconite," known as bis, bish, bikh etc.

The references of poison-damsels are not available in later period. Use of this technique was perhaps given up in the Post-Gupta period as except the occasional and traditional references in literacy works, there is no mention of 'poison-damsel' as an organised operation against adversaries. In the 'Nitivakyamratam'[17] a reference shows that the legend was alive in India around the 8th century AD.

But in modern period these poison-damsels came to world scenario in a different form. Lovely looks, captivating gait and cute figure of beautiful women had been a centre for attraction for man since a long time. In modern times they are frequently used for spying and killing the enemy. Matahari was a secret agent during first World War. Her activities reminds of 'Viskanya'.[18] She was born in 1876 in a Dutch trader's family. The meaning of the word 'Matahari' is 'Eye of heart' in Malaysian language. She was fond of spying since her childhood. She proved that she was the daughter of a dancer of south India. In the beginning she was a dancer, later on she got training in a German intelligence school. During World War First in 1914 she worked for Germany. She made contacts with the officers of France, Russia and England and gave their secrets to German intelligence department. Her method to convey the information was very different, She used to write the letters to her daughter in a very innocent and affectionate words and these words were full of dual meaning and secret messages. But she was assisinated in 15 Oct. 1917 by French army during a secret mission. Like her, her daughter Banda also had been a well known secret agent. She was unaware of her, mother's life. After her death, she got a letter and knew about her and then she left the home and reside with a Dutch officer and got the higher education. She was beautiful and sweet tongued, so she easily once in touch of higher society people and was invited in grand parties. During Second World War in 1939, her parties became the centre for attraction for the politicians, secret agents, reporters. She worked for Indonesian homeguards against Japanese. Later on she went China and worked for America. Then she was ordered to go Korea, there she was caught by Korean officers and asked for spying for Korea. But she denied and then she was shooted. Thus mother and daughter both were murdered.

One more famous lady spy was Tania. She was very efficient secret agent. She spied for three groups at a time.

She worked for a revolutionary warrior of Arjentiana. According to American reporter Danial James, Tania had been a spy of intelligence organization of previous Germany M.F.S. and a communist secret agent of Russian K.G.B. So she was a very shrewd, cuning, careful and intelligent secret agent of her time.

These modern women spies, though were not like the poisonous damsels of ancient times, but they used all the techniques of Visakanyas to trap their target. They use their beauty to know the secrets. They were given training in military style and the level of the training of these ladies was the same as the male army. So concept of Visakanya in ancient India is whether a myth or a killer truth but, so frequent references in religious, non-religious fiction, dramas, folklores and even in European a works like 'secretum secretosum' of Aristotle make it a most fascinating idea, of ancient Indian history. Though in later Gupta period references of the Visakanyas are absent but in Rajput era and later on in sultanate and Mughal period there are many references related to poison damsels. In modern times they come in a modified and different forn. During World Wars, the intelligence systems of world powers were benefitted with the strange works and tricks of beautiful women like Matahari and Banda. In present times also, secret operations are no less benefitted with the services of modern type of secret women agents with more dangerous and poisonous techniques.

The Visakanya could act in different ways on the person against whom she was employed. There was a belief that the look of a snake was poisonous, and hence it was known in Sanskrit as 'Dragvisa-drsavisa', poison in a glance. Perhaps Visakanyas who were fed on poison, their looks become so poisonous that they can kill a person by their fatal looks. Acharya Kautilya had given many tips to the kings for their security. He was aware of the fatal looks of Visakanyas. So he advised the king not to meet any lady without prior examination and they should see the prostitute after a proper bath with chemical water.[18]

The poison that was given to these women was named 'Sankhya'. It's scientific name is arsenic oxide (As_2O_3).

Another method of killing with the help of a Visakanya was through her fatal breath. They were given so much quantity of 'sankhya' from the age of ten and they were bitten by snake in the age of thirteen, that their nails, blood and even their breath become poisonous. Kautilya mentioned that birds can gave the indication if the *visa* was mixed in anything. 'Jivanjiva' bird becomes sad to see the poison. Nighttengale dies to see the poison and the eyes of a bird become red to see the *visa*. So kings can save their lives by these security measures. The Visakanya through her breath, can faint a person one more method of killing was by physical intercourse. This is proved by the story in *'Secretum Secretorum'* of Aristotle, when he warned Alexander not to have physical relation with unverified women of the orient. In case, he should be very alert by beautiful maidens in India. This type of practice which could lead to death was well known in the past. So special care had to be taken at birth and during the marriage to guard against any malign influences which might be at work seeking to cause him in physical relation.

The women who were born under certain configuration of planets, or suffering from some contagious disease, were expected to bring death and disaster.

References

1. Benjamin Walker, Hindu World, An Encyclopaedia Survey of Hinduism , Vol. 11, London, p. 222.
2. हन्ति स्प ग्रान्ति स्वेदेन गम्यमानाय मैथुने।
   पववं वन्तादिव फलं प्र ग्रायतीति मेहनतम्।।
3. Mudraraksasa of Visabadutta, trans, M.R. Kale, Varanasi, 1965, pp. 30-40.

4. कन्या तस्यविधाय या विषमयी गूढं प्रयुक्तामया।
देवात पर्वतकस्तया स निहतोपदस्तस्य राज्यार्धहृयत्।।
Mudraraksasa, Act I, 16.
5. N.M. Penzer, pp. 286-87
6. Brhatsmhita, p. II-XVIII, 24-25, 30-40, 60-62, 68-69.
7. Kamsutra, pt. I, Ch. V. 32, pt III ch, I, 11-13.
8. Susruta Samhita, Vol II, Ch I, p-673.
9. विद्धे विषकन्या च सैन्ये पव्यविलासिनीः।
प्राहिणोत्पुरुषां चैव नि ासुच्हद्मधातिनः।।
Kathasaritasagara, 3,5. 82.
10. Penzer, Ibid., p. 3.
11. M.N. Dutta (trans.), Srimad Bhagvata Mahapurana, Part 11, Discourse VI, Calcutta, 1895.
12. Ram Sharan Gaur, Bhautiya Prachin Katha Kosh, Anil Pub Delhi, 2001, p. 103.
13. Wendy Doniger O' Flatrerty 'women, Andreogeynes, and other Mythical Beasts, The University of Chicago, Press, Chicago & Landon, 1980, pp. 53-54.
14. *Ibid.,* p. 54.
15. A New Account of the East Indies, edited by sir William Foster Argonaut Press, Vol. I, 1930, pp. 138-139.
16. N.M. Penzer, Poison Damsels and Other Essays, London, pp. 9-10.
17. Nitivakyamratam, 24, 35-36.
18. B.K. Majumdar, Military System in Ancient India, Calcutta 1955, p. 37.

7

Diplomacy and Diplomatic Agents

The ancient Indian thinkers have accepted the utility and importance of the diplomatic agents or the ambassadors. They believed that it is the ambassador through whom two kings of the states talk with each other and he is the mouth of the king.

A king can conquer the world by means of diplomacy is a dictum of realistic politicians like Kautilya. The power of diplomacy was held to be the most far reaching one. 'An arrow of a zealous warrior may (even may not) kill only one person, but the policy of a diplomat may uproot a whole kingdom.' A successful ruler was considered to be one who conserved all his energies and forces for using them in extreme cases, and generally, depended on the art of diplomacy to secure the ends of the state. Narada, who also was well versed in the science of *Rajasartra* advises the king to destroy his enemy by diplomatic ways and to make peace and war at opportune moments.[1]

'Duta' originally means, 'to run on'. The root may be traced back to Indo-European 'du' to move forward. In the *Rigved* sometimes 'arati' also has been used in place of 'duta'. It signifies 'to move' or 'one who moves to and fro.' Duta conveys the meaning of 'carrier of news' as well. But whatever may be the etymological meaning of 'duta', it signifies a person who both moves as well as carries messages.

The diplomacy advocated by our authors is a curious combination of supremacy high ethical principals with treachery, deceit and calculated ruthlessness.

From the very dawn of human civilization, when one group of men wished to come to some kind of arrangement with another group so as to avoid the use of force, diplomacy, however crude or inept the manner of it, has come into existence. That is why, Sir Harold Nicholson, in his most scholarly work 'Diplomacy' remarks' 'diplomacy, in the sense of ordered conduct of relations between one group of human beings and another group alien to themselves, is far older than history.[2]

First reference of 'duta' can be traced from *Rigveda.* With the growth of tribal states and with the insistence on independence of the states was felt the necessity of agents for the exchange of communications among the states.

Agni is the acredited messenger of the gods. He is 'devaduta'.[3] He is a mediator between god and men and he is often requested to bring the gods to the sacrifice.[4] He is designated as messenger and herald,[5] the swift moving envoy.[6]

Though word 'Messenger' is applied to the divine 'Agni', it can form an idea of the then conception about an ambassador come like (royal) messenger in the land welcomed by many people (referred to Aswin) Agni was granted diplomatic immunities and privileges. This accounts for the fact that the gods "made the (Agni) their messenger, the disinterested bearer of oblations". It is very significant to note the term disinterested. It shows that an ambassador was expected to be above his personal baises and prejudices. His task was to convey the commissioned message disinterestedly. Diplomatic immunities were granted to those diplomats who were disinterested. In the *Rigveda*, Agni appears to be disinterested in his affairs. It shows that ambassadors were given public reception. They were honoured guests and were welcomed by the people.[7] One of the verses of Rigveda says,

> *"Between both races, Agni sage, well skilled*
> *thou passest to and fro*
> *As envoy to friendly mankind".*[8]

There is reference of *'Sarama'* in the *Vedas.* Although there is controversy about her designation whether she is a female deity or spy bitch of Varuna or a messenger of Indra. Macdonell points out that the name Saramaya indicates that they were regarded as descendent of Sarama, the messenger of Indra.[9] There is a hymn[10] in the form of a dialogue between Sarama and Panis as the messenger of Indra.

She was sent to Pani with an ultimatum for war but she was not manhandled by Pani. She was accorded welcome. Thus, the Rigveda gives us example of the granting of personal safety. Though the whole Rigveda atmosphere was surcharged with the evils of war, bloodshed, treachery, arson, loot and pillage, yet, diplomats were appointed and sent and they were given privileges and immunities for the smooth functioning of their diplomatic missions.

With the passage of time, the 'dutas' were associated more and more with new political duties. In Taittiriya Samhita[11], another term '*Prahita*' also mentioned besides 'duta'. '*Prahita*' also means an envoy but it appears to have different functions from that of 'duta'. According to the celebrated commentator Sayana while 'duta' is one who is skilled in collecting information about the enemy's forces, *Prahita* is an emissary sent by his master.[12]

B.A. Saletore, also considers 'Prahisa' a suitable messenger, who was sent by the king on a particular and secret errand.[13] In this sense only, the *Atharvaveda Samhita* uses these terms. The diplomatic agents were of two kinds: ambassadors (dutas) and spies (Chara or Guptacharas). Both aimed at the collection of information about the foreign states, although spies were employed to be watchful in the internal affairs as well.

In the post Yajurvedic period many instances of the appointment of diplomatic agents by rulers to represent them at each other's court, both in the time of peace and on the eve of war.[14] In later Vedic period some other officials are mentioned functioning as envoys viz *Palagala* (a messenger carrying errands from place to place) 'Suta' (carrying important diplomatic missions) to other states.

The epics speak eloquently about the 'dutas'. The epics assert that the king should appoint efficient persons as ambassadors. Because they are very important agency for carrying out the interstate-relationship. The *Ramayana* speaks of dutas as being sent out on important occasions to the enemy-kingdom for delivering master's message to others and reporting back their reaction or as carrying out a certain mission, as was the case with Hanumana who was sent by Sugriva to find out Sita who was leading a prisoner's life in Ravana's kingdom. He suggests it would be fatal to provoke war with the money king and describes the might of Rama. The forty-four verses of this fifty first chapter deserve most careful perusal as a model of advocacy by an envoy in a hostile court. The words uttered are wise, carefully chosen, and exhibit the utmost fact.

The *Mahabharata* contains a remarkable exposition of the well-known diplomatic concepts and categories, viz., the 'doctrine of *mandala*' of 12 states, the 'doctrine of trivarga' or threefold condition of a state, 'the doctrine of three powers', 'the doctrine of four political expendients' (Upayas) and the 'doctrine of six instruments of foreign policy' (Sadgunya).

In ancient India, ambassador was respectfully welcomed and accorded a seat of honour near the throne. The life of an ambassador was sacrosanct.

The *Ramayana* and the *Mahabharata* are also full of various instances of diplomatic immunities and privileges. Messengers were often to be sent from one state to another. These messengers served the purpose of the envoys. In the *Ramayana*, there are many instances of envoys being accredited to arrange for matrimonial alliances, i.e., envoys were sent by Raja Janaka to Dasaratha. The envoys were given hearty welcome in the court of Dasaratha. The king, Dasaratha gave seats to the dutas nearer to him. (This was a privilege). Dignified emissaries were also sent to invite various monarchs to the sacrifice arranged by Dasaratha for the propitiation of gods with a view to being blessed with sons. Sumantra, the chief envoy himself went to bring the monarchs. He was granted personal safety for the discharge of his function. He was honoured everywhere he went.

The Rakshasas were also conversant with the idea of diplomatic immunity. The person of the envoy was inviolable. He could not be killed when Ravana ordered for the execution of Hanumana, the envoy of king Sugriva, Bibhisana intervened and explained the Rajdharma to the envoys in' general. He said that an envoy should not be punished with death at all. Hanumana also claimed diplomatic immunity and he said, "A messenger, I came". But when question about the forms of punishment to be inflicted on guilty or obnoxious envoy, Bibhisana mentioned mutilation of certain limbs, beating and other forms of chastisement. Thereupon Ravana ordered Hanumana's tail to be burnt.

Another event that reveals the diplomatic immunity for envoys is concerned with Angada, the emissary of Rama, and Ravana. Angada pleaded his master and outwitted Ravana. Ravana became angry but he could not kill Angada. Being irritate he told that 'Niti' did not permit him to kill an envoy of other kings.

Thus there are various examples of diplomatic immunity in the *Ramayana*. The person of the envoy is regarded inviolable.

It has also been stated in the *Mahabharata* that, the 'dutas' are simply the mouth-piece of the king, who deputes him and as it is his duty to convey the message exactly that has been entrusted to him, he should never be killed. But the Udyog parvan[15] elsewhere states, that if he would transcend his jurisdiction, he was liable to be killed. But this injunction would apply only to ordinary ambassadors who were the mere conveyers of messages, as was the case with Ulaka, while there were others who enjoyed a greater degree of freedom. But inspite of these statements the epic lays stress on the inviolability of the ambassadors. It emphatically enjoins that any one who kills an ambassador, who delivers his message according to the very letter and spirit of his instructions, brings down untold sins not only on himself but even on his deceased ancestor.[16] His ancestors become guilty of embryocide. Even it was not advisable to make him capture. Lord Krishna as an ambassador of the Pandavas was sent to the Kauravas. When he reached the court of the Kauravas, Duryodhana proposed to make him captive. But Drtarastra opposed it saying that it was improper to make an ambassador captive. Side by side with this emphasis on the rights and privileges of the ambassadors, the *Mahabharata*[17] as well as the *Ramayana*[18] allow to punish or even to murder an ambassador, who is unfaithful or undutiful and if does not convey the message properly.

The epics decide some qualifications of an ambassador. In the *Mahabharata*, Bhisma advocates that an ambassador should possess seven qualifications. An envoy should come of a noble family, be modest, skillful and an eloquent speaker, capable of conveying the message, exactly as entrusted to him and should have a sharp and excellent memory.[19]

Those persons should be appointed as ambassadors who follow the 'Sita' and are very efficient. The duta was to be wise as he was to work among persons of different natures.[20] Further, he should be familiar with diplomatic policy, accustomed to espionage, fearless, royal and capable of understanding hints and innuendos which suggest intended policy. The story of sending the priest of Drupada as ambassador to the Kaurava court shows that much care was given to the selection of an ambassador.[21]

Similarly, the virtues and requisites of Sanjaya, the duta of Dhritrashtra to the Pandavas, also reveal the same thing.[22]

Vidura thinks that there are eight virtues to be sought in a person who is to be appointed as an ambassador. He should be egoless, fearless, active, kind, pure-hearted, honest, healthy and sweet in speech.[23] The ambassadors exchanged between kings Hiranya Varma and Drupada were well versed in the Vedas.[24]

Hanuman, the chief councillor and envoy of king Sugriva, was well versed in all arts and sciences. He was endowed with prowess, intelligence and skill of the highest order and had all the qualifications of an ambassador.

Purohitas (priests) also were deemed fit to play the role of an ambassador. Drupada sent his Purohita, a well versed Brahmana, in the same capacity to the Kauravas, on the eve of the war of Kuruksetra.[25] King Hiranya Varma also sent his Purohita as an ambassador to Drupada after knowing that Shikhandi, that so called son of Drupada and the son-in-law of Hiranya Varma was a female. The idea behind appointing Brahmanas as ambassadors seems to make their immunities and privileges more effective.

Hopkins[26] is of opinion that the ambassadors mentioned in the epics were recruited from amongst the priestly and the military communities.

The *Mahabharata* seems to imply that there were no permanent ambassadors in the contemporary period; persons of eminence were temporarily called upon by the king to carry his message or to conduct negotiations, on his behalf with a foreign king.

A perusal of the subject shows that they stayed in the king's court by the time their objectives were achieved. They returned to their countries after the fulfillment of the mission for which they were sent. Dhaumya, Krishna and Sanjaya were all urged to discharge their duties as ambassadors only on important occasions. Until recently, the idea of the permanent embassy was not in practice and the same thing is also seen is ancient India.

The *Mahabharata* is silent about the different categories of 'dutas'. The *Ramayana*, however, mentions three kinds of 'dutas'—Purusottama, Madhyamanara, and Purusadhama. The classification made there is not according to the qualifications of the envoys or works entrusted to them but according to the way in which they performed the tasks assigned to them. The *Yudhakanda*[27] mentions that, he, who performs even an desirable and insurmountable task, out of dexation and love is a **Purusottama**, the best among men. He, who does not act so as to enlist the love and affective of the king, but entrusted with a certain mission, and does it in his own way, is **Madhyamana**, the middling person. That man, though ordained does not carry it out in the proper manner is a **Purusadhama**, the lowest among men.

This division of envoys, as envisaged in the *Ramayana*, is in no way similar to the one referred to in the *Arthasastra*. There is, however, perfect agreement between the *Ramayana* and Kautilya's work in regard to the inviolability of the ambassador's person.[28] Commenting on Yajnavalkya, Vijnannesvara also lucidly explains three classes of dutas.[29] According to him, **Nisrstarrha**, who is a first grade ambassador, is capable of conditions of 'desa' and 'kala'. **Sandistartha** lacks the power to conduct negotiations independently. He can only present the messages of his master verbatim to the other party. **Sasanahara**, the third category of 'duta' is the carrier of royal letters or writs. In the modern period also different categories of 'dutas' exist. The powers assembled at the congress of Viena by an international agreement on March 19, 1815, decided to recognise three classes of envoys[30] in the following orders: (a) Ambassador, (b) Ministers Plenipotentiary or envoys extraordinary and (c) Charges d'Affaires. One more fourth class of envoys came to known in Aix-la-chapelle congress held on 1818, namely, Ministers resident, to rank between ministers plenipotentiary and Charges d' Affairs.[31]

Panini the great grammarian also gives the term *Pratiskasah* that denotes a messenger, a herald or an emissary. Another term is *'Yaujanika'* denoting a courier travelling one Yojna. But Katyayena adds '*Yaujanasatika*' a courier who is deputed to carry his message to a distance of one hundred Yojnas. So these terms possibly can be attributed to envoys carrying political messages.

Kings of the Sangam age also employed dutas. The dutas were representatives of one king in the court of another. They may called in modern language 'ambassador' or envoys.[32] Their function is called *'Dutu'*.

The *Tolkappian* says that the duta was a mediator also. According to it, *'Dutu'* can be undertaken by princes as well as Brahmin and other high-caste persons; and it was customary for kings or princes to undertake *Dutu* only as a mediator of honoured status and not as one employed by another. '*Dutu*' was a normal political activity; but generally dutas were busy during war time. Nachchinarkkiniar says: "The ministers, the priests, the generals, the envoys and the spies are the five great advisers".[33]

The *Kural* has a whole chapter[34] on the dutas, which gives the details of the qualifications of dutas. Parimelalagar, the commentator on the Kural, mentions three types of dutas.

First, who are placed in foreign court as to deal with the affairs of state and they are equal in status to a minister of state. Second, those whose range of argument in the foreign court is limited and they do not enjoy enough freedom to suit their arguments to fresh and unforeseen exigencies and third, those who transmit a sealed letter and also explain that message and sometimes they had to carry the reply (if any) to the message they had delivered. These are known to Sanskritists by different names like *Uttama*, *Madhyama* and *Adharma* who might correspond to ambassadors, envoys an messengers respectively. But in *Kural* text there is no such division of dutas as its commentator shows.

Orampogiyar, a Sangam poet, mentions a peculiar function of dutas; they went about crying aloud for support to their king and collected help for his cause.

The *Kural* also deals with the qualifications of the dutas, like they should have a good and stately personality, pleasing manners, eloquence, a good and high standard of education, ability to carry message without betraying fear or showing favour and courage even in the face of certain death. He should belong to a noble and high family and must be well-trained in administration and the secrets of the government. All these qualities shows that in the Sangam age when warfare was not infrequent, the dutas were frequently in commission and played an important and decisive role.

The *Silappadikaram*, a Tamil work also shows that envoys had to manage military affairs also during war time. Ambassadors were not permanently assigned to foreign courts with a regular and recurring routine of political activity; but were chosen and employed only when and if the need arose. "The system of accrediting ambassadors permanently from one court to another is of modern origin". One Jataka story indicates that 'dutas' have the right of free access to the king.

The Buddhist literature also shows that active intercourse among states were maintained through ambassadors. The Bhaddasala Jataka[35] refers to an envoy being sent by the Kosalen monarch Prosenajit to the Sakya who were urged to offer him one of their daughters in marriage. King Pukkasati or Pushkarasarin, the ruler of Gandhar, sent an embassy and a letter requesting help to his great Maghadhan contemporary Bimbisara. The embassy was graciously received by Bimbisara. The Teviyya Sutta and the Mahali Sutta, refers to the presence of Brahmana envoys of Magadha and Kosala at Vaisali.

The Jain literature also indicates that the states established and maintained diplomatic relations with one another through their respective ambassadors in times of war and peace.

The classical authors like Pliny, Arrian and Curtius also throw positive light on the position of ambassadors in the pre-Mauryan cpoch. Pliny's Anabasis of Alexander IV, for example, shows that ambassadors were an important part of the government in Indian kingdoms in the 4th Century BC. Arrian also mentions that; Abisarus, king of Taxila, also despatched envoys to Alexander with enormous presents. Another Indian king Porus, is believed to have tendered his submission to Alexander through the agency of envoys. Curtius also speaks of the tribal ambassadors of the Malavas and the Ksudrakas, who met Alexander consequent upon the defeat of their tribes at the hands of the foreign invader.

With the advance of time, the importance of diplomatic agents was realised in the section entitled '*Duta-Pranidhih*' of the *Arthasastra*, Kautilya has elaborately discussed the problem of dutas who were divided into three categories. His classification of dutas is similar to the Kamandaka's and Somdevasuri.

The first one *Nisrstarthas*, can be fitly compared to a modern ambassador. He possesses full powers of negotiation with the foreign rulers and endowed with the excellencies of a minister.

The second one is the *Parimitarthas*. These diplomatic agents are deficient in respect a quarter of the qualities expected to those belonging to the first. They are granted limited freedom in making negotiations with the foreign power, and entrusted with a definite mission, which they had to perform without deviating from the instructions given to them.

Third type of envoys are *Sasanaharas*, conveyers of royal writs and obtains the reply. They possess only half the qualifications of the officers of the first group.

Kautilya describes that an envoy would start only when there were excellent arrangements for carriage (*yana*, conveyance (*vahana*), servants (*purusa*) and subsistence (*Parivapa*).

Kautilya also laid stress on the qualifications of a duta. A duta should be high born, of good family, eloquent intelligent, sweet-tongued, faithful in delivering his message, and endowed with a good memory. Further, he should be familiar with diplomatic policy, accustomed to espionage, fearless, royal and capable of understanding hints and innuendos which suggest intended policy.[36] An ambassador should possess the same high qualities as a royal counsellor. A senior administrator must be assigned the post of a minor diplomat. Lord Krishna himself undertook diplomacy with the Kauravas on behalf of the Pandavas in the *Mahabharata* and Hanuman with Ravana on behalf of the Rama in the *Ramayana* the two great epics of the country.[37] Kautilya lays great emphasis on the moral character and personality of the men to be chosen. So well qualified men were appointed ambassadors to maintain inter-state relations during the Mauryan period. Females were not barred from holding diplomatic appointment in ancient India. In this connection, Krishnamurti rightly says that "appointing woman, as diplomat, is not new to modern international practices". During the reign of Asoka, after the Kalinga war, influenced by the tenants of Buddhism, he appointed his beautiful daughter, Sanghamitra, and accredited her to Lanka (Ceylon) and Svaranbhumi (Burma). She performed the function related to Dhamma mission as assigned to her.

While defining the functions of a *duta*, Kautilya sums up them in the following words, "transmission of missions, maintenance of treaties, issue of ultimatum, gaining of friends, intrigue, sowing dissension among friends, fetching secret force, carrying away by stealth relatives and gems, gathering information agents about the movements of spies bravery, breaking of treaties of peace, winning over the favour of the envoy and government officers of the enemy," these are the duties of an envoy.

Apart from these duties, a duta should find out the instigation of seducible parties, the loyalty or disaffection (of the enemy's subjects) towards their master and the weak points in the constituent elements (of the enemy's realm) through spies appearing as ascetics or traders, or through their disciples or other agents in disguised.

Besides it, most important duty of a diplomat was the maintenance of the peaceful diplomatic relations between different states. An ambassador was to manipulate that he could always make the forces favourable for his own state. He was to advise his master accordingly and advance the interest of his own state by successful manoeuvering in the diplomatic chessboard. An embassy was to be the control centre of the espionage in the another state.

An ambassador was given all facilities for his travel to another state. It was realised that, to add to the honour and prestige of such an official, a royal pomp was to be maintained round the ambassador. He was to enter the capital with the permission of the foreign ruler. A friendly relation, says Kautilya, was to be presumed from the nature of the reception given and also the talks. It was expected that, there would be natural exchange of good wishes from both sides. Kautilya mentions of 'respectful reception of the mission and respectful treatment of the envoy' as signs of friendly relations.

Kautilya warns an envoy to be always on his guard. He was always to be cautious and be on his safeguard lest, he should disclose his state secrets. Kautilya was fully aware of the dangers to which an envoy was sought to be put, by another state, through wine and women. He was even more cautious; he advised an envoys to sleep alone, lest in his sleep he would give out, his secrets in his dreams.

An ambassador was given right to decide whether he would stay any longer or not. But he could not leave the state to which he was sent without the permission of his ruler. He could be punished for violation of this rule. The only safeguarding clause to this was that he could return only if he could prove that he was threatened with imprisonment or that his life was in danger.

It was also in the area of an ambassador to study the situation and to decide upon breaking of the diplomatic relations. He was to consider whether delay was being deliberately made by the ruler and facilitate his own advantage, viz., if he was trying for new alignment of forces, or, of his master by instigating internal and external foes of his ruler or whether he was gaining time for preparation or delaying the season for attack. If he found the delay to be unfavourable for his master, he was to use a stricter ultimatum and return to his country. Any step should be taken with great care and after a thoughtful talk with his companions. Kamandaka advises an ambassador to be an observer, patient and persevering. He says, an intelligent envoy should not be depressed, confused and disappointed, if there is any interruption in his mission or projects, better way is to have wait for accomplishment, while it would be a long duration'.

From a passage in the *Arthasastra* it appears that Kautilya has stated about stationing permanent dutas and secret agents in the entire *rajamandala*.[39] In this connection it may be mentioned that in the chapter entitled '*bhrtyabharaniyam*', there is no mention about the salary of the ambassadors. It seems that Kautilya was not in favour of assigning any fixed salary of dutas. They possibly recieved salary in commensurate with the posts they held in the state. He says, "the average envoy (Madhyama category), who may possibly be equated with the '*parimitartha*' should receive a travelling allowance of ten 'panas' per 'yojna' for the first ten 'yojanas', and double the amount beyond ten yojnas up to one hundred 'yojnas'.[40] As the dutas of the first category enjoy the status of an 'amatya' his salary may be equal to that of an 'amatya'. They were paid 12,000 *panas* as salary. S.C. Banerji argues that as 'dutas' were not entitled to any fixed salary, there was no independent post of 'dutas' as such and that officers of different ranks were employed as occasions arose, to perform the duties of envoys. R.P. Kangle,[41] on the other hand, thinks that the duta was entitled to his regular salary, and the rates given in the passage cited would cover his travelling expenses.

Furthermore, dutas were granted lands[42] which were not transferable through sale or mortgage and they were also exempted from paying tolls while crossing rivers.[43] Thus it appears from Kautilya that different levels of envoys enjoyed status and salary according to their ranks.

In ancient India also the dutas were treated with respectful consideration and they enjoyed considerable privileges and immunities. Even if a duta conveyed an unpleasant message it was expected that he would be cordially welcomed considering the fact that he was simply the mouthpiece of the king.[44] A sharp controversy exists among indologists on the question of Kautilya's view on diplomatic privileges and immunities. Scholars like B.A. Staletore are of the opinion that Kautilya did not acknowledge the inviolability of the person of ambassadors. But such an opinion can not be upheld as Kautilya explicitly states them simply the mouthpiece of the king. Therefore, envoy speak out as they are told even when weapons are raised (against them). But it is a duty of an envoy.[45] They are not deserving death of them even the lowest born are immune from killing. Then there is no question of death punishment for Brahmins. But there are in the *Arthasastra* some statements,[46] which imply that its author was aware of ambassadors being subjected to discourteous treatment and capital punishment at the hands of foreign kings. Though they have not much fear of life, but they may sometimes be detained against their will. Thus Kautilya enjoins, 'After delivering an unpleasant message he should, for fear of imprisonment or death, go away even when not permitted, also he might be put under restraint.

Megasthenes, also says about some officers, who are in charge of the city are divided into six bodies of five each... Those of the second attend to the entertainment of the foreigners. To these they assign lodgings, and keep watch over their modes of life by means of those persons whom they give to them as assistants. V.A. Smith says that these officers who have been called '*astynomoi*' by Megasthenes, closely resemble those of the Greek '*Proxenoi*'. By the Megasthenes account, it is clear that these officers have two duties to perform first, to look after the foreigners while they remain at Patliputra, and second, to keep a close watch over their movements so that they cannot do any anti-state activity. So '*astynomoi*' can be called a 'duta' of Mauryan times but he may be regarded as resembling more a spy gathering information of and from the foreigners than an officer with consular duties.

The maintenance of diplomatic relations were considered as important as it is done today. In ancient India inter-state relations and negotiations rose as a natural sequel to the growth of a number of states. 'Messengers had often to be sent from one state to another. They were after entrusted with political functions also and they could well be compared to the ambassadors of modern times. Envoys were sent for different purposes, like matrimonial, political, religious, commercial etc. King Janka sent his messengers to the Dasaratha, seeking his permission for Rama's marriage with Sita. They were also responsible to invite the rulers of other states to the ceremonies held in their own state.[47]

Kautilya, for the first time, gives the most elaborate rules for the conduct of diplomatic relations. His B.K. VII give an exhaustive discussion of the problems connected with the foreign policy. His mandala concept, four doctrines to guide diplomatic relations, six types of foreign policy, cast the limelight on the fact that ancient India was very rich in diplomatic practices these instructions with little modification are valid even today to guide inter-state relations although they were formulated in 3rd or 4th century B.C.[40] When, we peep into the history of Magadha, it appears that states possessed the 'Right of legation'. Able and qualified persons having knowledge of time, place and conditions, were appointed diplomats. Bimbisara, ruled Magadh and maintained friendly relations by appointing able ambassadors and receiving others in turn.[49]

But the diplomatic relations of India with the rest of the world were established more systematically in Mauryan period. The intercourse, as described in various literatures, indicates that relations in ancient India were more commercial than political in character. But, political relations with foreign nations become a matter of importance from the days of Chandragupta Maurya. The ancient Indian epigraphic as well as literary sources bear testimony to the fact that ancient India remained in close touch with the outside world diplomatically and culturally, especially with the Western world, Central Asia, the Far East and South East Asia. During the reign of Chandragupta Maurya, many embassies, were received and sent to the outside world. One of the numerous examples which indicates the diplomatic matrimonial relation between Chandragupta and Seleucus I of Syria.

A conflict took place between both of them shortly after or rather shortly before 301 B.C. The quarrel is reported by Strabo (Geographica XV, 2,9), Appian (Romaika, Syrian Wars, XI, 55.), Plutarch (Lives, Alexander, 62) and Justin (XV, 4). It appears from their statements that Seleucus "crossed the Indus and waged war with Androkottos (Chandragupta), king of the Indians, who dwelt on the bank of that stream, until they came to an understanding with each other and contracted connection by marriage." (Appian, *op. cit.*, XI, 55), Strabo also speaks of giving away the territories on the terms of "the right to intermarriage". He states the terms of treaty.

"The area of the paropamisadai (to the south-east of the Hindu-Kush and in north-east Afghanistan bordering the Indian subcontinent, the land of the Aracholoi to the south of the Paropamisadai (Khandahar area in south-eastern Afghanistan), and the country of the Gedrosenoi on the sea-coast and to the south of that of the Arachotoi (in Baluchistan) were ceded by Seleucus to Sandrokottos, who gave away five hundred elephants in exchange." Strabo also speaks of giving away the territories on the terms of "the right to intermarriage". Plutarch, too, mentions about the presentation of five hundred elephants.

Chandragupta had already conquered the Greek Satrapies established by Alexander to the east of N.W.F.P, Punjab area and Sind territories. So with this annexation, the Maurya empire reached up to the Hindu-Kush, a natural frontier of Indian culture. More important was the "treaty" concluded between the two monarchs. By it "the right of inter marriage" or connection by marriage between the Greeks and Indians was officially recognised. Such a legal sanction had very important role to play in Arachosia, where the Indians and people of inter alia Hellenic origin lived together. Hence the international treaty had a clause catering to the social need of the time. The Mauryas, had the credit of concluding the earliest recorded international treaty involving India.[50]

Thus the conflict ended in friendship. Diplomatic relations were established between the Seleucus and the Mauryas. Chandragupta received Megasthenes in his court as a regular diplomatic envoy on behalf of his Greek contemporary Seleucus Nicator and thus cemented his relations with the Hellenic empire. Athenaeus (I, 32,18 D) refers to strange drugs sent by Sandrokottos to Seleucus.

Chandragupta Maurya was succeeded in or about the year 298 B.C. by his son Bindusara. He also possessed diplomatic insight and tried his best to maintain cordial relations with foreign governments. He appointed able and successful diplomats to cement inter-state relations. Bindusara was an able and competent administrator who tried his level best to be on friendly terms with his neighbouring kings. He received and sent several diplomatic missions to a number of western countries. "In his relations with the Hellenistic powers, Bindusara pursued a pacific policy. According to Athenaeus, Amitrochates (i.e. Bindusara Amitraghata, the father of Asoka) requested Antiochus I (280-261 BC), the king of Syria, to send a quantity of sweet wine, some figs and "a sophist to teach him argu." The wine and the figs were despatched as desired, but not the sophist, "since sophists were not marketable commodity among the Greeks." Antiochus I sent Diamachus of plateau as an envoy to the court of Bindusara (?). Ptolemy II Philadelphos (283-246 B.C.) of Egypt sent Dionysius as an ambassador to India. Probably to the court of Bindusara or his famous son Asoka.

Asoka also continued the same policy with frontier kingdoms and foreign powers. During the first thirteen years of his reign, Asoka seems to have carried on the traditional Maurya policy of expansion within India, and of friendly co-operation with foreign powers. Like Chandragupta and Bindusara, Asoka was aggressive at home but pacific abroad. The friendly attitude towards non-Indian powers is proved by the exchange of able and well qualified ambassador. The conquest of Kalinga was a great landmark in the history of Magadha, and of India. It marked the close of that career of conquest and aggrandizement which was ushered in by Bimbisara's annexation of Anga. It opened a new era—an era of peace, of social progress and of religious propaganda. The era of Digvijaya was over, the era of Dhamma-Vijaya was about to begin.

Asoka was aware of the importance of foreign relations and contacts with peoples outside his empire. Most of his contacts were to the south and the west. Asoka's missions to various parts of the Hellenic world must also have assisted him in establishing relations.

These missions were the main instruments of contacts that Asoka had with neighbouring countries. They can be described as embassies, though the mission is more appropriate. Their main purpose was to acquaint the countries they visited with the policies of Asoka, particularly that of Dhamma or propagation of his Buddhist mission as well.

The cumulative evidence of RE II and RE XIII of Asoka claims that medical missions for treatment of human beings and animals had been sent to and conquest of *Dhamma* had been affected in the frontier states like those of Kambojas, Gandharas, Nabhakas, Rstikas, Bhojas, Andhras and the Parinda paradas and in the courts of foreign kings as Antiochus Theos II of Syria (261-246 BC), Ptolemy II Philadelphos of Egypt (283-246 BC), Antigonus of Macedonia (278-239 BC), Magas of Cyrene, in north Africa (d. 258 or 250 BC) and Alexander of Epirus 272-255 BC, and in the countries "downwards" (i.e. Southern territories) like those of the Cholas, Pandyas, Satiyhaputra, Keralaputra (Mentioned only in RE II dealing with the medical missions) and Tamraparni or Sri Lanka.

As Asokas missions were primarily concerned with *Dharma-vijaya*, the conquest of the law of piety, Dr. Bhandarbar remarks in this connection are worth quoting. Says he, "What we have really to understand from the Rock edict VIII, is that Asoka was already in the habit of sending ambassadors to the Greek courts, but that he now thought of propagating his faith through these officers in the Greek kingdoms, just as he did in his own empire through his other officers.[51]

The missions appear to have been successful in Ceylon where Devanampiya became a firm adhvent of the Dhamma idea. According to the *Mahavamsa*,[52] Tissa and Asoka were friends for a long time. Once Tissa sent an embassy with gifts to Asoka and had himself consecrated for the second time as a king at his friend's request.

The use of Kharosthe in the Shabhazgarhi and Mansahra edicts in the north is an evidence of strong contact with Iran. The fragmentary Armaic inscription at Taxila and the Armaic inscription from Kandhar, point to continued communications between the two areas. The use of the Iranian words '*dipi*' and '*nipista*' in the northern versions of the major Rock edict, reinforces thjis idea.

The Mauryan period saw the development of trade and commerce with Babylon. This was of great assistance to communication between India and the west, since it kept the maritime route open.

Tibetan traditions maintain that Asoka visited Khotan 250 years after the death of the Buddha, in 236 B.C., also Asoka sent *Dhamma*-Mission to Khotan. Asoka appears to have had close connections with the area of modern Nepal. Traditions show that he was accompanied on this visit by his daughter Garumati and she was married to a Rsatrya of Nepal, Devapala. Nepali traditions maintain that Asoka actually visited Nepal. This may be a reference to the visit to Rummindei, or he may have journeyed farther into Nepal on the same occation. With the influence of Asoka, many embassies later passed between India and China also during the time of Sung-wanti. Their chief object was to congratulate the ruling emperor on the spread of Buddhism in his dominions and to pave the way for more frequent intercourse on the ground of identity of religion, the letter of an Indian monarch preserved in the history of their dynasty, expresses his admiration of the emperor Wanti, in glowing language. He adds that though separated by a wide sea, it was his wish to have embassies passing and re-passing between the two countries.[53]

It is, however, difficult to believe that such medical and *Dhamma-vijaya* missions could have been effectively sent to countries in Europe or even Africa, though there could have been formal diplomatic and economic relations between them and the Maurya empire. It was also possible for the Mauryan diplomats to urge upon the Greek monarchs to follow certain principles of Dhamma, like avoidance of self-restraint, impartiality and gentleness in their behaviour (in domestic and international fields). Regular contacts (of cultural and commercial types) were possible with the Seleucid domain, which had a common border with the Maurya empire till the rise of the Greek kingdom of Bactria in about the middle of the 3rd century B.C. But there is no evidence of diplomatic relations of the newly founded kingdom of Bactria with Asoka, though the Mauryan territory had to face the invasion of the Bactrian Greeks in a post-Asoka period.

Thus the Mauryas had diplomatic contacts at different levels with several countries and Indian kingdoms. In this regard they were among the pioneers in the sub-continent.

Besides the religious, cultural and diplomatic aspects, the Mauryan empire or contemporary India has also economic aspect behind its relations with outside world.

The references of the exchange of embassies are also traceable in the subsequent period of ancient Indian history. It is in the post-Maurya period that one comes across the earliest epigraphic reference to ambassadors. The Basnagar Garuda Pillar inscription, assignable to the last quarter of the second century B.C., speaks of a Greek ambassador (Yonaduta) named Heliodorus who visited the court of king Bhagabhadra at Vidisa in his fourteenth regnal year as a representative of Maharaja Amitalikita, identified with Bhadraka, the fifth Sunga king, as mentioned in the Bhagvata Purana. It may be presumed that the Bactrian Greeks cultivated friendly relations with their Sanga counterparts with the helps of envoys.

The Roman historian record the exchange of embassies time and again between the Roman empire and the Indian kingdoms during the post-Maurya period. Pliny[54] speaks of an embassy being sent to emperor Claudius from the kingdom of Taprobane which has been identified by some scholars with Cyclon, and located in south India by others. Again, the Roman emperor Trajan is said to have received an Indian embassy about A.D. 103.[55] and, if the opinion of Warmington is to be trusted, the embassy was sent out by the Kusana king Kanishka I to seek help against the Indians or the Chinese. Emperor Hardian likewise received an embassy from an Indian ruler. But there is no clear identification of that Indian king. B.A. Saletore identifies him with Kanishka I but this is not in agreement with the generally accepted chronology of the Kusana manarch. Still it would not be far from truth to surmise that these Indian embassies to the Roman court were like the modern missions of goodwill, offering presents to the heads of the governments concerned, and claiming some commercial concessions.[56]

Later on, the contribution of the Gupta dynasty to the diplomatic practice is laudable. But, unfortunately there is no reference to the dutas or ambassadors being sent from the imperial court to those of the vassals or the frontier chiefs or even foreign powers. Kamandaka no doubt provides some information on the role of the ambassadors or dutas and charanas who were spies. It is interesting to note that the great poet Kalidasa does not mention ambassadors at all in any of his works. This has given rise to the speculation that probably the work of these costly and comparatively useless and ornamental figureheads was more efficiently done by clever spies who were deputed to watch the activities of enemies in foreign territories.[57] So there will always remain a question on the silence of Kalidasa on the role and contribution of ambassadors in Gupta period.

Yajnavalkya Dharmasatra mentions the 'dutas', where the king is urged to consult his ministers on the issue of despatching his ambassadors. The Chinese author Wang-Hiuen-Tse gives the information of dutas, sent, to Gupta empire from Ceylon. 'Kamandakiya Nitisara' often utilize as reconstructing the history of Gupta period. In the *'Duta prakaranam Prakasarnam'* section of this work dutas appear as top ranking officers of the state, being recruited from amongst those few ministers who were noted for their astuteness in the sixfold policy of alliance, war, etc. Following in the footsteps of his illustrious predecessor Kautilya, Kamandaka has classified the dutas into three divisions, namely, the *Nisrstarthas*, the *Mitarthas* and the *Sasanaharakas*. In order to strengthen their master's position they maintained cordial relations with frontier guards and foresters.

According to him, an ambassador should he conversant with the rules and communications of the enemy's state and be bold enough to convey the message of his master to the enemy rulers. They should visit the capital and the court of the enemy at opportune moments and should gather all sort of information in regard to the strength and equipment of forts, official secrets, vulnerable points and financial as well as military resources. It was also the responsibility of ambassadors to inquire about the ruler and his relationship with the subjects. They should study the vantage points of the enemy's territories, the loyalty or otherwise of their people as also their discontent and praise the enemy as if he were their master. They should show lot of patience and put up with insults. They should be never reluctant to deliver their master's massage to the enemy even when such an act might, involve a threat to their life. *Kamandaka* advised to the dutas to avoid the influence of lust on all occasions. In order to guard themselves effectively against the unwilling revelation of secrets, they should sleep alone and avoid women and drinks. It was also the qualification and duty of dutas to appland the powers of their master in the presence of enemies with a view to striking terror in his enemies whose aggressive designs might thus be curbed. They should sow seeds of dissension among friends and relations of the enemy and trace out the routes of escape for the army in an exigency and should keep then alive to the machinations of a foreign envoy. So in short, *Kamandaka's* account of ambassadors strikingly agrees with that furnished by Kautilya centuries earlier.

It is from about this period and onwards that the word 'dutaka' being used time and again in both north and south Indian epigraphs. The term, which literally means 'a messenger', is a technical title of an officer who was employed in connection with formal grants. The Gupta inscriptions used the word 'duta' for the carrier of the royal sanction to a grant, though the person entrusted with this task sometimes included high dignitaries such as *mahabaledhikrita*. Nagar Simha of Majhgawan plates of Maharaja Hastin, Kumara Srichandra Gupta of the Nalanda Copper plate of Samudragupta, and the *dutaka* Gopasvamin the *akshapatadhikrita* of the Gaya copper plate inscription of Samudragupta, so these Dutakas, who carried not the actual charter itself but the king's sanction and order to the local officials, whose duty it was to have the charter drawn up and delivered in favour of the recipients of land grants, were evidently different from dutas as or envoy.

The Sukraniti, also includes the duta in the list of the ten principal officers of the king. It embassies on the prerequisites of the duta. They should be efficient in reading of emotions and gestures. They should have good memory, a sound memory of time and space. They should courageous and proficient in the six-fold means of peace (*Sandhi*), war (*vigraha*), march (*Yanam*), and neutrality (*asanam*), dual policy (*dvaidhibhavam*) and seeking refuse (*samsraya*). The Sukraniti is very clear about the fact that the dutas were generally Brahmana by caste, but sometimes a Ksatriya or even a Vaisya would have been tipped for the post.

Some inscriptions, mostly from Bengal mention about an officer called '*Duta Praisanika*'. The literally meaning of the term is one who sends out an envoy (*dutampresayati iti*). If this interpretation of the term is accepted, it would decide that the '*Dutapraisanika*' was a top-ranking officer who was authorized to supervise the work of envoys. Some epigraphic documents show another class of officer called *Gamagamika*, which literally means 'one who comes and goes'. The commentator Utpala has interpreted the term as 'an envoy'. They might have been the officers carrying out functions of an urgent character in connection with the diplomatic department of the state, requiring frequent visits to the neighbouring kingdoms or to the dominions of vassals.

The *Agni purana* also presents the classification of dutas into three categories, viz., the *Nisrstarthas*, the *Mitarthas* and the *Sasanaharakas*, each succeeding type being one fourth in qualities than the preceding one. This classification of dutas is similar to the previous classification. It is laid down that, intelligence, relentive memory, ingenuity, proficiency in the art of war and scriptural knowledge and eloquence of speech were the essential qualifications that were expected of an ambassador. The *Agnipurana* further points out ambassadors were 'open spies'. It shows that the ambassadors perform their duties with the help of secret agents. But the *Agnipurana* is silent on the status of these ambassadors or the caste barriers during the time of their appointment.

During the time of Gupta rulers these ambassadors were used to carry on their diplomatic relations. Diplomatic techniques and practices were frequently used to maintain the relations. The fundamental distinction between Asoka and Samudragupta regarding their diplomatic outlook lies in the fact that Asoka glorifies in the *'Dhamma Vijya'* while the latter glorified in the *'Yudha Vijya'*. Internally, the Gupta's principle of dynastic alliances was to enlarge the sphere of political power.

The administration under the Guptas with reference to interstate relations between the ruling power, as also with the other countries in the neighbourhood was based on the *Rajmandla* theory which was evolved by Kautilya a or even earlier by his predecessors like Valavyavadhi.

Samudragupta's approach in dealing with the contemporary powers was varied, quite in conformity with the rules, norms and injections prescribed in the texts on State-craft. He maintained a different type of diplomatic relations with the rulers and kept them under his authority like, he violently uprooted the rulers of Aryavarta-namely Rudradeva, Matila, Nagadatta, Chandravarman, Ganapatinga, Nagarseva, Achyuta, Nandin and Balavarman and many other rulers, and made all the kings of the forest countries (*ataviraja*) to be his servants. The rulers of the south (*Dakshinapatha*) who were, however, liberated after conquest (*Raja grahana-mokshaanugraha*) included Mahendra of Kosala, Vyaghraga of Mahakantara, Manteraja of Kaurala. Mohendragiri of Pishatopura, Swamidatta of Kottura, Damana of Erandapala, Vishnugopa of Kanchi, Nilaraja of Avamukta, Hastivarman of Vengi, Ugrasena of Palakka, Kubera of Devarashtra and Dhananjaya of Kushthalpur. It can no doubt be taken for certain that the Deccan, campaign by the Gupta monarch as a *Vijigishu* was not for aggrandisement, but for the exhibition and extention of his suzerainty.

Besides these rulers, Samudragupta defeated many frontier kings (Pratyantara nripati) who paid taxes and obeyed royal orders obeisance. These included Samatata, Devaka, Kamarupa, Nepala, Kartaripura and other countries and the republican states of Malavas, Arjunayas, Yaudhyas, Abhiras, Prajunas, Sanakanikas, Kalas and other tribes. Besides rendering obeisance, they brought presents of Maidens (Kanyo-Payadana), their emblems of regality (garutmadanka) surrendering the enjoyment of their territories and soliciting his commands etc. The last in the category of powers maintaining relations with Samudragupta were the descendants of the Kushanas known by the titles used by Kanishka and his successors—*Daivaputra-Shahi-Shahanushahi* and the Saka lords, and these rulers occupying all island countries, such as Sinhala (Ceylon) and others. Bhandarkar has remarked on his diplomatic relations that, the military achievements of Samudragupta must have spread his name and fame far and wide so that the neighbouring independent monarchs entered into diplomatic relations with him. The ways of soliciting his friendship were three fold, that of self-effacement (atmanivederana), offering of daughters in marriage (Kany-Opayana-dana), and with a request (Yachana) for the governance (sasana) of their own districts and province (Svavishaya bhukti) by means of the Garuda badge (Garotmadanika) the royal insignia of the Gupta family. It was by one or another of these means that they established friendly relations with the Gupta emperor. The foreign dignitaries noticed in this record included some descendant of the Kushanas living beyond Punjab somewhere in Afghanistan, but not beyond in the Oxus region, the Sakas and Murundas representing different regal families which are also noticed in the Purnas, as foreign tribes, living in contiguity with each other. The Murundas are, however, located in the eastern part of India. The Sakas rulers must be the western Kashatrapas of Kathiawar and north Gujarat. So Samudragupta used farsightedness and diplomacy to maintain his relation with the distant rulers.

Samudragupta not only sway his authority on inter state rulers but maintained diplomatic relations with external powers also. The foreign travellers that came to India in the Gupta and later Gupta periods, were more or less cultural ambassadors from their respective countries, but they were decidedly helpful in establishing diplomatic relations also between their countries and India. The particular passage in the Allahabad Prarsti describing the relations of these powers with Samudragupta is somewhat vague and uncertain. It may, however, be accepted that these rulers strived to win the favour of the Great Gupta emperor by personal attendance in the court, offering daughters in marriage and asking permission for the use of imperial coins or soliciting imperial charters confirming them in their territories. This approach on their part might have been the result of the tutelage, or just, a diplomatic move to save themselves from the brunt, of Gupta's onslaught. The discovery of some coins of the Kushana type with the name of Samundra and Chandra, and the use of the Gupta type of coins by some Scythian rulers of the west is taken by some historians to symbolize some sort of Gupta suzerainty over some of frontier states. The Saka and Kushana chiefs can be noticed in this relations, in the records of Samundragupta. Even the distant Simhala (Ceylon) and all other Islands bracketted with the Sakas and the Kushanas in this record. It is not unlikely that in view of Indian cultural expansion in South-East Asian countries, there was a deep impact of Gupta culture in these regions. So far as Ceylon is concerned, there is an independent piece of evidence recording political relationship between the ruler of this island and Samundragupta. The Chinese author Wang-Hiuen-Tse tells that the king of Ceylon named Chi-Mi-Kia-po-mo, i.e., Meghavarna (A.D. 352-379) sent two monks to Bodh-Gaya to visit the sacred spots, but they had to face some inconvenience for want of suitable accommodation. So Meghavarna decided to built a monastery there. He accordingly sent a mission to Samudragupta with rich presents soliciting his permission to do so. The Indian emperor granted this permission at once and Ceylonese king built a splendid monastery to the north of the 'Bodh tree.' By the time of Hiuen-tsang it had emerged as a magnificent establishment with more than 1,000 priests. This monastery is famous for its rich decorations and vastness. The pilgrim tracing the old history of the foundation records that the Ceylonese king gave in tribute to the king of India all the jewels of his country. It is likely that this rich presentation of jewels was by way of tribute or in lieu of the grant of permission to build the monastery at Bodh-Gaya as an appropriation for charter, confirming him in the enjoyment of his territorial rights, it being one of the forms of acknowledging the suzerainty of the paramount ruler.

The neighbouring States in the Islands might have been similarly maintain their relations with the Gupta Emperor. These were Hindhu States in Indo-China at Funan-Kambiya and Champa (Annam), as also in Indonesia and Malaysia and cultural and political contacts with the motherland were not wanting. The prarastikara Harishena, however, places them in the category of Vassals which might be rather rhetoric in the absence of any other independent evidence. The performance of the Asvamedha-Horse sacrifice-recorded in the inscription, as also the coin legend, having the prowess of a tiger, wielding the axe of Kritanta (the god of death), the unconquered conqueror of unconquered kings having protected the earth, wins heaven, suggest the expansionist zeal of the ruler and his achievements.

Later Samundra Gupta successors also maintained the interstate relations. His successors, Ramagupta-although his historicity is accepted yet it is clear he had to face a difficult situation so soon after the death of his illustrious father. In the course of war with the Saka king, he was closely besieged and place in such a difficult and awkward position that in order to save his people he agreed to surrender his queen to the Saka, king. His younger brother Chandra Gupta protested against this act of dishonour, and using the diplomacy he personally went to enemy's camp in the guise of queen Dhruvadevi and killed the hated Saka ruler. He also killed his brother and married his widow without discussing the historicity of this episode one might review Chandragupta's relations with the Sakas who had accepted tutelage of Gupta sovereignty in the father's time. Records shows that Chandragupta waged a war against the Saka ruler of Gujarat and the Kathiawar peninsula. The details of the compaign are not known, but there are indication that

Chandragupta with this feudatory chiefs and ministers, had to make aprolonged stay in Malwa for waging war against the Sakas. The Gupta ruler was successful in his campaign. The Saka ruler Rudrasinha III was not only defeated but his kingdom was annexed. The line of western Satrapa thus ended after more than there hundred years.

The king 'Chandra' of the 'Mehrauli pillar inscription' is identified with Chandragupta II, that adds a new dimension to the expansionist policy pursued by this Gupta monarch. He led his military expedition towards the eastern as well as the western regions of his empire. After conquering the Saka in western Malwa, Gujarat and Kathiawar, he, rounded off the Gupta imperial hold in northern India in all directions.

Gupta rulers also maintained matrimonial diplomatic relations to being to powerful ruling families under his influence. Chandragupta I, the founder of Gupta, rejuvenated the glories of Magadha by contracting matrimonial alliance with a princess of Lichchhavis, a connection of which his son Samudragupta always felt proud. Chandragupta II Vikramaditya followed the same policy. He married Kuberinage of the Naga family, and had a daughter named Prabhavati Gupta by her. This daughter was married to the Rudrasena II, the great Vakataka king in Deccan to have listing peace in the South.[60] According to Dr. Smith "Chandragupta adopted a prudent precaution in giving his daughters to the Vakataka prince and so securing his subordinate alliance.[61] The geographical location of the Nagas and the Vakatakas was definitely favourable for the military campaign against the Sakas, and their containment was necessary for any military expedition. Over all, after this marriage the two imperial dynasties were knit together in still closer ties of friendship, which resulted in establishing a long era of peace and prosperity in India, an era rightly known as the golden period of the ancient Indian History.[62] The inscription of the powerful Kadamba ruler

Kakusthvarman of Kuntaka records the marriage of his daughter in the Gupta family and elsewhere. This points to the traditional matrimonial diplomacy which was quite a normal and routine business for establishing political friendship between contending or rival powers.

The policy pursued by this Gupta monarch as also by his father Samudragupta was motivated by consideration of conquest and consolidation as evolved by Kautilya and equally endorsed by Kamandaka of Gupta period. This political philosopher accepts and approves the 'mandala theory' of his predecessor. Kamandaka refers to the conquest of the earth as the legitimate duty of a monarch. He is, however, advised to take into account the time, place and circumstances involved in military expedition. He also favours for consultation with the chief war minister, before venturing on any military expedition. So matrimonial relations as well as diplomatic missions and their establishments were of great importance for cementing inter-state relations in the early as well as the later ancient Indian history.

Later on in Seventh century A.D. ambassador were employed by Indian kings to cultivate diplomatic ties with foreign powers. King Harsavardhana of Thanesar is known to have sent a Brahmana envoy to 'Tai Tsung', the emperor of China, in A.D. 641, where upon the latter reciprocated by sending a mission, carrying his reply to Harsa's dispatch. According to Dr. V.A. Smith,[63] "the mission remained in India for a considerable period till A.D. 645". Again, in the early part of A.D. 648, the Chinese emperor sent an ambassador named Wang-Hiuen-tse to Harsa, who had, however, passed away before the envoy arrived in India.

Bana's narrative would indicate that ambassadors visited courts with presents were honorably treated and they delivered their commission in confidence. Dutas were further employed by Indian kings to establish friendly relations among themselves. The *Harsacarita* records that Bhaskaravarman, king of Kamarupa, dispatched on envoy to Harsavardhana in order to conclude an alliance, presumably against Sasanka, their common enemy and king of Bengal.[65]

Besides Harshavardhana, some other Indian kings of the seventh century A.D. are known to have maintained diplomatic relations with foreign powers. The Arab historian of 9th century A.D., Tabari tells that Paramesa or Paramesvara, the king of India, sent an embassy to the court of Persian king, Khusuru II. This king Paramesa has been identified as Pulakasin II of the early Chalukya dynasty of Badami. But scholars like R.C. Majumdar have traced that this king is not Pulakesian II, but Harsavardhana Pushyabhuti dynasty of Kanauz. Some scholars surmise that a painting in one of the Ajanta caves depicts the Persian embassy presenting Khusru's reply to Pulakesian II but this is far from being certain. Later in A.D. 692 an embassy was sent to China from the Chalukya court at Badami. After the death of Harsavardhana, till the ascendancy of the Muslims, the history of ancient India is a history of several Principalities mainly dominated by the Rajputas. During this period (8 century A.D. to the 13th century A.D.), the exchange of diplomats became purely the internal matter and the relationship with the outside world, to a great extent, suffered a set-back still we have references of the exchange of embassies with China, Tibet and the western countries.

Among other Indian rulers to have maintained friendly relations with foreign courts, mention may be made of the Pallava king Narasimhavarman II who is known to have sent an embassy to the Chinese Court. T.V. Mahalingam observes : "The Chinese emperor received the ambassador with all kindness and issued instructions to his officers that they must look after him with greatest care till his departure and act in such a way that his hopes might be fulfilled, when he left China, the Ambassador was given a robe of flowered silk, a golden girdle, a purse with an amblem in the form of a fish and the seven objects.

In A.D. 731, as Chinese authorities would have us believe, a king of Central India named I-Chafon-mo dispatched the envoy Seng-Po-ta-to China. The Central Indian ruler has been identified with Yasovarman, of Kanuaj. The identification of the Indian ruler may not be incorrect but it is not possible in the present state of our knowledge to trace the circumstances in which the embassy was sent.

In A.D. 972, forty four Indian monks went to China, next year, Dharmadeva, a monk of Nalanda was received by the emperor of China with great honour. There were political relations between South India and China during the *Sung* period, a Chola embassy visited the imperial court in 1015 A.D. Chinese annals provide the full information about their journey. The Chola king is said to have sent as presents among other thing twenty one thousand ounces of pearls, sixty elephants, Turks etc.

This great Chola king was Rajaraja. He cultivated relations with Culamani Varma, the Sri Vijaya king of the Malay Peninsula, who commenced, apparently with the approval of his Indian counterparts, the construction of a Buddhist Vihara at Nagapattinam in Tanjavur district. Culamani died soon after, leaving the Vihara to be completed by his son Sri Maravijayottungavarman who named it after his departed father. King Rajaraja made a grant of the village of Anaimangalam for the upkeep of this monastery in A.D. 1006. The construction of this monastery by these foreign kings in the dominions of an Indian ruler must have been preceded by the exchange of embassies between the two courts. Rajraja's son and successor Rajendra Chola sent an embassy to China in A.D. 1033. Kulottunga I is, likewise, known to have sent an embassy to China in A.D. 1077, 'The embassy consisted of seventy two men who carried with them as tributes glass, camphor, brocades, rhinoceros horns, ivory, incense, rose water, borax, cloves, etc. each of the value of a dollar. There are references to the exchange of diplomatic contracts between India and Tibet during this period. During Pala period Tibet was in close touch with India inscriptions from Bengal of about the ninth and tenth centuries A.D. seem to prove the prevalence of the office of ambassadors in the Pala kingdom, although historian B.B. Mishra[67] put his view that they were permanent offices in the Pala government, may be considered too exaggerative. Pandhukeswar Copper plates of the ninth century A.D. and the Indra inscription of the Kamboja dynasty also provide the information about these officers. B.C. Sen presented his different opinion that according to latter records Dutas were helped in their work by a number of secret agents. We have abundant references to close contacts between India and the Muslim world. During this period, South East Asian countries i.e. Java, Sumatra and Malay Peninsula (Yavabhumipalah), also remained in close touch with India, especially with South India. The Sailendra emperor of South East Asia named Balputradeva, had intimate relations with Pala emperor Devapala.

The Sailendra monarch sent an ambassador to the Pala king. The object of this embassy was to secure a grant of five villages with which the Sailendra king proposed to endow a monastery, he had built at Nalanda. A great patron of Buddhism, Devapala granted to request of the Sailendra king. As early as 782 A.D., Kumar Ghosh, an inhibitant of Bengal as the royal preceptor (Guru) of the Sailendra kings who were followers of Mahayan Buddhism and an inscription on a copper plate bears testimony to the fact.

References

1. Mahabharata, XII, 56, 12.
2. Harold Nicholson, Diplomacy, Oxford University Press, New York, 2nd ed. 1958, p. 117.
3. R.V. I. 12, 1. Tr. Griffith.
4. R.V. VIII. 44, 3.
5. R.V. I. 12, I.
6. *Ibid.,* I 60, 1. Tr. Griffith.
7. T.B. Mookerji, Inter State Relation, in Ancient India, p. 24.
8. R.V. II, 6, 9, Tri Griffith.
9. A.A. Macdonell, A Vedic Mythology, Strassburg, 1897, p. 151.
10. R.V. X, 108.
11. Taittiriya Samhita, IV, 5,7.
12. S.L. Roy, Diplomacy in Ancient India, Charu Pub, Co. Calcutta, pp. 164-65.
13. B.A. Salctore, Diplomatic Relations with the West, 1958, p. 334.
14. I. Dutta, Sharma, Theory and Practice in Ancient Indian International Law, Siddha Bharati, Part II, 1950, p. 283.
15. Udyoga Parvan, 37, 25.
16. Mbh, Shantiparvan, LXXXV, 26-27.
17. Mbh, Udoga Parvan, LXXII, 7.
18. Ramayana, Yudhakanda, 20.19.
19. कुलीनः कुलसम्पन्नो वाम्मी दक्षः प्रियंवदः।
    यथोक्तवादी स्मतिमान् द्मतः स्यात् सप्तभिगुणैः।।
    Shantiparvan, LXXXV, 28.

    अस्तब्धमक्लीवमदीर्घसूत्रं सानुक्रो ं लसणमहार्य मन्यैः।
    अरोगजातीयमुदारवाक्यं द्मतं वदम्त्यष्टगुणोपएमान्।।
    Udogya Parvan, XXXVIII, 27.
20. Udogya, 1. 23-24.

21. *Ibid.,* 4.26, 5.8, 6.2-3.
22. *Ibid.,* 30. 3-5.
23. *Ibid.,* 37.25.
24. *Ibid.,* 193.22.
25. Udyoga, VI.
26. JAOS, XIII, 1889, 95.
27. Yudhakanda, I, 7-9.
28. D.K. Ganguly, Aspects of Ancient Indian Administration p. 215.
29. Yajnavalkya I, 328.
30. Classification of envoys started in the 16th century: Oppenheim, international law, Vol. I (1966). pp. 776-777.
31. S.L. Roy, Diplomacy in Ancient India, pp. 170-71.
32. 'Duta' is a Sanskrit expression, there is no corresponding expression in Tamil.
33. N. Subramaniam, Sangam Polity, Asia Publishing House, Bombay 1966, p. 97.
34. Kural, Chap. 69.
35. Jataka, IV, p.145, No. 465.
36. P. Saran, Ancient Indian Thought, p. 528.
37. T.N. Ramaswamy, Essentials of Indian State craft. p. 16.
38. Chamber's Twentieth Dictonary, edited by William Geddle (New Delhi) Allied Pub., Revised edition, 1970, p. 853.
39. Kautilya Artha. VII, 13.
40. *Ibid.,* V, 3.19.
41. R.P. Kangle, *op. cit.,* pp. 351-52
42. Artha. V, 3.18.
43. *Ibid.,* II.18.
44. Artha, I.16.
45. *Ibid.,* I. 16, 13-17.

46. *Ibid.,* I. 16, 10.
47. P. Saran, *op.cit.,* pp. 529-30.
48. Bharti Mukherjee, Kautilya concept of Diplomacy, p. 8.
49. S.L. Roy, *op.cit.* p. 102.
50. B.N. Mukerjee, The Character of the Mauryan Empire, pp. 80-81.
51. Bhandarkar, 'Asoka' p. 162.
52. Mahavamsa, XI, 20-26.
53. Indra, *op.cit.,* pp. 86-87.
54. B.A. Saletore, *op.cit.,* p. 228.
55. The Cambridge Ancient History, Vol. XI, p. 238.
56. D.K. Ganguly, *op.cit.,* p. 218.
57. S.A. Sabnis, Kalidasa, His style and His Times, Bombay, 1966.
58. Fleet: Corpus- *op.cit.,* p. 108.
59. Bhendarka, *op.cit.* pp. 227-28.
60. Ganga Prasad Mehta, Chandragupta Vikramaditya, Hindustan.
61. Harold Nicolson, 'Diplomacy', p. 62.
62. Epigraphica Indica, Poona plates, p. 150.
63. V.A. Smith, *op.cit.* p. 352.
64. The Harsacarita of Bana, Trans, by E.B. Cowell and F.W. Thomas, Delhi, 1961, p. 212.
65. R.C. Majumdar, History of Ancient Bengal Calcutta, 1971, p. 52.
66. D.K. Ganguly, *op.cit.,* p. 221.
67. B.B. Mishra, Polity in the Agni Purana, Calcutta, 1965. p. 118.
68. K.V. Rangaswami Aiyangar, Krtyakalpataru, XI, Rajadharmakanda, Introduction, p. 49; text, p. 34.

8

Position and Contribution of Spies

The department of spies occupied a very important place in the administration of a state in ancient India. A complete network of spies used to spread throughout the length and breath of the country. Their work was considered to be of utmost importance.

It kept the rulers posted with the activities, affections and operations of political adversaries, disloyal and disgruntled elements, fifth, columnists and foreign powers.

There is reference of spies of gods in the *Rigveda* which wander upon earth never stop, never close their eyes.[1]

Spies were advised to be planted everywhere so that they could visit every place and watch everything unceasingly. On the basis of the employment of spies by *Varuna*, the divine counterpart of the human king, that spies were often employed by the Vedic monarchs with a view to keeping themselves well informed of the happenings of various kinds within their kingdom.[2]

The evidence indicate not only that spies existed, but that they were numerous and formed an important part of the government and got a high position.

The *Mahabharata*[3] mentions that "spies are the base of a state. A king is called like the sun who look-after his subject and provide them security with the help of *caras*.[4]

Spies are considered one of the eight limbs of army.[5] These evidences show the clear picture of the great position of spies in the epic *Mahabharata*.

The *Ramayana* shows the important position of spies when Rama enquires of Bharata if the latter was keeping an eye on the fifteen *tirthas* of the kingdom through *caras*.[6]

Supernakha says to his brother Ravana that without confidant spies no king can rule the kingdom. In early period, people could not imagine a king without spies.[7]

The *Ramayana* mentions that, the kings who have not controlled over secret agents, treasury and policies, they are like the common people.[8]

The position of spies can be judged by the incident that no king could be dear to the people if he rejects the statements of spies. As Rama had abducted the Sita, hearing to the spies.[9]

Kautilya had given a high position to spies. He once mentioned that ministers should work on the forecast of '*Tapas*' spies.

Their work is so important that the king is obliged to give a daily audience to the reports of these agents.[10] These periods from the traditional daily routine of the king's duties were not apart for attention to work in connection with the department of espionage viz. a portion of the time 12 to 1.30 p.m. was devoted to understanding the secret reports from spies written in cryptic characters, 6 to 7 p.m. to interview with spies, and a portion of the period from 3 a.m. to 4.30 a.m. to sending out spies on their errands.[11] It is evident that king was always in contact of spies and spent a long duration with them. King was fully depend upon the information of spies.

Megasthenes considered the spies a special class of society. Of them he says, "the sixth class consists of the 'overseers' to whom is organised the duty of watching all that going on and making reports secretly to the king. Some are entrusted with the inspection of the city, and other with that of the army.[12]

By this passage of Megasthenes, there appears a complete picture of existing and flowering secret services and their special position in the state.

In the *Yajnavalkya smriti*, spies are given same position as in the *Arthasastra*. It was the duty of king to contact with the spies in his daily routine. After the battle, king at once met the spies to know the condition. In evening, after the worship, king used to hear the secretive talks of spies and then decide the programme.[13]

Yajnavalkya says that the king is to protect subject against scribes, check on officers with spies. Manu also gave similar idea.[14]

In Sangam polity, espionage was a permanent institution and was not suspended during peace-time.[15] Although spies were regarded very reliable persons, yet a ruler was advised to verify the information supplied by a secret agent from other sources.[16] A report was identified by three different spies unknown to each other. The treatment of spies was very hard if they bring wrong news.

There is a little difference in the position of spies and *dutas*. Duta has been called the 'licensed spy' and he can assume any role for the benefit of his country and advancement of the interests of his master.[17]

Dr. Chakravarty has commented that "An ambassador in ancient India, like his modern prototype, was nothing more than an honourable spy acting under the protection of customary laws".[18]

Although sometimes their functions seems to overlap, yet there is difference in their states.

Spies did not enjoy any diplomatic immunity as was the case with ambassadors.[19]

In Sangam polity, *Dutas* were considered superior to the *Orrar* (spy); and that while the king looked upon *dutas* as part of his court, he considered the *Orrar* as a part of his personal guards and information service.

The spies had no official status in foreign courts like ambassadors or envoys, while the latter were public servants and were to be treated honourably, the former secret service and, if caught, would be summarily executed.[20]

There is an instance of the treatment of spies in *'Manimekhalai'*. A 'merchant' named Sangama, from Kapila, went Simhapura, there in course of his business he was arrested by a police official of the state, and was shown up before the monarch as a spy. Under royal orders he was beheaded.[21]

Sometimes a more cruel punishment was in store for spies. The *Rajatarangini* (VIII, 2200) mentions the eyes of *tiksna* spies being torn out by enemy against whom they were employed.[22]

Thus, in ancient India spies were given a high position. They were considered an integral part of administration but diplomatic immunity was not provided to them.

The kings in ancient India which was studded with small states, constantly threatened by external aggressions, plagued by internal dissension and which was witnessing the growth of an 'imperial tradition' had developed an efficient machinery to collect and collate political intelligence.

Secret agents played an important role in political field. Existence of the system of espionage can be traced back to the early Vedic period. The spies seem to have been largely employed then not merely to ascertain validity or invalidity in the statements of parties and witnesses, but also to gather correct and reliable information as to the movements of tribal settlements of inimical tendency or disposition.[23]

Kautilya gave an institutionalised form to the 'secret service' to maintain and to watch over seducible and non-seducible elements in the state.[24]

His secret agents were quite active. They used to identify the opposing and dissatisfied groups, to placate them and win them over, and if needed they eradicate the target.[25]

Spies not only collected the information by overhearing converSation or through sources but also they provoked the people and get their secrets.[26]

The bureaucrats and ministers had to be cultivated, and their weak movements were exploited by secret agents.

Sometimes spies frightened the enemy's subjects by giving publicity to '*Vijigisu's*' power of omniscience and his close association with gods[27] so spies tried to enhance the king's impression as well as terror among the enemy's. They adopted various covers to gain the confidence of officers and kings whom they sought to cover.

Secret agents provided their services not only on their own land but in foreign countries also. For intelligence abroad, the *Ubhayavetenas*' (special agents) were employed, 'who got salary from both the countries'. These agents manage to secure service with the ruler or some high official in a foreign state, when they have won the confidence of the latter, they are in a position to collect and pass on valuable information secretly to their native land and thus render a useful service to it.[28] So they played a crucial role.

In relation to foreign states, political form of espionage involved an attempt to get into touch through secret emissaries with the discontented or disloyal elements in the hostile state, and utilize their services for the destruction of the latter. Various forms of political espionage have been elaborated by Kautilya in BK I, Ch. 14, BK VIII and XI, I. Some of these have a curious resemblance to methods employed by Hitler and Mussolini on the eve of the Spanish Civil War.[29]

In the *Mahabharata*, spies are called the 'eyes of king'. In actual, king through spies perceives the acts and intentions of foes, friends and neutrals. The epic reflects the contemporary political condition in which, a king is advised to be ever vigilant and cautious towards frauds, fools and the wicked. In such atmosphere of conspiracies, political espionage became more important.

Spies were presented everywhere in the cities, provinces and feudatory dominions. No one could escape their glance, not even the king's sons, friends and counsellors.

Manu mentions a "special branch" collecting political intelligence that plays most important role in an efficient administration. They rendered security to the state by observing dissatisfied and discontented elements, who could not only create unstable conditions in the state but may destroy the king himself.[30]

Kamandaka[31] also lays the importance of the political information collected by spies.

Matsya Purana considers intelligence reports indispensable to assist the king in the formation of state policies. "The state is said to depend upon spies as the king sees through them, i.e. they gather varied information through spies, through them he knows what acts pleased the people and which displeased them, so that he could pursue or abandon them".[32] So spies were associated with every sphere of political life of state.

The military intelligence wing of 'secret services' was an inalienable part of the war machinery in ancient India.

In fact espionage developed with the evolution and advancement of the technique of war. It became necessary to know the troop concentrations of the enemies and to provide against surprise attacks or shock tactics. This was also necessary to make an estimate of the strength of an enemy[33] and to ascertain the nature of a hostile country, its army and fortified places.

These spies and their work had military significance, can not be doubted. Spies are the secret agents of a state sent abroad for the purpose of obtaning clan destinely information in regard to military on political secrets.[34] The Rigveda speaks of spies, or presumably reconnoiting troops, going forward in on unambiguous content of war and this is corroborated by another passage.[35] As the opposing armies approach to each other, the spies try to find the exact position of the enemy and messenger keep the king informed of the latest happening.[36] In thc thirteen chapter of Yajurveda, spies are entrusted with the job to inquire about the activities of the enemies. They were used during the war time. The earliest traces of military espionage are to be found in the Epics and the *Puranas*.[37]

In the *Ramayana*, a king mentions the wise adage that "the enemy, whose secrets have been known through espionage, can be conquered without much effort".[38] The spies had attained so much importance that in the *Mahabharata* they figure as one of the 'eight constituents', of the army.[39] It laid emphasis on the employment of spies in army for the guidance if army is marching from the jungle, because the spies who were living in jungle for the information, they had full knowledge of short and safe routes of forest.[40]

In the war scenes the spies of the *Mahabharata* they are always taken for granted as forming part of a camp. It says "with only this kind of force, an enemy from within the fort can affect the whole army of even a powerful and prosperous king".[41] The Virata Parva refers to spies sent by the Kurus to trace the where about of the Pandavas.[42] Spies are always present in the camp and the army.

In the *Udyoga-parva*, Yudhisthira says : "the spies I had placed in the army of Dhritarastra's son brought me this news in the morning". From them he learns everything about Drona's intention to capture him alive.

In the *Dronaparva* (73, 27), Krishna says, "I had sent some spies into the camp of Dhritarastra's son. These spies quickly returning, gave me this information". They bring the news of the formidable military army to be formed next day by the Kurus. Spies were also allowed on the battle field. The Kuru king made proper arrangements for them along with other spectators.[43]

The news of Arjuna's vow is likewise carried across by spies to the other camp.[44]

It shows spies importance in military field that the *Mahabharata*[45] praises a king who details clever spies for ascertaining enemy's secrets, and seeks to win over enemy's officers by ingenious methods, "by employing trusted agents, a king would render the enemy forces inefficient through disunion".

The epic suggests measures to thwart enemy attempts at collecting intelligence from the fort. Besides this, the counter-espionage staff was detailed to discover enemy's agents.

The *Ramayana* is repleted with instances where espionage was perfected both as a science and art. Rama[46] was advised to depute his agents to collect intelligence about the strength of Ravana, his troops, their deployment and fighting capabilities. These agents tracked Sita to Lanka and collected intelligence about Ravana's operational plans.

Secret agents were also deployed to Lanka to ascertain the background and antecedents of Vibhisana. It is a very remarkable function of spies, as even today preventing of diplomatic personnel is undertaken by the receiving states.

Ravana sent his spies to Rama's camp to discover the nature, number and disposition of the enemy troops.[47] But he was unsuccessful in his intelligence missions and the *Ramayana* vividly portrays the annoyance of Ravana. It provides the first historical record of numerous intelligence agents by name viz., *Suka*, *Sarana*, *Sardula*, *Ahala*, *Sarbha*, *Sampati* and *Pradhasa.*

During Buddhist period spies played a very important part in peace and war. In one of his talks with the Buddha king Basenadi speaks of his spies and informants, and on other occasion refers to the counsellor at his court and the weavers of spells aimed to arrest the advancing enemy. Magic and sorcery helped to prop the morale of the credulous king and his army.[48]

These examples show the importance and their valuable contribution in the war time. In throwing fresh light on diplomacy, military espionage, secret war (*Kutayudha*) and new conceptions of strategy, the *Arthasastra* surpasses all writers.[49]

In the *Arthasastra*, Kautilya speaks of "spies who are residing as traders in enemy's villages as well as those who are residing as cow-herds or ascetics in the district borders of the enemy's country". Like the German agents in the eastern department of France during the Great War, these were apparently expected to transmit news of military importance to the king.[50]

Kautilya elaborately elucidates measures for the collection of defence intelligence and means to defuse defence efforts of the enemy.[51] He advocates the employment of spies alongwith the marching army in the camp and also in the fighting line.

The prime responsibility of the envoys was to poisoned the minds of enemy kings or to demoralised them so that their energies frittered away, and their capacity to sustain a war diminished. They were to keep up the morale of the troops, by declaring the success of their own operations and the failure of those of the enemy.

They also harassed the enemy, created divisions in their ranks and demoralise the hostile king "by telling him that his own fort was burnt, stormed or that some one of his family or an enemy or wild chief rose in rebellion".[52]

The army chiefs and civilian officials were lured and infatuated by prostitutes, and later killed by secret agents. Agents, appearing as mendicants caused poison to be administered to army commanders on to the pretext of love-winning medicines. The astrologer agents secretly instigated senior officials by pointing out in them 'the marks' of a king.

The 'female agent' infiltrated as wife of a senior officer poisoned the ears of the officer by complaining that the king had eyes on her and had approached her by sending ornaments.

To a weak king, menaced by a strong neighbour, spies wage the 'battle of intrigue' (*mantra-yudha*) and secret war (*Kutayudha*). The spies were to practise all kinds of fraud, artifice, incendiarism and robbery.[53]

In capturing a fort, Kautilya advises the invading king to "infuse enthusiastic spirit among his own men and frighten the enemy's people by giving publicity to his power of omniscience and close association with gods".[54] The circulation of this precious information was to be entrusted to spies disguised in various covers.

Secret agents were also used in a variety of ways to create disaffection and revolt against army officers of the enemy or to win them over for espionage. They were also permitted to assassinate the chiefs of infantry, cavalry, chariots and elephants, kings relations or disturb the supply lines and reinforcements.[55]

Kamandaka also described the 'military intelligence' these spies were employed in the army camps and marched along with the army. They not only foiled enemy intrigues, and exposed his manoeuvres but also kept up the morale of their own troops by forecasting the success of their king, and the inevitable failure of the enemy.[56]

Although very few information of espionage is available of Gupta and post Gupta period, yet it is only reasonable to assume that there was no sudden reversal of the old strategy and that spies continued as an important feature of Indian Civil and Military administration through succeeding ages.[57]

In early India, military police was also existed as an integral part of defence forces Kautilya[58] lays down rules for organising military order and discipline in the army, and for ensuring security when the troops were on the march or engaged in war.

Much of the police control was by means of informants who sometimes acted as agents provocateurs. If the person suspected, was an officer of rank, the police officer would approach him and address him by talking him into his confidence. He would offer the officer a sum of money as bribe for letting his friend out of the trouble he was in. If this were accepted, the officer was at once reported as charged with corruption and banished out of the land. The function attributed to the informants, such as shadowing the suspected, find a parallel in the modern secret police organization.[59]

So military espionage was treated in various ways. Emphasising, its importance Kautilya states, "intrigue, spies, winning over the enemy's people, siege and assault are five means to capture a fort".[60]

Spies thus formed a regular feature of the military administration.[61] And it was the most important duty of the spy, as mentioned in the *Mahabharata*, to get information about the military strength of the enemy.[62]

In ancient India, political thinkers had intelligently appreciated the importance of treasury which was considered as one of the 'saptangas' of the state. As Kautilya[63] had mentioned, "All undertakings are depended on the treasury (*Kosa*) the king therefore, should ensure his economic resources".

To ensure the economic resources, spies played a very important role. *Economic intelligence* is an indispensable feature of administrative machinery with a charter to ensure the coverage on economic offenders, investigation of cases of economic bungling, defalcation of government funds in financial institution.[64]

Secret agents were also responsible for assisting the king during an economic emergency when the treasury was depleted owing to human or divine considerations.

In the *Arthasastra*, it is mentioned that officers concerned with state revenues, particularly those preparing budget accounts should be watched by secret agents.[65]

Samaharta exercised his sway over the whole range of the rural area. Besides directly dealing with his subordinates he sent out special intelligence officers who were to go on.

Circuit round the country in disguise especially those of householders,[66] they reported him about the area and output of the fields, the title and the remissions in respect of the tenements, the caste and the occupation as well as the income and the expenditure of members of families and their strength.

These secret agents also used to spy on the work of various officials, detecting those living above their means or falsifying accounts and acting as income tax inspectors, assessing the productivity of fields.[67]

These spies checked the report about the detailed village records prepared by the '*Gopa*' or '*Sthanika*'.[68] The Controller General or chief administrator ascertained through spies the honesty or dishonesty of the heads of department.[69]

The king's spies were favoured with money and honour to ascertain the integrity of the kings servants. Even the king's wives and princes were spied upon in financial matters.[70]

The *Nagaraka* was authorised to direct the spies for similar works within the town, as *Samahartra* in rural areas.[71]

Secret agents were responsible to find out the quantity and price of king's goods produced in his own country, obtained from mines, water works, forests, factories and fields. They also spied upon the counterfeiters of coins, adulters, robbers, farmers, cowherds, traders and judges.[72]

The king was informed about the trade routes where foreign or native merchants may be harassed by royal favourites, departmental officer, robbers and frontier chiefs and this was ensured through the secret agents of the 'revenue department'. Strict security measures depending on the observation reports of secret agents, working under the '*Sulkadhaksa*' were taken against tax evaders.[73] On the report of spies, the persons who were found guilty of tax-evasion, strict measures were taken against them.

Secret agents also collected advance intelligence on those seeking to take out any of the unexportable articles, viz. weapons, armour, coats of mail, metals, chariots, jewels, grains and cattle.[74]

In no uncertain terms, Kautilya placed the responsibility of surveilling economic offenders and collection of intelligence about fraudulent businessmen on the 'Special Branch' of police.[75]

Manu, also advised to king to keep the watch on the activities of '*Loka-kantakas*' or 'Public thorns' by secret agents. Because these type of persons made money by openly deceiving and cheating people, and caused incalculable damage to the government.[76]

Besides these, spies assisted the king in replenishing his treasury in times of financial stringency.[77] It was suggested that a king without adequate financial resources should seek to raise funds while difficulties concerning money have arisen. But polity thinkers suggest not only legally accepted methods but also unorthodox means for replenishing a depleted treasury, and secret agents played a significant role in such operations.

Kautilya was of the view that men may not be willing to part with their money voluntarily. But they have to be made to contribute on false ideas.[78]

He suggests that spies will move about masquerading as honest citizens and spread calumnies against those who contribute less than expected. The wealthy people will be asked to contribute their '*biranya*' to the best of their capacity and they should be tempted with the reward or honour by the state. It is a procedure by which money is raised with the help of spies in collusion with some people who allow themselves to be falsely announced as donors.[79]

Sometimes spies played with the religious faiths and superstitions of the people and used the methods regardless of all moral considerations. These ways succeed in an atmosphere of secrecy and make-believe. They include appropriation of the wealth of duties brought to the central place after being collected from different localities of their worship as a seemingly. Protective measure under the direction of the '*Devatadhyaksha*', i.e. the officer in charge of religious affairs, whose sincerity being above suspicion, this method is most likely to succeed with the people left completely ignorant of the manner of its loss.

Secret agents may collect entertainment fee from unwary public by showing them a serpent with several heads in a well which has earlier been connected with a subterranean passage.

Sometimes a secret service agent posing as trader may start business with another person, and after enough money has been collected as sale proceeds, deposits and loans, he may cause himself to be robbed. A merchant spy may borrow or take on pledge vast quantities of valuable or commodities or borrow from corporations gold or gold-coins, and later may allow himself to be robbed thus by cheating to another person, the spies used to seize their money.[80]

Prostitute spies also enamoured rich and amorous seditious persons and later get their property confiscated to the government on complaint.

A spy who is appointed to murder a claimant, but the responsibility for the commission of the crime will be laid at the door of the person, aimed against, who will be punished with a confiscation of his property. In short, the trap is to be laid in such a clever manner that the victim, when caught, can be held guilty of complicity in murder, manufacture of counterfeit coins, and other similar criminal activities to justify in the eyes of the public the states measure for his financial, ruin.[81]

The *Mahabharata*[82] supports the policy of acquisition of finances by taking away individual property by force during emergency situation.

Thus spies helped the government in the economic distress. They not only kept the watch over revenue officers, market, cheaters and merchants but also confiscated the extra money from rich and greedy people.

Secret agents provide their services in the social field also. In line with the contemporary civilizations of the ancient world which were threatened by antisocial elements because of large uninhabited areas affording shelter to fierce criminal tribes, the ancient Indian society was also constantly disturbed.[83]

The Vedic literature, Buddhist and Jain cannons, the folk literature and the *smritis* provide copious evidence in this regard.

T.N. Ramaswamy has mentioned about a particular type of spies that are “social spies they are state’s orphans, fed and educated by the state and trained in general science, magic various orders of religious life”. They collected the information by wondering in the state.[84]

Spies were used to eradicate the corruption in society. They were made responsible to kept the watch over the conduct of the people as well as ministers.

They spied upon the adulteration, counterfeiters etc. moved problems that could affect the society.

Secret agents protected society from the dacoits also. It would not be an exaggeration to say that all sorts of conceivable crimes were in evidence in ancient India. There are reference of dacoits like Angulimala. The *Arthasastra* and the Epics, the Buddhist and Jain folk literature mentioned about the regular criminal settlements. In view of these dangers to social life it had become necessary for the law givers to evolve elaborate arrangements for the collection of intelligence to ensure internal security. Secret agents were engaged by the state to detect criminals, agent provocateurs were detailed to incite suspects and potential offenders, and then to bring them to justice.[85]

Police also worked by means of informants and acted as agent provocateurs to arrest the corrupted people.[86]

Kautilya[87] explains various techniques adopted by spies in the disguised manner for the prevention of crimes.

Megasthenes observed intelligence men working for crime control in the society. He wrote 'overseers' to the secret service men and put them in the sixth class, they were assigned the duty of watching all that goes on making reports secretly to the king. Some were entrusted with the inspection of the city.[88] This description show the ubiquitous presence of secret agents and also that they worked for the society.

In Mauryan dynasty, king used the secret services not only for his safety but also for the welfare of his people.[89] Public security and discipline was ensured by the spies.[90]

Spies were used in ancient India as the means of communication, as they were not developed in that time. They reached the news from part of a kingdom to other parts.[91]

Manu[92] enumerates thirteen categories of anti-social elements who include shady characters, persons taking bribe, fortune tellers, cheats and confidence tricksters, exploiters, quacks, artisans, calculating prostitutes etc. They cheated the innocents in broad daylight. The king was advised to collect intelligence on these persons. Thus secret agents reported the king the conduct of these malefactors or 'public thorns'. These defraud the people, harm the society by adopting unethical means, and make easy money.

Thus, spies were appointed to check the corruption, robbery, cheating, exploitation etc., moral degradation social problems in the society. Moreover, the secret services grew out of the requirements of protection originating in the philosophical concept of '*Rta*' or moral order, which pervaded the entire socio-religious and economic structure of the Vedic society.

Secret agents played a very important role in every walk of life viz., is political, military, economic or social life. They achieved a high position in the state and considered the eyes and ears of the king. Indian political writers have very systematically and assiduously established that the success of all governments depend on their capability to effectively implement the 'rule of law', which in turn depends on the performance of 'spy system'.

References

1. T.B. Mukherjee, Interstate Relations in Ancient India, Meerut, 1967, p. 25.
2. D.K. Ganguly, Aspects of Ancient Indian Administration, p. 282.
3. राज्यंमणिर्धमूलं हि मन्ससांर प्रचक्षते। 83/51
   Mahabharata, Shantiparvan, 83/51.
4. यदा प यति चारेण सर्वभूतानि भूमियः।
   क्षेंम च कत्वा प्रजाति तदा भवति भास्करः।।68/43
   Ibid.,
5. *Ibid.,* 59/41.

6. The *Ramayana, Ayodhya Kanda*, 100-36.
7. Vimla Chaudhary, *op. cit.*, p. 33.
8. येषां चारा च कोषा च नय च जयतांवर।
   अस्वाधीना नरेन्द्रणां प्राकतैस्ते जनैः समाः।।
   Ramayana, Aranya Kanda, 33/9.
9. Vimla Chaudhry, *op. cit.,* p. 38.
10. Aradhana Parmar, Techniques of Statecraft—A Study of Kautilya's *Arthasastra*, p. 240.
11. N.N. Law, I.H.Q., 'Machinery of Administration in the Kautilya', Dec. 1929, p. 631.
12. J.W. Macrindle, Ancient India as Described by Megasthenes and Arrian, pp. 85-86.
13. हिरण्यं त्यापतानीतं भाण्डागारेषु निक्षिपेत।
    प येच्चारांस्ततो दूतान्प्रेषयेन्मन्त्रि संगतः।।328, 13।
    Shri Narayan Mishra, *Yajnavalkya Smriti* (trans.), Kashi Sanskrit Series'.
14. I.W. Mabbett, Truth, Myth and Politics in Ancient India, New Delhi, 1971, p. 50.
15. N. Subrahmaniam, Bombay, 1966, p. 100.
16. S.L. Roy, Diplomacy in Ancient India, Calcutta, p. 198.
17. Aradhana Parmar, *op. cit.*, p. 232.
18. B.K. Majumdar, Military System in Ancient India, p. 93.
19. D.K. Ganguly, *op. cit.*, p. 290.
20. N. Subrahmaniam, *op. cit.*, pp. 102-103.
21. P.C. Chakravarti, The Art of War in Ancient India, 1972, p. 74.
22. *Ibid.,* p. 75.
23. S.L. Roy, *op. cit.*, p. 183.
24. *Arthasastra*, 1. 13.26.
25. *Arthasastra*, 1. 13.26.

26. *Ibid.,* 1. 13.2.
27. S.L. Roy, *op. cit.*, p. 190.
28. Aradhana Parmar, *op. cit.*, p. 238.
29. P.C. Chakravarti, *op. cit.*, p. 70.
30. *Manu Samhita*, IX/266.
31. M.N. Dutta, Kamandaka, *Nitisara*, VI.
32. S.D. Trivedi, *op. cit.*, p. 129.
33. T.B. Mukerjee, *op. cit.*, p. 46.
34. L. Oppenheim, International Law, Vol. I, p. 862.
35. Rigveda, IV. 4.3, RV. VIII 47.II.
36. S.D. Singh, Ancient Indian Warfare with special reference to the Vedic Period, Leiden, E.J. Brill, 1965, p. 144.
37. B.K. Majumdar, Military System in Ancient India, Calcutta, 1955.
38. P.C. Chakravarti, *op. cit.*, p. 68.
39. *Mahabharata, Shantiparvan*, 100/12.
40. चारैः सुविदिताभ्यासः कु ।लैर्वनगोचरैः।। 13
न ह्यरण्येन ।क्येत गन्तुं मगगणैरिव।
तस्मात सेनासु तानेव योजयन्ति जयार्थिनः।। 14
Ibid., 100/13-14.
41. *Mahabharata, Shantiparvan*, CXL.
42. Mbh. 4.24.5, 4.25.8-12
43. S.D. Singh, Ancient Indian Warfare, p. 163.
44. P.C. Chakravarti, *op. cit.*, p. 68.
45. *Mahabharata, Santiparvan*, CIII, CVII.
46. S.N. Vyas, India in the Ramayana Age, Delhi, 1967, p. 40.
47. *Ramayana, Yudhakanda*, 25.1, 29.24.
48. S.D. Singh, Motilal Banarasi Das Pub., Delhi, 1965 *op. cit.*, p. 146.

49. B.K. Majumdar, *op. cit.*, pp. 92-93.
50. P.C. Chakravarti, *op. cit.*, p. 71.
51. *Arthasastra*, 12.1.5.
52. *Arthasastra*, X 6.
53. P.C. Chakravati, *op. cit.*, p. 71-72.
54. *Arthasastra*, Bh. XII.
55. S.D. Trivedi, *op. cit.*, p. 133.
56. M.N. Dutta, *Kamandaka Nitisara*, X 3, 51; XII 29.48.
57. P.C. Chakravati, *op. cit.*, p. 72.
58. *Arthasastra*, 1.2.17.
59. V.R.R. Dikshitar, Hindu Administrative Institutions, Madras, 1929, p. 235.
60. *Arthasastra*, XIII, 4.
61. V.R.R. Dikshitar, *op. cit.*, p. 99.
62. B.P. Roy, *op. cit.*, p. 366.
63. कोषपूर्वाः सर्वारम्भाः ।
    तस्मात्पूर्वं कोषमवेक्षेत ।। *Arthasastra*, 2.7. 1.
64. S.D. Trivedi, *op. cit.*, 138.
65. V.R.R. Dikshitar, *op. cit.*, p. 320.
66. I.W. Mabbett, *op. cit.*, 971, p. 49.
67. I.W. Mabbett, *op. cit.*, 1971, p. 49,
68. एवं च जनपद चतुर्भागं स्थानिकः चिन्तयेत। 7।
    गोपस्थानिकस्थानेषु प्रदेष्टारः कार्यकरणं बलिप्रगहं च कुर्युः ।।
    Arthasastra, 11.315, 7-8.
69. B.P. Sinha, Reading in Kautilya *Arthasastra*, 1976, Delhi, p. 59.
70. *Arthasastra*, 1. 17. 1.
71. N.N. Law, I.H.Q., Machinery of Administration in the Kautilya, 1929, p. 631.
72. D.K. Ganguly, *op. cit.*, p. 287.
73. *Arthasastra*, 2.21.22.

74. *Arthasastra*, 2.21.20.
75. S.D. Trivedi, *op. cit.*, p. 140.
76. Manu, IX.
77. D.K. Ganguly, *op. cit.*, p. 287.
78. B.C. Sen, Economics in Kautilya, Sanskrit College, Calcutta, 1967, p. 124.
79. B.C. Sen, *op. cit.*, p. 125.
80. B.C. Sen, *op. cit.*, p. 126.
81. *Ibid.*, p. 127.
82. *Mahabharata, Shantiparvan*, 134.
83. S.D. Trivedi, *op. cit.*, p. 144.
84. T.N. Ramaswami, Essentials of Indian Statecraft, 1962, p. 56.
85. R.P. Gupta, Crime and Punishment in Ancient India, Calcutta, 1930, pp. 50-53.
86. V.R.R. Dikshitar, *op. cit.*, p. 235.
87. *Arthasastra*, 4.5.18.
88. J.W. Mccrindle, Ancient India as Described by Megasthenes and Arrian, pp. 85-86.
89. B.N. Puri, History of Indian Administration, Bombay, Vol. I, p. 68.
90. J. Auboyer, Daily Life in Ancient India, p. 124.
91. Bharti Mukherjee, Kautilya's Concept of Diplomacy, p. 41.
92. Manu, VII, 153.

9

Conclusion

Espionage, intelligence, investigation and prosecution have traditionally formed the part of the state security system. The states in ancient India were inclined to regard the spies as highly indispensable and their work was considered to be of utmost importance.

Spying was an integral part of an efficient administration and of a sound and strong foreign policy. It kept the rulers posted with the activities, affections and operations of political adversaries; disloyal and disgruntled elements, fifth columnists and foreign agents besides the strength and intentions of foreign powers.

Existence of the system of espionage can be traced back to the early Vedic period. Vedic literature testify the origin of secret services. Spying was practised in the Vedic period, for the security of the state, to uphold the moral order and for the eradication of criminals. In Epic period the system of espionage was a permanent and prominent feature of the state and secret services were used in a diplomatic way. The *Mahabharata* refers to a mythological tradition on the origin of *dandaniti* and art of espionage which was handed down from the past.

The Sangam age in South India show an institution of secret services that was an important component of the state machinery. Spies were considered the eyes of a king where with he can see.

Espionage was masterly used in the time of king Ajatsatru. But the virtues of organising the spy system was greatly adulated in the *Arthasastra* of Kautilya.

There is no section of the people that does not come under the preview of Kautilya's obnoxious system of espionage, which touches every one but the king.

The only plausible explanation that could be offered in connection with this terrible system of spying into the character and activities of citizens and officials alike is that perhaps the age. Which witnessed the rise to power of Chandragupta Maurya was one of the disloyalty at home and perfidy abroad... there were the numerous adherents of the old royal house of the Nandas in Magadha, and the sympathizers of the Macedonians in the north-western parts of the country. Perhaps it was to solve this double danger that faced the new rising Mauryan state that Kautilya introduced a system of espionage, which had no parallel anywhere in its working, its extentive powers, and its destructive hold on the administration.

It is elaborate in its treatment and emphatic about its use. It has therefore, given rise to some theories as to its real nature in all times and throughout the whole range of India's ancient history. He considers the espionage as an indispensable adjunct of foreign policy and also as an important instrument of serving the government. The security measures for the king as enunciated by Kautilya could be considered ideal even by modern standards.

Noticing such a frequency of inspections and the existence of spies in Maurya empire, Romila Thapar views that there must have carried with it the flavour of a totalitarian state. Since there was no elected representative body to assist the king in governing, he could have recourse only to such menas of eliciting public opinion. When used with caution and in a responsible manner they may have served them purpose well.

A good deal of criticism raised in relation to the Kautilya's concentrations on espionage system. Dr. V.A. Smith identified the *Arthasastra*, 'Machiavellian in spirit' and quoted the Bana, described the science of Kautilya as 'merciless in its precepts and rich in cruelty. But A.L. Basham rejects the view and states that "the function of the secret service was not confined to the suppression of criticism and reduction, and it was looked on not as a mere Machiavellian instrument for maintaining power, but an integral part of the state machinery." It is an application of *Dharma* to national defence.

But it may be said that over all picture of Kautilya espionage was not perhaps applicable with equal exactness to all the periods of ancient India. The system was not meant exclusively for the extension and maintenance of the authority of the state.

But, whenever 'spy system' slackened, India become a hunting ground of barbarians and foreign hordes. The mighty Mauryan empire disintegrated when Briahadratha failed to observe the basic precautions propounded by Kautilya. Pushyamitra Sunga easily murdered the Mauryan in open court. Later on Sungas also failed to maintain its strictness:

History was repeated during Gupta period, when Chandra Gupta assassinated the Saka ruler in the guise of a woman. It was due to the failure of intelligence of Saka rulers. In Gupta administrative machinery, espionage existed in a rising condition.

As a general view, espionage was an important and successful institution in ancient India. Indian polity writers have very systematically and assiduously established that the success of all governments depend on their capacity to effectively implement the 'rule of law', which in turn depends on the performance of 'espionage system'. This was particularly important in ancient India in view of the special geopolitical factors, racial diversities and foreign inroads. It greatly contributed to the security and stability of the empire.

Spies were called the eyes and arms of the ruler of the earth. King used to look through their medium, that is why, whole of the administrative fabric was woven with the thread of these *caras*. Even when occasional embassies were not on visit in a neighbouring state, spies-cares or gupta caras were always at work to fish out the information.

Spying was endemic. Espionage was a science in its own right. Secret agents were divided in different categories by different polity makers. They had created several terms for spies and agents depending on their suitability and situational requirements. Kautilya mentions two wings of secret services, viz. '*Samstha*' (stationed) and '*Sancara*' (moving). These were again sub-divided into different types of spies. Generally this classification has been followed in India through the successive centuries.

As spying needed utmost secrecy the success of the spies depended very much upon the secrecy with which they could carry it out, and the way in which they could clothe it in a grab of superficial sincerity and naturalness. So they adopted various covers such as pupil, ascetic, physician, joker, musician etc. The spies were drawn from both sexes and from all grades of society, saints, householders and warriors, scoundrels and prostitutes, Brahmans and outcastes, all found themselves in the same service. Before recruitment they were examined thoroughly and they required some qualifications. Brahmans were supposed to be most worthy trustful as spy. Secret agents were given different grades and scales of salaries.

The work of espionage department was so vast that it was not possible for the king to accomplish the whole of it unaided. So '*Samahartr*', *Nagarka* and other officers as '*Mahamatyasarpa*', '*Rahasyadhikrita*', etc. were entrusted with the power to direct the spies employed in different missions. The report submitted by a single spy was not considered true still it was not justified by three different sources independent of one another. If it was false, spy was punished.

A very interesting as well surprising aspect of ancient Indian spy system was its secret information system or means of communication of intelligence. Spies had developed 'coded language', secret script or '*gudhalepka*' and signals. A relay system for transmission of message through sounds by blowing conches, beating drums and smoke was developed. Spies used various techniques to study the weaknesses and liabilities of their targets. Some of them were dissension, or to create '*bheda*' misinformation, motivation, temptation, blackmailing, etc.

The range of the duties of the secret emissaries touched every department of government. The tentacles of espionage were spread far and wide. Spies were called veritable 'News paper'. In a way, spies provide the political stability to a state. As king was informed about the intentions and minds of his subjects and officers and the opinions of ministers, enemies, soldiers, members of royal family, queens relations and women in the palace by the spies. So he was aware of any disturbance and could took security measures. Spies were the one of the eight constituents of the army. The military intelligence and economic intelligence wing of spy system were important parts of war machinery and government treasury respectively. The spies not only prevent the tax evasion, adulteration, stealing but also assisted the king during an economic emergency and replenish the state treasury.

Spies were also responsible to have a penetrating eye on human behaviour, character and the persons who were inimical to public morality are called 'public thorns'. They watched and controlled the evils prevailing in society such as corruption, robbery, harassment of weak people, moral degradation, extortion, sedition etc. The welfare of subjects was the ultimate objective of secret agents. Spies who helped in collecting all possible facts about the case and witnesses. Judges pronounced their judgement on the basis of the information by secret agents.

In South Indian polity, espionage was considered as an honourable profession, where as in the north, the spies were sometimes considered low grade officers. But the official status of these '*orrar*' or spies was not so high as the ambassadors in foreign lands. There is also distinction between *duta* and 'spy'. On the pattern of the Sanskrit words, duta is called an 'open spy' and a 'spy' works in 'dark or in cover'. Spies were not enjoyed the diplomatic immunity while dutas were always respected and apologised. But sometimes, the distinction was overlapping and the functions assigned to these two categories were in distinguishable. In all ages, diplomatic agent has been called a licensed spy.

It is surprising to observe that many aspects of ancient Indian spy system are relevant in modern times and also practised in its developed form. As espionage was an integral part of efficient administrative machinery and of a sound and strong foreign policy, still today 'intelligence' is very important department of administration.

The regular departments of espionage of ancient period can be correlated with the modern C.B.I., the 'criminal branch' of spies, and with the 'Criminal Intelligence Department' of India.

'*Samstha*' and '*Sancara*', categories of spies according to Kautilya can be corresponded to the 'Secret Intelligence Department' of a modern state and the other to the Department of Secret Emissaries, whose service are needed for military department and the department of foreign affairs.

The functions attributed to the informants, such as, shadowing the suspected, find a parallel in the modern recent police organization. Modern intelligence services generally resort to three main sources of recruitment, the academic world, the armed services and the under world. This was also the pattern followed in ancient India. Like competitive exam spies had to gone through a right test, possessing sterling qualities of character and sharp intelligence, soft spoken and swift in action, equipped with sharp memory, presence of mind etc.

The means of secret communication such as '*gudhalakha*', secret alphabets, signals, by beating drums, smoke producing different voices and use of birds and animals are still used in advanced forms of technology such as Radar etc. Western security services consider the use of birds and animals as their innovation, while these techniques were prevalent in our Vedic period with the help of pigeons and 'Sarama' the 'spy bitch of Varuna'.

The techniques of disinformation or misinformation that was used by spies to know the public opinion, is widely used as an effective technique by modern intelligence services to create disharmony and distrust among friends, ill-will among allies.

As to work in disguised way, was the distinctive feature of ancient spy system even modern times, occasionally secret agents use the various covers to hide their personal identity. These agents could be present at any place to gather the information, female agents were also employed in this task.

There are many references in ancient literature to took precautionary steps before arrival of any diplomatic envoy. In recent times also, before arrival of any diplomatic envoy many precautionary steps are taken about his background, character and his intentions.

In modern times too, a secret agent does not enjoy diplomatic immunity. If he is caught, that country can take any step against him. The functions of the '*Duta*' and 'spy' are not entirely different even today, and are in fact, similar in as much as an ambassador in somewhat of an honourable spy acting within the laws of the host country.

Spies played a very important role in economic field. Like this economic intelligence is an indispensable feature of modern governments with a charter to ensure the coverage on economic offenders, investigation of cases of economic bungling, defalcation of government funds in financial institutions and collection of intelligence against tax evaders. It is also surprising that all the departmental heads of Kautilya employed secret agents much on the same pattern as in the modern world.

In a way, spies performed the duty that falls to the lot of Journalists at presents. As they had to submit to the sovereign daily reports on public feeling on the doings of the government in the cities and provinces. So ancient Indian spies were the journalists of modern times and '*Waqiah Nawais*' or the news recorder of Mughal empire. They may be called the 'Veritable Newspaper'.

So ancient spy system is accepted and maintained by the modern intelligence system in its developing stage. But one great difference that distinguishes this ancient system of espionage from the modern ones is that unlike the latter, the former is not on principle tied down in any case to only the collection of information helpful to government. The guilty with in the state being sought to be punished through open trials and those outside it through the recognised over procedures. The harassment of persons really innocent but yet suspected, and the persecution of them through court trials etc. are some of the abuses to which even the modern system is liable, apart from the question of any sinister policies or personal motives that may have a play in the actual working.

Though the spy system of today is perhaps better organised, more powerful, much larger and more influential than it ever was before, yet the spies, then as now were found necessary for purpose of security and collection of information otherwise difficult together.

The general treatment accorded to spies in certain periods of ancient Indian chronicle was dictated by good sense and moderation. All ancient writers on political science and art of government were not dark politicians, ready to recommend security and consolidation of royal power by unscrupulous and violent means. In spite of some occasional deviations from strict morality in the domain of state craft as in the *Arthasastra* and the great Epic, the spy system in ancient India formed only the necessary part of the governmental organization.

'Espionage' in ancient India was not a passive bureaucratic agency but *played* active role in the governance of the country with the welfare of the people as their role objective. Their contribution in the domain of internal security, administration and diplomacy was unique. It was a comprehensive and wide ranging organization of various disciplines involved in the investigation and collection of intelligence. It is very difficult for a government at any time to be able to function without secret agents of some sort and probably every ancient civilization had its spies. The thoroughness with which the *Arthasastra* and the Epics treat the spy system, however, appears to be unique the ancient Indian spy system, unique in the annals of ancient world.

Bibliography

Original Sources

Arthashastra, (Kautilya), R. Sharana Sastri, Mysore, 1967.

Atharvaveda, S.P. Pandit, Bombay.

Jataka, Annanda Kausalayan.

Kamandaka Nitisara, M.N. Dutta, Calcutta, 1896.

Kiratarjuniam, Dr. Krishna Kumar, Sahitya Bhandar, Meerut, 1975.

Mahabharata, (Santiparvan), Kesari Mohan Ganguli, Delhi, 1981.

Mahabharata, (Virataparvan), Kesari Mohan Ganguli, Delhi, 1981.

Manusmriti, G.N. Jha, Calcutta, 1922-29.

Mudraraksasa, J.C. Misra, Varanasi, 1972.

Ramayana (Ayodhyakanda)—Trans. Pandey Pandit Ram Narayan Dutta, Geeta Press, Gorakhpur.

Ramayana (Yudhakanda)—Trans. Pandey Pandit Ram Narayan Dutta, Geeta Press, Gorakhpur.

Sukraniti, B.K. Sarkar, Calcutta, 1890.

Yajnavalakaya Samhita—Trans. Shri Narayan Mishra, The Kashi Sanskrit Series.

Journals

I.H.C., Vol. 19, 'Role of Secret Services in Ancient India', Dr. B.K. Majumdar, 1956.

I.H.C., Vol. 33, 'Varuna Hymns and the origin of Monarchy' by Raghuvendra Vajpayi, 1972.

I.H.Q., 1930, N.N. Law, 11 Part.

Journal of Bihar Research Society, Vol. LIX, 'Facets of Prostitutes' by Vijay K. Thakur, 1973.

Journal of Indian History, 'System of Espionage in the *Nitisara* of Kamandaka', by R.K. Dikshit, Vol. 38, 1960.

The Indian Historical Quarterly, 'Espionage in Kautilya's Arthashastra', Vol. 36, edited by N.N. Law, 1960.

The Indian Historical Quarterly, 'The Machinery of Administration in the Kautilya', Vol. 1, edited by N.N. Law, 1929.

Secondary Sources

Agarwal, V.S., India as Known to Panini, 1953.

Agnihotri, P.D., *Patanjali Kalin Bharat*, Allahabad, 1963.

Aiyangar, K.V. Rangaswami, Aspects of the Social and Political System of Manusmriti, Lucknow, 1949.

Annand, Anvita, *Guptakala Mei Nariyo Ki Isthiti*, Radha Prakashan, Delhi, 1992.

Auboyer, J, Daily Life in Ancient India, Asia Publication House, 1961.

Altekar, A.S., State and Government in Ancient India, Motilal Banarasi Dass, Delhi, 1977.

Bhandarkar, D.R., Some Aspects of Ancient Hindu Polity, Banaras, 1925.

Bhandarkar, D.R., New Light on the Early Gupta History, Malaviya Commemoration, Vol. 1, 1982.

Bhandarkar, R.G., A Peep into the Early History of Mauryan Dynasty to the Fall of the Imperial Gupta Dynasty.

Bandhopadhyaya, N.C., Development of Hindu Polity and Political Theories, New Delhi, 1980.

Banerjee, S.C., Aspects of Ancient Indian Life, from Sanskrit Sources, Punthi Pustak, Calcutta, 1972.

Banerjee, S.C., Indian Society in the *Mahabharata*, Varanasi, 1976.

Barthakuria, A.C., India in the Age of Panchatantra, Punthi Pustak, Calcutta, 1992.

Bhakari, S.K., Indian Warfare, M.M.L. Pub. Pvt. Ltd., New Delhi, 1981.

Bhargava, L.P., Chandragupta Maurya, Lucknow, 1935.

Bhargava, P.L., India in Vedic Age, Ed. - 11, Lucknow.

Basham, A.L., The Wonder That was India, Calcutta, 1967.

Bhatia, H.S. (ed), Political, Legal and Military History of India, Vol. II, Deep and Deep Publication, New Delhi.

Bongard, G.M. Levin, Mauryan India, New Delhi, 1985.

Brill, E.J., Trans. by S.D. Singh, Ancient Indian Warfare with special reference to the Vedic Period, Leiden, 1965.

Chand, Tara, Short History of the Indian People from Earlier Time to the Present Day, London, 1953.

Chhangani, Shantiprasad, Interstate Relations in Ancient India, S.K. Publications, Delhi, 1986.

Chandra, Mohan, *Jain Sanskrit Mahakavya Mei Bhartiya Samaj*, Eastern Book Linkers, 1970.

Chakravarti, P.C., The Art of War in Ancient India, Oriental Pub., Delhi, 1972.

Chatterjee, M.L., International Law and Interstate Relations in Ancient India, Calcutta, 1958.

Chattopadhyay, Bhaskar, Kushan State and Indian Society, Punthi Pustak, Calcutta, 1975.

Chaudhary, H.C. Roy, Political History of Ancient India, Oxford Univ. Press, Delhi, 1996.

Dandekar, R.N., The Age of the Guptas and other Essays, Delhi, 1982.

Dharma, P.C., The Ramayan Polity, Madras, 1941.

Dikshit, Prabhakar, *Valmiki Ramayana mei Rajnitik Vichar*, Parimal Pub., N. Delhi, 1991.

Dikshitar, V.R.R., Mauryan Polity, M.L.B.D. Pvt. Ltd., Delhi, 1993.

Dikshitar, V.R.R., Hindu Administrative Institution, Pub., Univ. of Madras, 1929.

Ganguly, D.K., Aspects of Ancient Indian Administration, New Delhi, 1979.

Ghoshal, U.N., A History of Hindu Public Life, Part 1, Calcutta, 1945.

Ghoshal, U.N., A History of Hindu Political Theories, London, 1923.

Goyal, S.R., Kautilya and Megasthenes, Kusumajali Prakashan, Meerut, 1985.

Gupta, R.P., Crime and Punishment in Ancient India, Calcutta, 1930.

Indra, The Status of Women in Ancient India, M.L.B.D., Benaras, 1955.

Iyengar, P.T.S., Life in Ancient India, Madras, 1912.

Jain, T.C., Life in Ancient India as Depicted in the Jain Bombay, 1947.

Jauhari, Manorma, 'Politics and Ethics in Ancient India', A Study based on the Mahabharata, Bhartiya Vidya Prakashan, Varanasi, 1968.

Jayal, Shakambari, The System of Women in the Epics, M.L.B.D., Delhi, 1966.

Law, N.N., Aspects of Indian Polity, Calcutta, 1960.

Mabbett, I.W., Truth, Myth and Politics in Ancient India, Thomson Press, India Ltd., Pub. Division, New Delhi, 1971.

Majumdar, B.K., The Military System in Ancient India, Ferma K., Calcutta, 1955.

Macdonell, Vedic Mythology.

Majumdar, R.C., The Vedic Age, Vol. 1, Vidya Bhawan Series.

Majumdar, R.C., The Age of Imperial Unity, Vidya Bhawan Series.

Mecrindle, J.W., Ancient India as described by Megasthenes and Arrian, Bombay, 1877.

Michael, Edward, Everyday life in Early India, London, 1967.

Mookerjee, R.K., The Gupta Empire, Delhi, 1969.

Mookerjee, R.K., Chandragupta Maurya and His Times, M.L.B.D. Publications, Delhi, 1943.

Mookerjee, T.B., Interstate Relations in Ancient India, Meenakshi Pub., Meerut, 1979.

Motwani, Kewal, Manu Dharam Shastra, Madras, 1958.

Palmer, Encyclopaedia Britannica, Vol. 9, 1982.

Pannikkar, K.M., A Survey of Indian History, Bombay.

Parmar, Aradhana, Technique of Statecraft—A Study of Kautilya's Arthashastra.

Prabhu, P.H., Hindu Social Organi*Sati*on, Bombay, 1979.

Penzer, N.M., Poison Domsells and other Essays, London, 1952.

Prasad, Beni, Theory of Government in Ancient India, Central Book Depot, Allahabad, 1926.

Puri, B.N., History of Indian Administration, Vol. I, Bombay, 1968.

Ramaswamy, T.N., Essential of Indian Statecraft, M.M.L. Pvt. Ltd., 1962.

Rapson, E.J., The Cambridge History of India, Vol. 1, Delhi, 1955.

Renou Louis, The Civilization in Ancient India, Calcutta, 1959.

Roy, Brajdeo Prasad, Political Ideas and Institutions in the Mahabharata, Punthi Pustak, Calcutta, 1975.

Roy, S.L., Diplomacy in Ancient India, Charu Pub., Calcutta.

Sabnis, S.A., Kalidasa, His Style and His Times, Bombay, 1966.

Saha, B.P. and Behera, K.S., Ancient History of India, New Delhi, 1988.

Saran, P., Ancient India Political Thought and Institution, Delhi, 1983.

Sarkar, D.C., Society and Administration of India, Calcutta, 1967.

Sarkar, D.C., Some Aspects of the Earliest Social History of India, London, 1928.

Sen, B.C., Economics in Kautilya, Sanskrit College, Calcutta, 1967.

Shah, T.L., Ancient India, Vol. II (B.C. 900-A.D. 100) Shashikant & Court., Baroda, 1938.

Sharma, S.R., Ancient Indian History and Culture, II edition, Hind Kitab Ltd., Bombay.

Sharma, S.P., History of Ancient India, New Delhi, 1996.

Shashi Rekha, P., Ancient Indian Administration with special reference to Arthashastra, Manu and Yajnavalkya, New Delhi, 1996.

Shastri, K.A. Nilkantha, Age of the Nandas and Mauryas, Bihar, 1967.

Shastri, K.A. Nilkantha, The Cholas, Madras, 1955.

Shastri Nemichandra, Mahakavi Bhasa, U.P. Hindu Academy.

Shastri, H.P., The Ramayana of Valmiki, London, 1959.

Singh, Baldev, The Early Kushanas, Delhi, 1973.

Singh, Lallanji, *Ramayan Kalin Yudhkala*, Abhinav Pub., Agra, 1982.

Sternback, S.L., Juridicial Studies in Ancient Indian Law, Delhi, 1965.

Spellmen, J., Political Theories of Ancient India, Clarenden Press, Oxford, 1964.

Subramaniam, N., Sangam Polity, The Administration and Social Life of the Sangam Tamil, New York, 1966.

Shukla, H.L., *Mudrarakshasa Ka Sanskritik Anushelan*, Nagpur, 1976.

Thapar, Romila, A History of India, London, 1975.

Udgaonkar, Padma B., The Political Institution and Administration, M.L.B.D., Delhi, 1969.

Upadhyaya, Vasudeva, *Gupta Samrajya Ka Itihasa*, Allahabad.

Vidyalankar, S.K., *Mauryan Ka Itihas*, New Delhi, 1980.

Vidhyarthi, M.I., India's Culture Through the Ages, Meerut, 1970.

Vyas, S.N., India in the Ramayana Age, Delhi, 1967.

Walker, Benjamin, Hindu World, Vol. 1, George Allen & Unwin Ltd., Pushkin House, 1968.

Index

F

G

H

I

J

K

N